REMEMBERING THE SOUTH AFRICAN WAR

Remembering the
South African War

*Britain and the
Memory of the Anglo-Boer War,
from 1899 to the present*

PETER DONALDSON

LIVERPOOL UNIVERSITY PRESS

First published 2013 by
Liverpool University Press
4 Cambridge Street
Liverpool
L69 7ZU

British Library Cataloguing-in-Publication data
A British Library CIP record is available

ISBN 978-1-84631-968-6 cased

Typeset in Gill Sans and Adobe Garamond by Carnegie Book Production, Lancaster
Printed and bound in the United States of America

Dedication

Elizabeth Buchan Donaldson

Contents

List of Illustrations

Images taken from James Gildea, *For Remembrance and in Honour of Those Who Lost Their Lives in the South African War 1899–1902*, published by Eyre and Spottiswoode, 1911.

Acknowledgements

I AM grateful to a number of people for their help in the preparation of this book. I would like to thank the staff of the various libraries and archives used in my research. All members of staff were unfailingly helpful and supportive. The School of History at the University of Kent was generous with financial assistance and the granting of study leave to complete the manuscript. I would like to thank Rodney Constantine at the Anglo-Boer War Museum in Bloemfontein and the editorial staff at *History and Memory* for permission to reprint portions of articles that appeared in their publications. Alison Welsby from Liverpool University Press and Sue Barnes from Carnegie Publishing have been especially helpful in preparing the manuscript for publication. A particular debt of gratitude is owed to my colleague, Professor Mark Connelly, who acted as co-researcher on a pilot study and whose insights illuminate the chapters on memorialisation. Needless to say, the mistakes are all mine. Finally, I would like to thank Gina and Jamie for their forbearance when the memory of the South African War loomed larger than it should.

Introduction

The South African War has spawned a substantial bibliography covering an extensive range of aspects and topics. In Britain, the historiography was reinvigorated in the late 1960s when the conflict was rediscovered after years of neglect in such works as T. C. Caldwell's edited collection, *The Anglo-Boer War: Why Was it Fought? Who Was Responsible?*[1] A second significant landmark came in 1972 when Richard Price's *An Imperial War and the British Working Class: Working-class Attitudes and Reactions to the Boer War, 1899–1902*, was published.[2] This work was part of a new generation of histories which attempted to break away from the high political and military assessments to studies of popular perceptions of the conflict. Such studies did not, however, mark the end of the grand, narrative histories, for in 1979 Thomas Pakenham's hugely influential study, *The Boer War*, was published.[3] A year later the broadening out of South African War studies was confirmed in Peter Warwick's edited collection, *The South African War: The Anglo-Boer War, 1899–1902*, which contained essays on a diverse range of issues including women and the war, the poetry of the war and the role of black people in the conflict.[4] Unsurprisingly, the centenary anniversaries brought forward a fresh spate of work. Much of this built upon and extended the earlier trend in which the forgotten voices and discourses were subjected to close attention. This approach was encapsulated in Cuthbertson, Grundlingh and Suttie's edited collection, *Writing a Wider War: Rethinking Gender, Race and Identity in the South African War, 1899–1902*.[5] However, there remains an important gap

---

[1] T. C. Caldwell, *The Anglo-Boer War: Why Was it Fought? Who Was Responsible?* (Lexington: D. C. Heath, 1968).

[2] Richard Price, *An Imperial War and the British Working Class: Working-class Attitudes and Reactions to the Boer War, 1899–1902* (London: Kegan Paul, 1972).

[3] Thomas Pakenham, *The Boer War* (London: George Weidenfeld and Nicolson, 1979).

[4] Peter Warwick (ed.), *The South African War. The Anglo-Boer War, 1899–1902* (Harlow: Longman, 1980).

[5] Greg Cuthbertson, A. Grundlingh and M-L. Suttie (eds), *Writing a Wider War: Rethinking Gender, Race and Identity in the South African War, 1899–1902* (Athens, OH: Ohio University Press, 2002).

in research in the form of the conflict's memorialisation in Britain. Almost nothing has been written on this subject; by contrast, there is much work on the memory of the war in South Africa and the participating Dominions of Australia, Canada and New Zealand.[6]

The experience of the South African War sharpened the desire to commemorate and remember for a number of reasons. The combination of an increasingly literate public and a burgeoning populist press embedded the war firmly in the British national consciousness. Just how deep this interest went can be gauged from the flood of war-related literature that was published during and in the immediate aftermath of the conflict. It has been estimated that between 1899 and 1914 over 500 books and pamphlets on the war were published in the English language.[7] Among the more notable of the authors who rushed into print were Rudyard Kipling and Sir Arthur Conan Doyle. The former wrote five short stories about the conflict while the latter, who served on the staff of a private field hospital, produced two histories: *The Great Boer War* in 1900 and, having discovered that Boer resistance had not ended with the occupation of Pretoria, *The War in South Africa* two years later.[8] Not only did these works guarantee the popular appeal of the fighting in South Africa but they also provided a high public profile for the army. This fascination with the military was buttressed by the waves of volunteers that came forward following Black Week in December 1899. For the first time the gulf that existed between the civilian and military worlds was bridged, at least temporarily, as the respectable middle classes saw themselves reflected in the ranks of khaki.

Late Victorian and early Edwardian British society was, then, captivated by events in South Africa. The scale of the war and its costs, both human and financial, clearly dwarfed earlier colonial conflicts. Although later overshadowed by the fighting of 1914–1918, the conflict with the Boers seemed to a British public unencumbered by hindsight to be the first one that deserved the epithet 'Great'. The size of the armies, the involvement of civilian populations and the

---

[6]   See, for example, Ken Inglis, *Sacred Places: War Memorials in the Australian Landscape* (Melbourne: Melbourne University Press, 1998); Chris Maclean and Jock Phillips, *The Sorrow and the Pride: New Zealand War Memorials* (Wellington: GP Books, 1990); Michael Rice, *From Dolly Gray to Sarie Marais: The Boer War in Popular Memory* (Noordhoek: Fischer Press, 2004).

[7]   Figure complied from Fred R. Van Hartesveldt, *The Boer War: Historiography and Annotated Bibliography* (Westport, CT: Greenwood, 2000).

[8]   The five short stories by Rudyard Kipling are: 'The Outsider' in the *Daily Express*, 19–21 June 1900; 'The Captive', 'A Sahib's War' and 'The Comprehension of Private Copper' in *Traffics and Discoveries* (London Macmillan, 1904); 'The Way that He Took' in *Land and Sea Tales for Scouts and Guides* (London: Macmillan, 1923); 'A Burgher of the Free State' in *The Sussex Edition* (London: Macmillan, 1937). Arthur Conan Doyle, *The Great Boer War* (London: Smith, Elder and Co., 1900); *The War in South Africa: Its Cause and Conduct* (London: Smith, Elder and Co., 1902).

employment of modern technology all seemed to signal a break with the 'small wars' of the past. Moreover, many contemporary commentators couched the sacrifices of 1899–1902 in the same language that their counterparts (sometimes, in fact, the same people) were to use in the 1920s and 1930s. Just as Winston Churchill and David Lloyd George, hardly uncritical observers, viewed the Great War as a necessary fight for national survival so Conan Doyle could conclude his 1900 history, *The Great Boer War*, by asserting that, 'The Empire was at stake'.[9] These parallels are instructive. It is a given that the memory of the Great War permeated society in the interwar years and this is an area that has attracted much attention from social and cultural historians.[10] Yet, there has been little detailed work carried out on the ways in which the war in South Africa was commemorated and remembered. This glaring historiographical omission is made all the sharper when contrasted to the degree of research dedicated to Afrikaans' and black memory explored in such works as Stowell Kessler, *The Black Concentration Camps of the Anglo-Boer War, 1899–1902*.[11]

One of the most striking ways in which communities in Britain chose to commemorate the fallen of 1899–1902 and 1914–1918 was through the construction of war memorials and it is here that parallels between the two wars are especially apposite. In the South African War, as with the Great War, the fighting dragged on for a lot longer than anyone initially estimated and resulted in much higher casualties. Although in South Africa, unlike the Western Front, vast numbers of men died as a result of sickness rather than enemy action: 22,000 British and imperial troops died in the campaign against the Boers, 16,000 from sickness and 6,000 from enemy action. However, no matter how death came to the British soldier on the veldt, as in the Great War, it did so in a foreign land not easily accessible to family and friends. Therefore, missing graves in Britain around which to mourn, remember and celebrate, those left behind in the aftermath of both wars required other forms of commemoration.

Yet, the parallels between the two wars break down when it comes to scale of course. Death, as David Cannadine has noted, was universal in the 1920s and 1930s and the need for the bereaved to receive some form of solace seemed

---

[9] Winston Churchill, *The World Crisis* (London: Penguin, 1938, first published 1927), pp. 1091–1092; David Lloyd George, *War Memoirs* (London: Nicolson and Watson, 1936), p. 321; Conan Doyle, *The Great Boer War*, p. 742.

[10] See, for example, Angela Gaffney, *Aftermath: Remembering the Great War in Wales* (Cardiff: University of Wales Press, 1998); Adrian Gregory, *The Silence of Memory: Armistice Day, 1919–1946* (Oxford: Berg, 1994); Jay Winter, *Sites of Memory, Sites of Mourning: The Great War in European Cultural History* (Cambridge: Cambridge University Press, 1995); Alex King, *Memorials of the Great War in Britain: The Symbolism of the Politics of Remembrance* (Oxford: Berg, 1998).

[11] Stowell Kessler, *The Black Concentration Camps of the Anglo-Boer War, 1899–1902* (Bloemfontein: War Museum of the Boer Republics, 2012).

greater than ever before.[12] In the light of such overwhelming grief, to many civic leaders in the interwar years, the memorial movement at the turn of the twentieth century no longer appeared so significant. This certainly seems to have been the case in Canterbury. As debates over the form that the city's memorial to the fallen of the Great War should take rumbled on into 1919, the chairman of the city's war memorial committee, Mr H. A. Wace, chose to make a direct comparison with Britain's last imperial war to emphasise the size of the task he and his fellow committee members faced. The municipal authorities had, he reminded a gathering of civic dignitaries, 'erected a memorial in Dane John Gardens in commemoration of those who fell in the Boer War. That was an important event, but, great as it was, it was small in comparison to the Great War.' The mayor of Canterbury, Mr R. A. Bremner, agreed that the South African memorial did not serve as a suitable blueprint for their present project. 'Very few people,' he pointed out to the committee, 'now took the trouble to find out what the Dane John statue stood for; they said "What is that soldier for?"'[13]

The assumption that underpinned the concerns of Wace and Bremner, that the memory of the South African War would be eclipsed by the mass commemorative activity of the First World War, seems to have been borne out by the recent historiography of the subject. Although the South African War has been the focus for intense research by political and military historians, little work has been carried out on the way in which the conflict has been remembered. Studies such as Richard Price's, *An Imperial War and the British Working Class* and the collection of essays edited by John Gooch, *The Boer War: Direction, Experience and Image*, fail to make any reference to the widespread and socially significant memorial construction work that engulfed Britain once the Treaty of Vereeniging had been signed in 1902.[14] This omission becomes even more surprising when one considers the wealth of research that has been undertaken on the nature and form of remembrance in the aftermath of the Great War. Frequently, historians working in this field have identified the South African War as an important moment of transition in commemorative practice but, while raising some interesting issues, have been content to treat this earlier period as a brief prologue to the memorial movement of the 1920s and 1930s.[15]

[12]   David Cannadine, 'War and Death, Grief and Mourning in Modern Britain', in Joachim Whaley (ed.), *Mirrors of Mortality: Studies in the Social History of Death* (London: Europa, 1981), p. 195.

[13]   *Kentish Observer*, 20 March 1919.

[14]   Price, *An Imperial War*; John Gooch (ed.), *The Boer War: Direction, Experience and Image* (London: Frank Cass, 2000).

[15]   See, for example, Alan Borg, *War Memorials: From Antiquity to the Present* (London: Leo Cooper, 1991), pp. ix, 106–107; Stefan Goebel, *The Great War and Medieval Memory: War, Remembrance and Medievalism in Britain and Germany, 1914–1940* (Cambridge: Cambridge

Over the last few years there has been an attempt to test some of the assumptions contained in the current historiography by extending the debate on Great War memorialisation through an exploration of its antecedents in the South African conflict. These efforts are, however, still at an embryonic stage. Martin Staunton has surveyed memorials in Ireland and Andrew S. Thompson has included a brief survey of remembrance activity in his co-edited work, *The Impact of the South African War*.[16] More recently Edward Spiers and Elaine McFarland have written on the importance of South African War commemoration in Scotland, while Mark Connelly and the current author have carried out a similar regional survey for the South-East of England.[17] Valuable though these works are in filling in some of the gaps in our knowledge about how communities engaged with the war in South Africa and how they chose to define themselves in the light of the memory of the fighting, there is still much work to be done. General agreement with Alex King's judgement that, 'Commemoration of those who died in the Boer War foreshadowed that of the Great War' has not so far resulted in a detailed overview of how the sacrifices of those who served in South Africa were remembered.[18] It is the intention of this work to deploy the methodology used in my earlier monograph on remembrance of the First World War in Kent to explore this foreshadowing more completely by providing the first in-depth survey of the construction and evolution of the memory of the war in South Africa following the cessation of hostilities in 1902.[19] Key in initiating this process was the wave of memorial building that swept the country in the immediate aftermath of the fighting and the first four chapters will focus on this socially and culturally significant movement. However, memory did not stand still, was not enshrined in the bronze and marble of monuments to the fallen, and so the final two chapters will provide case studies of how the war was represented in print and on screen. The penultimate chapter will look at the two histories that came to dominate the written representation of the conflict for much of the twentieth century,

---

University Press, 2007), p. 21; Gaffney, *Aftermath*, p. 23; King, *Memorials of the Great War*, pp. 42–44, 68–70, 185–186.

[16]   Martin Staunton, 'Boer War Memorials in Ireland', in Donal P. McCracken (ed.), *Ireland and South Africa in Modern Times*, Vol. 3 (Durban: Southern African-Irish Studies, 1996), pp. 290–304; David Omissi and Andrew S. Thompson (eds), *The Impact of the South African War* (Basingstoke: Palgrave, 2002), pp. 99–123.

[17]   Edward M. Spiers, *The Scottish Soldier and Empire, 1854–1902* (Edinburgh: Edinburgh University Press, 2006), pp. 204–206; E. W. McFarland, 'Commemoration of the South African War in Scotland, 1900–1910', *Scottish Historical Review*, 89 (October 2010), pp. 194–223; Mark Connelly and Peter Donaldson, 'South African War (1899–1902) Memorials in Britain: A Case Study of Memorialization in London and Kent', *War and Society*, 29: 1 (May 2010), pp. 20–46.

[18]   King, *Memorials of the Great War*, p. 42.

[19]   Peter Donaldson, *Ritual and Remembrance: The Memorialisation of the Great War in East Kent* (Newcastle: Cambridge Scholars Press, 2006).

Leo Amery's *The Times History of the War in South Africa* and Sir Frederick Maurice's official *History of the War in South Africa*, while the final chapter will concentrate on the television documentaries of Kenneth Griffith, which were equally influential in shaping the modern memory of the fighting.[20]

In terms of memorialisation, the conflict in South Africa provides a fascinating stepping-stone to the outpouring of public commemorative effort provoked by the Great War. During the course of the nineteenth century war memorials had gradually altered in form and function. At the start of the century the overwhelming function of war memorials was to commemorate either individual battles or campaigns and usually served to glorify the commander. The struggle against Revolutionary and Napoleonic France saw major memorials erected in London: Nelson's column and Trafalgar Square, and the memorials to Wellington in the form of an equestrian statue of the general, a statue of Achilles and Wellington Arch on Constitution Hill. By mid-century, a significant shift in memorial function was beginning to occur as was seen in the wake of the Crimean War, 1854–1856.[21] The conflict saw genuine engagement with the army by Britain's emerging middle classes, many volunteering to serve in the popular cause, and this helped the army gradually to erode its highly pejorative image summed up in Wellington's notorious phrase, 'the scum of the earth'.[22] With Queen Victoria showing an immense regard for her soldiers, encapsulated in the striking of a new medal, the Victoria Cross, for supreme bravery on the battlefield, a new interest in the fate of the common soldier developed. In memorial terms this was most clearly seen in the Guards' Crimea memorial in London. Situated at the bottom end of Lower Regent Street at the junction with Pall Mall, it consisted of figures of ordinary guardsmen in a pose of stoic endurance rather than the lionisation of a commander. Running alongside this trend was that of the ever-increasing rituals of death and mourning in civilian life. For the middle classes, especially, concrete expressions of a virtuous life through a lavish funeral and a fine grave became extremely important.[23] The South African War was to bring these two forces together.

At the heart of the debates over the memorialisation of conflict is the question of where the balance should lie between the political and aesthetic significance of war memorials and their function as sites of individual and communal mourning. Bob Bushaway has argued that the intensive commemoration of the

---

[20]　Leo Amery (ed.), *The Times History of the War in South Africa* (London: Sampson Low, 1900–1909); Sir Frederick Maurice, *History of the War in South Africa, 1899–1902* (London: Hurst and Blackett, 1906–1910). The three documentaries by Griffith are: *Soldiers of the Widow* (BBC2, 1967); *Sons of the Blood* (BBC2, 1972) and *Against the Empire: The Boer War* (BBC2, 1999).

[21]　For further discussion on this shift in emphasis see Borg, *War Memorials*, pp. 104–124.

[22]　See Olive Anderson, *A Liberal State at War: English Politics and Economics during the Crimean War* (London: Macmillan, 1967).

[23]　See Pat Jalland, *Death in the Victorian Family* (Oxford: Oxford University Press, 1996).

First World War amounted to a 'deliberate construction of remembrance' that effectively resulted in 'the denial of any political critique of the Great War or of post-war society from the perspective of popular aspiration or expectation'.[24] David Cannadine, by contrast, has claimed that British war memorials of this period 'were in large part spontaneously generated by the bereaved for their own comfort'.[25] This line received support from Jay Winter in his immensely influential 1995 work, *Sites of Memory, Sites of Mourning*. The proliferation of commemorative artefacts and rituals of remembrance were, he suggested, first and foremost reflections of the depth of the trauma of 1914–1918 and the overpowering sense of grief felt by the post-war generation.[26] More recently, Alex King has stressed that, notwithstanding the insistence of contemporary civic leaders that memorials should and did have precise and immutable meanings, a true understanding of a commemorative site can be attained only by examining fully the relationship between the symbol and the community which it served.[27] Daniel Sherman is equally keen that commemoration should be connected securely to its roots within a locality. In his wide-ranging examination of the memorialisation process in interwar France he has claimed that, 'commemoration seeks to reinforce solidarity of a particular community … by forging a consensus version of an event or connected series of events that has either disrupted the stability of the community or threatened to do so'.[28] Ashplant, Dawson and Roper have built on these earlier approaches, noting how memory of war is, to a large extent, shaped by past experiences and pre-existing narratives. These 'templates of war remembrance' are, the authors contend, best understood not by surveys at the dominant national level but through more contextualised discussions of community practice.[29]

The works of King, Sherman and Asphalt, Dawson and Roper are very much an inspiration for the first four chapters of the current study as it aims to build on their approaches to provide a comprehensive insight into commemoration at a micro-level. Thus, by siting the war memorial movement securely in its context, these chapters will examine just how various communities attempted to arrive at a consensual vision of the past and explore what light this sheds on the shared traditions, beliefs and values of Britain in the early twentieth century. The approach will go beyond the simple deconstruction of memorial iconography and, instead, look at the often tortuous and lengthy gestation of

---

[24] B. Bushaway, 'Name upon Name: The Great War and Remembrance', in R. Porter (ed.), *The Myths of the English* (Cambridge: Polity Press, 1992), p. 145.
[25] Cannadine, 'War and Death', p. 219.
[26] Winter, *Sites of Memory*, chapter 3
[27] King, *Memorials of the Great War*, p. 3.
[28] Daniel Sherman, *The Construction of Memory in Interwar France* (Chicago: University of Chicago Press, 1999), p. 7.
[29] T. G. Ashplant, G. Dawson and M. Roper (eds), *The Politics of War Commemoration* (London: Routledge, 2000), pp. 34–36.

remembrance sites, from the formation of committees to the raising of finance and debates over form. In the process both Edwardian Britain's sense of self and the contested memory of the conflict in South Africa will be thrown into relief.

In many ways the war in South Africa was an evolutionary moment in civil–military relations as the rush of volunteers in the aftermath of Black Week saw, for the first time, the direct engagement of civilian society with the professional army. Communities, both civic and military, throughout the country were keen to record, remember and celebrate this unique manifestation of patriotic self-sacrifice. The opening two chapters will examine just how this sense of transition impacted on, and was highlighted by, the memorialisation process as the services of professional as well as citizen soldiers were commemorated with an admixture of pride and grief. A range of civic communities will be examined in the first chapter, covering a wide geographic and socio-economic mix, to build up a comprehensive picture of civil society's response to what was an extended period of national introspection. The second chapter will move the discussion on to the military world. Here there was a long tradition of memorial construction from which to draw. Yet, with the public's interest and involvement in military affairs at an all time peak, those tasked with overseeing commemorative activity found themselves under ever greater scrutiny. This was regarded as both an opportunity and an inconvenience. While a war memorial could be used to advertise a regiment's worth and cement community relations, it was also a highly sensitive site where the sensibilities of the local populace had to be taken into consideration. By exploring the memorialisation process in full, considering who was included in and who excluded from the rituals of remembrance, these two chapters will look to uncover the local and national issues surrounding class, political consciousness and military reform that the South African War brought to the surface. Next, the study will examine the ways in which the service of former pupils was remembered by their alma maters. Memorials built in communities of the young played a different role from those erected elsewhere. Invariably seen as an extension of, and adjunct to, classroom instruction their primary function was didactic. As such, the construction and unveiling of these memory sites provides a fascinating insight into the values and ethos of the school system in the early twentieth century. The fourth chapter will conclude the examination of the war memorial movement by investigating the construction of memory at the more intimate level of family, workplace and religious institution. For the vast majority of the population of late Victorian and early Edwardian Britain, the three key components in their sense of identity and belonging were family, employment and faith. It was, in many ways, at this immediate level that those being commemorated were defined as individuals. Yet, though the needs of bereaved relatives, friends and work colleagues often took precedence for the organisers of these tight-knit schemes, a wider agenda could also come into play. Institutions regularly seized on the memorialisation process as an opportunity to advertise their worth both to their own members and the wider community, with unveiling ceremonies frequently being used to stress wider points about core values and national direction. By studying the sometimes heated debates over inclusion, funding and form, the tensions that existed between the competing concepts of identity and belonging in late Victorian and Edwardian England will be revealed. To this end, the chapter will include a case study of the raising, by Devonians, of a memorial to Sir Redvers Buller, the disgraced commander of the British forces in the early stages of the war. His lionisation, in the face of official condemnation, provides a fascinating insight into the friction that could occur when the forces of local pride ran counter to the national political consciousness.

As already mentioned, however, the memorial movement in the aftermath of the South African War did not operate in isolation. While communities were constructing monuments to the memory of those who had served and died, so the public image of the war was being shaped by other forms of *lieux de memoire*. At the forefront of these alternative memory sites were literary representations of the conflict. Even before the Peace of Vereeniging had been signed the history of the war was being presented to an eager public, more often than not in the form of edited collections of despatches from war correspondents. These were quickly followed by a spate of war memoirs and detailed campaign histories. However, two key works stand out; the official *History of the War in South Africa* by Sir Frederick Maurice and Leo Amery's *The Times History of the War in South Africa*. These two comprehensive, multi-volumed histories were immediately recognised by contemporary critics to be of lasting significance and they came to dominate the popular memory of the war for much of the twentieth century. The penultimate chapter will examine the protracted and complicated genesis of these two monumental works. To avoid what Dan Todman has called 'the sin of psychological anachronism', the analysis will go beyond simple textual deconstruction to investigate both the production and reception of the sources.[30]

Finally, the study will move forward to conclude with an examination of the representation of the war on television. In the 1960s and 1970s, a renewed interest in imperialism and the British Empire in Africa combined with a rediscovery of the Great War and its roots encouraged scholars to revisit the war in South Africa. This historiographical reawakening was given a further boost at the close of the millennium as the fusion of a rapidly altering political landscape in Africa and the centenary of the war against the Boers encouraged new analyses of themes such as race, gender and the construction of national identity. Although these new lines of enquiry were largely restricted to the academic world and rarely percolated through to the lay public, one documentary film-maker did manage to introduce a wider television audience

---

[30]   Dan Todman, *The Great War: Myth and Memory* (London: Hambledon Continuum, 2005), p. xiv.

to this renaissance of interest in the war and to some aspects of the new research. Between 1967 and 1999, Kenneth Griffith wrote and presented three documentaries on the war in South Africa for the BBC. These, as was the case with most of Griffith's work, adopted a deliberately provocative viewpoint and challenged much of the received wisdom. The production and reception of these three documentaries will be explored to uncover how the conflict was reconfigured to suit the changed cultural context of Britain in the latter part of the twentieth century.

Chapter 1

Civic War Memorials:
Public Pride and Private Grief

$\mathcal{L}$ATE Victorian and Edwardian Britain was a society obsessed with social class and stratification, yet the war in South Africa had been a crucial evolutionary moment for the British middle and working classes. Emerging from the shadow of the aristocracy, the middle classes, and lower middle classes in particular, made up the majority of the initial volunteers for the army and thus often perceived themselves to be the instruments of victory. The war validated and confirmed their importance, status and respectability. Working-class volunteers had also come forward in large numbers, although historians debate the extent to which the motivation was patriotic or economic.[1] To many, such an egregious manifestation of patriotic service demanded some form of permanent recognition. Thus, civic leaders throughout the country took it upon themselves to begin the process of memorialising their locality's contribution to the imperial cause. This chapter will explore how civic communities went about the business of constructing memorials in honour of their citizen-soldiers and, in the process, will attempt to shed light on the extent to which such commemorative sites can be said to have embodied a collective memory of the war.

Although it was common for the inscriptions on civic and county memorials to claim collective ownership by declaring that a monument was raised through public subscription, determining the extent to which commemorative projects were genuinely expressions of popular demand is very difficult. Frequently organising committees simply emerged from pre-existing hierarchical patterns, legitimising their membership and role by claiming that they were giving concrete form to the desires felt by their own particular communities. As might be expected, leadership tended to come from those either already in a position of influence or unencumbered by other demands and therefore able to dedicate time and energy to a memorial project. This, in practice, effectively meant

---

[1] See Price, *An Imperial War.*

those in a comfortable financial position. Indeed, so embedded was the idea of paternalistic public service in late Victorian and early Edwardian society, with Victoria's Golden and Diamond Jubilees and Lansdowne's South African War Fund having provided the most recent opportunities for displays of civic largesse, that the formation of an organising committee rarely involved much in the way of preparatory work. At county level this resulted in the lead being taken, more often than not, by the Lord Lieutenant who gathered around him a mixture of civic and military notables to take the project forward. Typical was the experience of Pembrokeshire, where the Lord Lieutenant, Earl Cawdor, convened a meeting in the Shire Hall, Haverfordwest, to 'consider the arrangements to be made for the erection of a memorial to Pembrokeshire men who lost their lives in active service during the South African campaign'. With the meeting unanimously agreeing 'that such a memorial was desirable', Cawdor proceeded to 'invite ladies and gentlemen to join a committee' to oversee the work.[2]

In towns and cities, the civic authorities were usually the main inspirations behind war memorial schemes. However, in contrast to the frantic bout of civic memorial construction that took place following the Armistice in 1918, many civic communities in the aftermath of the South African War were content to either be subsumed by the county scheme or to leave the memorialisation of the fallen to the military authorities. Where a scheme was established, not infrequently the guiding hand of one or two particularly influential individuals with links to the military can be discerned. In Folkestone, the fact that Viscount Folkestone, the largest landowner in the locality, had served as a volunteer must have played an important part in the town council's decision to have 'a tablet placed in the town hall to commemorate the yeomen and volunteers from the borough who went to the Front'.[3] The impetus in Dover was provided by the town clerk, Sir Wollaston Knocker, who commanded the 1st volunteer battalion, The Buffs; in Wigan, Councillor Thomas Fyans, who 'had himself borne a part in the field of battle in honour of his country', was the moving force behind the town's memorial; while in Tonbridge, the organising committee included retired army tutor, John Le Fleming, who had been instrumental in establishing a volunteers corps in the town in 1859.[4]

Although the evidence suggests that in the vast majority of cases committees at civic and county level were self-forming and self-perpetuating cliques which made little or no attempt to seek genuine public affirmation, it was, nonetheless,

---

[2]   Pembrokeshire Record Office (PRO), HDX/94/1, *Booklet on the Pembrokeshire South African War Memorial*, 1908, p. 2.
[3]   *Folkestone Express*, 23 April 1904. Indeed, Viscount Folkestone's name, who on the death of his father had become Lord Radnor, appears at the head of the roll of honour.
[4]   East Kent Archives (EKA), Do/CA17/1/17, South African Memorial Committee, minutes, 6 May 1904; *Wigan Examiner*, 11 February 1903; *Tonbridge Free Press*, 15 April 1904; A. H. Neve, *The Tonbridge of Yesterday* (Tonbridge: Tonbridge Free Press, 1933), p. 195.

not uncommon for committee members, aware that reciprocal bonds of duty and loyalty were based on nothing more than location, to look to validate their authority through the calling of a public meeting. However, even when it was felt necessary to make this nod towards democratisation, it was, almost without fail, no more than that. Although the committees which oversaw the construction of the Kent, Leicestershire and Bedfordshire county memorials were nominally elected at public meetings, these were, to all intents and purposes, self-selecting groups. For Earl Stanhope, the Lord Lieutenant of Kent, who presided over the open meeting at Maidstone Town Hall to discuss the county proposals, service appeared to be simply a matter of aristocratic duty rather than the result of any public mandate. Although the gathering was held with 'the object of electing a large and representative committee', no vote was taken and the nominal purpose of the afternoon's business was only achieved at the end of proceedings when a select list of 'noblemen and gentlemen desired that their names be placed on the committee'.[5] The unchallenged right of the county elite to assume control was equally evident in Leicestershire. The initial public meeting at the County Rooms in Leicester on 3 January 1903, convened by the Marquess of Granby, the Lord Lieutenant, was immediately followed by the inaugural meeting of the memorial committee, the members of which had been pre-selected from a list of leading military and civic figures. Unsurprisingly, the first action of the committee was to elect Granby to the chair.[6] The careful choreographing of public debate also attended the open consultation for the Bedfordshire scheme. Chaired by the Lord Lieutenant of Bedfordshire, Earl Cowper, on 10 July 1902, the meeting was immediately faced with a resolution from Cowper's deputy, the Duke of Bedford, that 'the whole matter [of a county memorial] be placed in the hands of a committee'. With the resolution duly passed, the usual array of civic leaders, politicians and local dignitaries were co-opted to serve on the committee and further discussion was restricted exclusively to methods for raising funds.[7] Occasionally, the veneer of public consultation was abandoned completely and the whole matter remained the preserve of municipal officials. Exeter's memorial scheme was initiated by the estates committee of the city council, the form was chosen at a full meeting of the councillors and the £30 costs was defrayed from the local rates. Even the unveiling of the commemorative

[5] Royal West Kent Regiment Archives, *Queen's Own Gazette*, Vol. XX, No. 6 (June 1902), p. 1759
[6] Leicester and Rutland Record Office (LRRO), DE171, The Leicestershire South African War Memorial Committee, minutes, 12 January 1903.
[7] Bedfordshire and Luton Archives (BLA), L/c/Cha, Bedford County Lieutenancy, county meeting, minutes, 10 July 1902.

plaque remained in-house, with the ceremony in the Guildhall on 22 February 1905 organised and orchestrated by the council alone.[8]

It was not only the management of these public meetings but their timing that invariably put the lie to any claims about open consultation. In all three county cases cited above the meetings were held on weekday afternoons, thus precluding attendance by those without the time, influence or money to leave work early. The Earl of Carlisle went one step further in placing obstacles in the path of those who wished to attend the public meeting to consider proposals for the Yorkshire county memorial. Not only was the meeting held on a Thursday afternoon but it took place in London. Unsurprisingly, the list of those present was restricted to the great and good of the county.[9] In the small Scottish town of Alyth, fifteen miles north of Dundee, Provost Johnston's choice of Thursday afternoon as the best time to hold an open consultation on how to commemorate the three local men who had died in the war, one of whom was the Earl of Airlie, the local laird, resulted in an attendance of just twelve. Despite this disappointing turnout, and a suggestion from the town clerk that no final decision should be reached until more views had been canvassed, a resolution fixing both the form and location of the memorial was passed and 'most of those present were appointed to the committee'.[10]

In the London borough of Islington, one resident, A. T. Gould, used the apparent lack of openness in consultation to launch a strident attack on the memorial committee's management in general. In a bad tempered letter to the *Islington Daily Gazette* he implied that a deep schism had grown up between leaders and led, claiming that the initial public meeting to explain the war memorial committee's ideas was a sham as it 'seemed simply to consist of a specially selected and favoured few', particularly as it started at 5 p.m., a time which excluded 'masters and men' still at work and suitable only for 'drones'. He went on to urge the funding of a practical scheme such as a hospital which would be especially useful to poorer people and cited examples in Scotland. The best service of the memory of the dead was by 'sustaining the helpless ones some of our men have left behind'.[11] The editorial of the *Islington Daily Gazette* gently mocked Gould's suggestions for their over-ambitious nature reminding readers of the great costs involved in establishing a hospital. However, this slightly facetious attitude misunderstood Gould's commitment and passion, which was shown most forcefully at the next public meeting. After listening to the opening

---

[8]   Devon Record Office (DRO), ECA 12/20, Exeter City Council Estates Committee Reports, 1894–1906, pp. 277, 282, 285, 289, 291, 313, 320, 344.

[9]   Meurig Jones, 'The Yorkshire County Memorial: A History of the Yorkshire County Memorial, York, for the Second Anglo-Boer War, 1899–1902', *York Historian*, 12 (1995), pp. 63–64.

[10]   *Dundee Courier and Argus*, 19 July 1900.

[11]   *Islington Daily Gazette*, 13 October 1903.

I Islington Memorial,
Highbury Fields.

remarks, Gould returned to his agenda and pointedly stated his desire 'that the movement should be made as democratic as possible, and representatives of the working classes added to the committee'. Wishing to at least appear inclusive, Gould was duly elected to the committee. Howell Williams, one of Islington's representatives on the London County Council, seemed to support Gould's sentiments for he called upon them to endow a nursing home or medical centre. Distinct tensions then erupted when Gould passed a written resolution to the mayor which he asked him to read. The mayor declined to do so stating that he did not wish the meeting to descend into discord. Gould pressed his case and asked bluntly, 'Will you read the resolution?', to which the mayor equally bluntly replied, 'No, I will not, for if I do, you will have the satisfaction of getting what you desire', which brought forth applause from the floor.[12] Left with the sense that he was being branded a politically motivated agitator, Gould sent his resolution to the *Islington Daily Gazette*:

> This meeting suggests to the committee that the best method of perpetuating the memory of Islingtonians who lost their lives through the war in South

---

[12]   *Islington Daily Gazette*, 14 October 1903.

Africa is to establish a permanent fund with the object of assisting the most necessitous cases among the widows and orphans created by the late lamentable war, and that (memorial) tablets be placed inside and outside public buildings.[13]

'I have read and read this resolution', he added, 'and I positively cannot see anything political in it'. However, he then placed himself within a particular socio-political context, albeit perhaps subconsciously, by concluding that his position was 'that of every workman ... so I cannot but regret that the mayor refused an opportunity to the meeting to decide for or against my proposal'.[14] Accusations of political motivation were clearly regarded as extremely grave insults in relation to memorial activity. Significantly, neither side in the dispute saw themselves as acting in a political manner and were at least claiming to be oblivious to the underlying implications of their positions.

Not only were such rifts viewed as a slight on the memory of the fallen but they were also seen as an affront to civic prestige. For many communities the decision to persevere with the construction of a remembrance site to the conflict in South Africa was underpinned by a strong sense of collective pride. Although the justness of Britain's involvement in the war had not been, by any means, universally accepted at the outbreak of hostilities, the military reverses of what became known as 'Black Week' in December 1899 had resulted in a rush of volunteers to the colours.[15] Over 500 men joined the 1st volunteer battalion of The Queen's Own Royal West Kents in 1900 and, later the same year, there were sufficient new recruits for an additional company to be formed in the regiment's 2nd volunteer battalion.[16] Leaders of civic remembrance projects were keen to celebrate this display of patriotic devotion by their communities' members and, thus, frequently stressed the voluntary nature of service. Dover's notables not only determined to erect a memorial plaque to those local men who had died in the war but 'to combine with it a Roll of Fame in honour of those who volunteered for service and on whom the Corporation conferred the Honorary Freedom of the Borough'.[17] In Folkestone, the town councils chose to exclude professional soldiers from their plans and commemorate only those local men who had volunteered for the war, making no differentiation between those who died and those who returned.[18] At a public meeting in Salford town

---

[13] *Islington Daily Gazette*, 15 October 1903.
[14] *Islington Daily Gazette*, 15 October 1903.
[15] Will Bennett, *Absent-Minded Beggars: The Volunteers in the Boer War* (Barnsley: Leo Cooper, 1999), pp. 9–18.
[16] H. D. Chaplin, *The Queen's Own Royal West Kent Regiment* (Maidstone: Queen's Own Regimental History, 1959), p. 108.
[17] EKA, DoCA17/1/17, South African War Memorial Committee, minutes, 6 May 1904.
[18] *Folkestone Express*, 23 April 1904. Catherine Moriarty has noted that the tendency to privilege the sacrifice of volunteers ahead of regulars continued into the Great War. One

hall on 17 September 1902, the mayor, Samuel Rudman, insisting that 'Salford should be exceedingly proud that she had put forward her quota of men', was similarly inclined to restrict the roll of honour to the 119 Salfordians who had volunteered.[19] It was only when the Conservative MP for Salford South, James Grimble Groves, gently reminded those present that it was both regulars and volunteers who had 'represented the town of Salford so nobly in the late war' that an amendment to extend the scope of the scheme to include 'all Salford men who have fought for the King and country' was accepted.[20]

Civic pride continued to inform the memorialisation process in Salford as the scheme worked its way towards completion. With the King and Queen due to visit Manchester to open a new dock in the Manchester Ship Canal, Salford's civic leaders were eager that the unveiling of the town's war memorial should be included on the itinerary. The editor of the *Salford Chronicle* neatly captured the sense of civic rivalry (and civic inferiority) that now suffused events when reporting that the initial approach by the memorial committee had been rebuffed: 'In consonance with their ordinary custom and the general treatment meted out to Salford by Manchester in connection with such events as these, the city authorities entirely ignored the existence of the borough'.[21] However, a second delegation to the King's private secretary, Lord Knollys, met with more success and although the royal visit on 13 July 1905 lasted no more than six minutes, during which time neither the King nor the Queen stepped out of their carriage, this was enough for the unveiling to be transformed into day of civic rejoicing, with 45,000 schoolchildren being given a souvenir mug and 3,500 over-sixty-fives provided with a celebratory meal.[22] For Salford, the construction of what was its first major outdoor war memorial was a prime opportunity to assert its civic identity. Having been granted county borough status by the Local Government Act of 1888, and with a population approaching quarter of a million by the turn of the century, the town's civic leaders had

---

reason she suggests for this is that death for the professional soldier was frequently regarded as no more than an 'occupational hazard'. Moriarty, 'Christian Iconography and First World War Memorials', *Imperial War Museum Review*, 6 (1991), p. 65.

[19] *Salford Reporter*, 20 September 1902. Once again the public meeting was held on a weekday afternoon (this time a Wednesday) and once again the committee was almost entirely composed of civic dignitaries.

[20] *Salford Chronicle*, 20 September 1902. Despite the acceptance of Groves's amendment, the inscription on the memorial still privileged the contribution of the volunteers. It reads: 'Erected by the county borough of Salford to the many townsmen who served their sovereign and country in South Africa 1899–1902 and particularly in honour of the volunteer active service companies of the Lancashire Fusiliers: daring in all things'.

[21] *Salford Chronicle*, 15 July 1905.

[22] *Salford Reporter*, 15 July 1905; T. Wyke, *The Public Sculpture of Greater Manchester* (Liverpool: Liverpool University Press, 2004), p. 176.

seized on the chance presented by the sacrifice of its citizen-soldiers to emerge from the shadow of neighbouring Manchester.[23]

Pride in the sacrifice of local volunteers also played a part in initiating commemorative activity in Halifax. Prompted by the return of the volunteers of the 1st battalion, the West Riding regiment, on 18 June 1902, the *Halifax Courier* reminded its readers in the very next edition that over forty men 'lie buried 'neath the veldt in that far off clime, their graves marked by crude monuments erected by sorrowing comrades' and urged the authorities to construct 'something permanent at home … to show [the fallen] some honour'.[24] Yet, once again, civic rivalry was to the fore. Under the sub-heading 'What other towns have done', the article concluded by archly observing 'how promptly and nobly our neighbours at Elland have recognised that they have a duty to fallen townsmen. Contrast this with the loss Halifax has sustained – 2 sons to our 31'. Across the border in Lancashire, the mayor of Rochdale used a similar argument to justify the town's decision to embark on a memorial scheme over three years after the war had ended. It was, he explained to those present at the unveiling in June 1907, only after his appointment as mayor two years earlier that the council was persuaded 'that Rochdale should not be behind other towns in commemorating the services of the citizens in South Africa'.[25]

Occasionally it was the local press that led the way in ensuring that civic prestige was maintained by initiating commemorative schemes. This was the case in Birmingham, Nuneaton and Middlesbrough where the memorial movements were established and sustained by the *Birmingham Daily Mail*, the *Midland Counties Tribune* and the *North East Daily Gazette* respectively.[26] During the course of the war, provincial newspapers had been keen to distinguish themselves from the national press and, in the process, sustain interest in lengthy and often uneventful campaigns, by printing letters from serving soldiers with local connections. Thus, having championed local pride in volunteerism during the conflict, it was hardly surprising that, in the immediate aftermath of the fighting, some editors thought it only right that they should continue to take the lead in honouring the sacrifices of local men who had served.[27]

A civic war memorial was not only a site of collective tribute but also a key symbol of community worth. The civic leaders of both Alyth and Ely were anxious that their commemorative projects should not be subsumed by larger

---

[23]   Tom Bergin, *Salford: A City and its Past* (Salford: City of Salford Cultural Services Department, 1975).

[24]   *Halifax Courier*, 21 June 1902.

[25]   *Rochdale Observer*, 6 June 1907.

[26]   J. Gildea, *For Remembrance and in Honour of Those Who Lost Their Lives in the South African War, 1899–1902* (London: Eyre and Spottiswoode Ltd, 1912), pp. 217, 220, 245.

[27]   Edward M. Spiers, *The Victorian Soldier in Africa* (Manchester: Manchester University Press, 2004), p. 8.

regional schemes. In Alyth, the death of the local laird, the Earl of Airlie, at the battle of Diamond Hill on 11 June 1900, triggered the authorities to act. Eager to claim the Earl as one of their own, and concerned that a competing plan had already been launched in neighbouring Kirriemuir, where Airlie was a major landholder, a hastily convened meeting in Alyth town hall overruled the suggestion that 'no memorial should be gone on with until after the war ... as the fighting might claim more victims', and resolved to press ahead with the construction of a commemorative obelisk in Market Square immediately.[28] With the unveiling taking place in July 1901, a full ten months before the signing of the Peace of Vereeniging, the editor of the *Alyth Guardian* felt it necessary to explain to his readers, in terms redolent with civic pride, why the town required its own memory site. It was, he wrote, because 'Alyth had suffered in so special a manner from the South African war that, instead of joining with neighbouring communities in commemorating the fallen it was fitting it should have a local monument to commemorate its own gallant dead'.[29]

In Ely, the recent redrawing of bureaucratic boundaries invested the memorial project with even more significance. Initially designated to be part of the Suffolk regiment and county memorial scheme, which included Cambridgeshire, a traditional recruiting ground for the Suffolks, the administrative county of Ely appeared to be under threat of being overshadowed by its more populous neighbours. This threat became a reality when the memorial committee, chaired by the Marquess of Bristol, the Lord Lieutenant of Suffolk, proposed that there should be three memorials located in the county towns of the three administrative counties of Cambridgeshire, East Suffolk and West Suffolk.[30] Having only had its incorporation into Cambridgeshire following the local government reforms of 1888 revoked as a result of last minute intervention by Charles Selwyn, MP for Wisbech, Ely's leaders moved quickly to rectify this apparent slight to its independence.[31] At its very next meeting, the members of the county committee were presented with a petition declaring that it was 'the unanimous wish of the subscribers of Ely' that a separate memorial to 'the men of the Isle of Ely' be erected in Ely Cathedral. The committee acquiesced and £50 was apportioned from the collective funds.[32]

---

[28] *Dundee Courier and Argus*, 19 July 1900.

[29] *Alyth Guardian*, 9 August 1901. Fortunately for the civic authorities of Alyth, the Earl of Airlie and the two other men commemorated on the monument in Market Square remained the total war deaths suffered by the town.

[30] Although Ipswich was the headquarters of the administrative county of East Suffolk, it was, by the terms of the 1888 Act, a county borough in its own right. As will be seen, this was to cause some tension.

[31] *Victoria History of the County of Cambridge and the Isle of Ely, Volume IV* (London: Institute of Historical Research, 1953), p. 27.

[32] *Bury Free Press*, 12 November 1904.

Similar tensions held back Ipswich's participation in the Suffolk scheme, although this time it was the decision to site a memorial in the town that caused the difficulties. Serving as the administrative headquarters of the newly formed county of East Suffolk, Ipswich was, by the terms of the 1888 Act, also a county borough in its own right. That this was more than just a bureaucratic nicety can be discerned in the protracted negotiations over a suitable location for the memorial that took place between Captain J. Mayne, the chief constable of East Suffolk and honorary secretary of the county memorial committee, and Ipswich town council. Rejecting the council's opening offer of a position on the edge of the market as 'too restricted', Mayne requested a prime site abutting the town hall. Aware that this may involve a reconfiguration of existing street furniture, he looked to play up the bonds of common identity by noting that, 'in the list of Suffolk soldiers who died in the war there are a number whose native place was Ipswich'.[33] Apparently impervious to such tactics, the council's use of the personal pronoun when proposing an alternative site was telling of its lack of any sense of ownership of the project. The council could, Mayne was informed in a letter from the town clerk, 'offer a site near the entrance of Christchurch Park instead in which the statue to her late Majesty Queen Victoria will shortly be erected, and *your* memorial would be largely seen there by many visitors'.[34] As discussions rumbled on, the failure to find an acceptable compromise threatened to undermine the whole scheme. It was not, in fact, until June 1906, over two years after Mayne's initial approach, that an attempt to politicise the issue finally prompted the town council to arrive at a solution. Emboldened by his colleagues' continued intransigence during a debate in the council chamber to discuss an alternative site in the Cornhill, Councillor J. W. Christie, chairman of the Westgate Ward Liberal Club, seized on the moment to make a wider political point about the war in general. 'In his opinion', he told his fellow councillors, 'the less that was said about the war in connection with which this memorial was to be, the better. That war was not to the credit of the nation. Gentleman might cry "oh" but those with whom it was waged had now become our compatriots, and a monument should not be put up to commemorate it'. This move to open up old wounds seems to have been just the jolt the Conservative dominated council needed. With the collapse of the scheme now a distinct possibility, the mayor, Blundell Henry Burton, called for an immediate vote on the proposed site to be taken and the resolution was passed, with only Christie in opposition.[35]

---

[33]   Suffolk Records Office (SRO), 352.1409/Ips, Ipswich town council minutes, 22 June 1904, p. 102.
[34]   SRO, 352.1409/Ips, Ipswich town council minutes, 22 June 1904, p. 102 (emphasis in original).
[35]   SRO, 352.1409/Ips, Ipswich town council minutes, 20 June 1906, p. 109; *Suffolk County Handbook, 1906* (Ipswich: East Anglia Daily News, 1906).

Clearly, if a memorialisation project was to be a success, and if expectations about civic prestige were to be met, then it was essential for significant funds to be raised. In contrast to schemes in workplaces and religious institutions, it was much more common for memorials at civic level, where the bonds of association were looser and any sense of belonging was simply based on residence rather than a shared profession or faith, to be financed by public subscription. More often than not, funds were raised in the traditional manner: appeals in the local press, house to house collections, military concerts and a variety of other charitable entertainments. Subscription lists were regularly published in local newspapers with eminent citizens leading the way with substantial donations. Typical is the example of the Suffolk regiment and county memorial where the Marquis of Bristol, the Lord Lieutenant of the county, Sir Cuthbert Quiller, MP for Sudbury, and Lord Cardogan, whose seat was Culford Park outside Bury St Edmunds, opened the fund with a donation of fifty guineas each.[36] Implicit in such donations, and in the publication of subscribers' names in the local press, was the message that it was the responsibility of all citizens to match such charitable acts if not such extravagant amounts. In Halifax, the editor of the *Halifax Courier* ensured that the paper's readers were left in no doubt exactly where their duty lay. Not content with simply publishing the first subscription list, headed by the mayor with a £10 donation, readers' consciences were pricked further with a letter from a bereaved mother thanking those who had already given for their kindness and an article, under the heading 'A Little Child's Help', recounting how a four-year-old boy had collected 10s 4d.[37] Such shameless appeals to sentiment clearly worked and, by the time of the unveiling, the committee's original target of £1,000 had been surpassed.[38]

However, notwithstanding the support received from leading citizens and the editors of local newspapers, by no means all memorialisation projects met their financial goals. Successfully raising subscriptions for memorial schemes depended in part on making a clear appeal to the relevant community based on an equally clear objective. Subscribers wanted to know what they were contributing towards and delays either in deciding a final form or in explaining it to the public often caused difficulties for fund-raisers. The civic projects of Dover, Islington and Rochdale reveal this problem most fully.

Having already tested the charitable reserves of the local populace with public appeals to finance the South African War Fund in January 1900 and the Queen Victoria memorial project in June of the following year, Dover's civic dignitaries managed to compound the financial difficulties facing what was the port's third publicly funded scheme in four years by adopting an approach which was, at one and the same time, precise in its financial ambition and vague

---

[36]　*Bury Free Press*, 12 November 1904.
[37]　*Halifax Courier*, 21 June 1902.
[38]　*Halifax Courier*, 12 November 1904.

in its conceptual realisation.[39] The press release for the launch of the scheme best illustrates this point: 'It is the intention of the civic authorities to raise an indoor memorial in St Mary's Church, at a cost of £200, and an outdoor monument, at upwards of £300, to the memory of the men who fell in the recent war in South Africa. The type of memorials will depend on the amount of money raised and the wishes of the subscribers'.[40] Dovorians were being asked to contribute to two costly schemes while being given no indication of the final form either would take. Predictably, the appeal did not elicit an enthusiastic response and it was not until nearly a decade after the war had finished, by which time financial shortfall had resulted in the outdoor monument being abandoned, that a commemorative tablet in St Mary's Church was unveiled.[41] Reviewing the debacle of the memorial's lengthy gestation for his readers on the day of the unveiling ceremony, the editor of the *Dover Express* was of the opinion that the port had ended up with little more than a civic white elephant. Insisting that 'the very undesirable and unexplained delay in completing the memorial' had undermined any didactic purpose that the memory site might once have had, he was adamant that, 'as to the younger generation the South African War is entirely a matter of history, they have no personal recollection of the time of stress through which this country passed and the grave defects that it revealed in our Army'.[42]

Islington left its appeal until the summer of 1903, which caused some to doubt whether the scheme was already doomed. An editorial in the *Islington Daily Gazette* bemoaned the fact that the mayor's call to action was too late, and many

[39] EKA, DoCa/10/5/7, South African War Fund Committee, minutes 13 November 1899; EKA, Do/AMS/3, Queen Victoria Memorial Committee, minutes, 19 June 1901. Lord Stanhope, the chairman of the public meeting held to discuss moves for a county relief fund and memorial scheme, made plain just how real the danger of donor fatigue was when he told those assembled at Maidstone Town Hall that 'he had no doubt there would be a large fund in time, even though it was the year of the Coronation and there were funds for bonfires and feedings and all kinds of rejoicing'. *Queen's Own Gazette*, Vol. XX, No. 6 (June 1902), p. 1760.
[40] EKA, Do/CA17/1/17, South African Memorial Committee, minutes, 6 May 1904
[41] Although financial difficulties clearly played a part in the extraordinary delay in the completion of Dover's memorial scheme, one can't help thinking that there must have been more to it. One possible explanation may lie in the competing demands on hard-pressed civic officials' time. Certainly Alderman Mowll, the mayor of Dover, was quick to present this excuse for the late launch of the scheme. In a letter to the editor of the *Dover Express*, he explained that the delay had come about 'because the Proclamation of Peace had been followed by the serious illness of the King, his own ill-health, the welcoming home of the troops and other duties which had made it impossible at that time to consider the matter'. *Dover Express*, 13 May 1904. This, of course, doesn't explain why it took another eight years before the memorial was ready to be unveiled and here the records hold no clue.
[42] *Dover Express*, 19 April 1912.

had now shamefully forgotten the sacrifice made by their fellow Islingtonians.[43] When the fund was launched in September it met with a desultory response, which was hardly surprising given the lack of advanced publicity over the public meeting, the subsequent controversy over the composition of the committee and the complete lack of any public announcement as to the precise nature of the scheme. In effect, the Islington war memorial committee asked people to subscribe to nothing and expected them to continue doing so. As has been noted, the committee then made no formal decision until the spring of 1905 and only exhibited a sketch of the memorial in May 1905, just two months before the unveiling.[44] Inevitably, the local newspaper carried many comments on the very slow progress of the memorial fund. The target was vaguely set at between £700 and £800, and this was thought easily achievable with a population of 345,000, but only £370 was collected by October 1903.[45] For this reason, the *Islington Daily Gazette* and the memorial committee thought it was absolutely vital to get the support of the borough's businessmen and major employers, and indeed the timing of the public meetings was set with a deliberate eye to avoid business hours.[46] The onus was on the leading citizens of Islington to make a public statement of commitment and an early subscriptions list shows contributions from fifty-six individuals including one clergymen and three JPs; seven businesses also contributed communal amounts and others acted as groups including the employees of the council's bathhouses and a sports club.[47] Fearful that the working classes of Islington were uninterested in the project, both the mayor and local MP stressed the cross-class nature of the appeal and urged all to contribute according to their ability.[48] Thus, regardless of protestations of apolitical status, the memorial scheme was inherently bound up in local (and national) forces of class and political consciousness. Confusion continued to reign, however, with little done to confirm a target amount or form until the sum of £1,000 was finally announced in January 1905 well over a year later.[49] 'Merrie Villager', the author of the 'Islington Bells' column in the *Islington Daily Gazette*, commented mournfully: 'My little collection for the Memorial to Islington's Dead Braves still goes on, but so slowly that it almost discourages me, and makes me think unkind things of a great patriotic community that so easily forgets the brave deeds of her sons and brothers'.[50] With little clarity emerging from the committee, the collection inched forward reaching £728 in

---

43   *Islington Daily Gazette*, 7 July 1903.
44   *Islington Daily Gazette*, 17 May 1905.
45   *Islington Daily Gazette*, 7, 14 October 1903.
46   *Islington Daily Gazette*, 1, 7 October 1903.
47   *Islington Daily Gazette*, 4 September 1903.
48   *Islington Daily Gazette*, 14 October 1903.
49   *Islington Daily Gazette*, 4 January 1905.
50   *Islington Daily Gazette*, 17 September 1903.

July 1905. In order to reinvigorate the scheme, a children's fund was established in May 1905 with a target of £50 or 1,000 three-penny pieces. The *Islington Daily Gazette* printed the proud letter of Master T. W. Saint who enclosed eighteen three-penny pieces on behalf of himself and his eight brothers and sisters.[51] By July 814 three-pennies had been collected, which prompted a Miss Tice to note: 'I am surprised at the children of Islington not showing a more patriotic spirit'.[52] It is not known whether the final target was reached. On the eve of the unveiling the editorial of the *Islington Daily Gazette* reflected on the evolution of the scheme. The problem of commencing late was acknowledged, but the committee were then praised for persisting and conquering all difficulties; at the same time, 'for the small section of Islingtonians who try to throw discredit upon the Memorial we have the utmost contempt'.[53] Clearly, the passage to the memorial had been anything but smooth.

As we have already seen, Rochdale was even later in initiating its remembrance plans with the first appeal for subscriptions not made until a public meeting on 21 November 1906.[54] Again, as one might expect, local residents were disinclined to contribute towards a memorial commemorating a war that had finished more than five years ago and by the time of the unveiling in June 1907 only £325 had been collected.[55] Yet, for the civic leaders, of even greater concern than the meagre sum raised was the paucity of actual donors. More than half the total had come from just five subscribers with a further 135 subscriptions accounting for all but forty pounds of the remainder; this from a total population of 120,433.[56] At the unveiling ceremony such manifest evidence of public disengagement threatened to reignite bitter political infighting. Thanking Brigadier-General Fry, commanding officer of the Lancashire grouped districts, for officiating, the chairman of the memorial committee and, until 1906, Liberal Unionist MP for neighbouring Heywood, Colonel George Kemp, chose to eschew conventional pleasantries and instead called into question the loyalty of the local populace:

> The memorial committee hoped to have had a stone cross, pillar or monument erected in some public place in memory of those who had fallen, so that all people might see it from every side. To accomplish this no effort was spared. At private houses, in factories and workshops, and every place the appeal was made known, and the committee hoped that a generous response would be made to it. I am ashamed to say that no response in any degree worthy of the

51 *Islington Daily Gazette*, 17 May 1905.
52 *Islington Daily Gazette*, 14 July 1905.
53 *Islington Daily Gazette*, 14 July 1905.
54 *Rochdale Observer*, 25 November 1906.
55 *Rochdale Observer*, 6 June 1907.
56 *Rochdale Observer*, 6 June 1907; for population figure, see *Victoria County History of Lancashire, Volume V* (London: Institute of Historical Research, 1911), p. 188.

occasion was made to that appeal. Had it not been for the determination and support of the mayor they would not even have had that tablet to show their gratitude to those who had laid down their lives for the county. I maintain therefore that it is a sad day … because it is not the amount they want, but that everyone should show in some way that they cared for that patriotism.[57]

This attack received a barbed response from Rochdale's Liberal MP, Gordon Harvey. From the radical wing of the party, Harvey had fought and only narrowly lost the 1900 Khaki election on an anti-war platform, and in the process had seen his Conservative opponent's majority reduced from 1,463 to just nineteen votes.[58] Reluctant to now allow support for the war to become a litmus test for patriotism, he reminded Kemp, when seconding the vote of thanks to Fry, that, 'there were many people in Rochdale who, although they may not have subscribed to the memorial, had an affectionate regard for the men who had served their country'.[59] Harvey's views were echoed in the *Rochdale Observer*'s coverage of the unveiling ceremony. Forefronting the fact that Kemp had spoken 'strongly about the small support given to the memorial by the townspeople', the paper left its readers in no doubt which side in the Liberal rift it supported:

> It is a fact that more than half the total of the sum subscribed was given by five individuals, and that the plans of the memorial committee had to be curtailed because of lack of support. The gossips are saying that this is a reflection on the 'Pro-Boers'. But there are enough imperialists and 'patriots' in Rochdale to raise ten times £325, if their hearts were really stirred. It should be borne in mind that before the fund was opened, £5,666 was subscribed by the townspeople for the relief of the families of men at the Front. As was said in Wednesday's *Observer*, whatever additional sum had been required for that object would have been raised without difficulty … It is undoubtedly true that some held aloof because of the belief that the war could have been prevented, and the feeling that if there was to be a monument it should be one to the folly and incapacity which led to such woeful sacrifice of life and treasure.[60]

In Rochdale then the failure to raise an acceptable sum, the primary cause of which was most likely the delay in launching the scheme, created sufficient tension for the act of subscribing to the memorial to be viewed as a political statement. In order to avoid this politicisation of commemorative work, civic dignitaries were frequently keen to stress that their work crossed class boundaries.

---

[57] *Rochdale Observer*, 6 June 1907; John Cole, *Rochdale Revisited: A Town and its People, Volume II* (Littleborough: George Kelsall, 1990), p. 30
[58] Paul Laity, *The British Peace Movement, 1870–1914* (Oxford, Oxford University Press, 2002), p. 183.
[59] *Rochdale Observer*, 6 June 1907.
[60] *Rochdale Observer*, 6 June 1907.

By 1902 Britain was a nation increasingly aware of the middle and working classes. Indeed, as already mention, the South African War can be seen to have been a key moment of transition for these classes. With tens of thousands of men volunteering for active service between 1899 and 1902, the war had, in many ways, served to legitimise claims for greater political representation. Yet, at the same time, the British people remained acutely sensitive to hierarchical boundaries and largely accepting of the rigid stratification of society. Both these phenomena played a part in a political scenario in which increasing uncertainty and creeping democracy created ever greater sensitivity to the issue of class.[61] As the debacle over funding has already intimated, this evolving tension was felt very keenly in the borough of Islington. By 1901 the population of Islington stood at 335,238 making it one of the most populous of the London boroughs.[62] At a parliamentary level the borough was represented by a Conservative MP, but the borough was declining in terms of its residential complexion.[63] Once a smart and wealthy London suburb, the affluent areas had retreated to pockets around Highbury and Canonbury.[64] Nonconformity was strong in the borough, which had created some tensions during the war as many Nonconformist ministers and congregations had remained unconvinced by Britain's cause.[65] The editor of the *Islington Daily Gazette* was therefore particularly keen to support the mayor's insistence that the memorial was for 'all classes' and implied that the bulk of the troops had come from the working and lower middle classes, stating the scheme should be 'as interesting to the humbler citizens from which our soldiers sprang as to the leaders of our social life'.[66]

By appealing to all classes, memorial committees were also seeking to foster a sense of collective ownership in commemorative activity. If a memory site was to have any resonance within a community, and if it was to function successfully as a symbol of civic worth, it was vital that all citizens felt some engagement with the process of construction. The members of the Bedfordshire memorial committee attempted to draw in all sections of society.

---

[61] See Jose Harris, *Private Lives, Public Spirit: A Social History of Britain, 1870–1914* (Oxford: Oxford University Press, 1993), pp. 194–195; P. Thompson, *Socialists, Liberals and Labour: The Struggle for London, 1885–1914* (London: Routledge and Kegan Paul, 1967), pp. 5–16.

[62] *Victoria County History of Middlesex, Volume VIII* (Oxford: Oxford University Press, 1985), p. 13.

[63] Mary Cash, *A History of Islington* (London: Historical Publications Ltd, 2005), pp. 325–329.

[64] *Victoria County History of Middlesex*, p. 11.

[65] *Victoria County History of Middlesex*, pp. 13, 101–115; Cash, *A History of Islington*, pp. 235–249. See reports in *Islington Daily Gazette*, 10 June 1902 for the reaction of Nonconformist communities to the war. For a wider discussion of Nonconformity and the South African War see Alan Wilkinson, *The Church of England and the First World War* (London: SPCK, 1978), pp. 10–11, 16, 30, 176, 202, 295.

[66] *Islington Daily Gazette*, 13 October 1903.

The press release giving notification of the initial public meeting stressed that 'the attendance of all classes is invited', although the choice of a Thursday afternoon somewhat undermined the sincerity of this invitation, while the deputy-chairman of the committee, the Duke of Bedford, was insistent that, 'opportunity should be given for all classes to contribute in order that the memorial may be representative of the whole county'.[67] In Yorkshire, the act of giving was thought to be as important as the amount given. Concerned that a few wealthy donors would account for a large percentage of the final total, the county memorial committee initially decided to impose a ceiling of £10 on subscriptions. Although the cap was lifted when a £2,000 shortfall on the original target of £3,500 was discovered in 1902, the original resolution does, nevertheless, reveal the proprietorial sub-text that many members of organising committees felt underpinned fund-raising.[68] Further evidence of this can be found in the frequency with which inscriptions on civic memorials proclaimed the fact that sites were 'erected by public subscription'. Even in Rochdale, where, as we have already seen, the public's failure to subscribe caused something of a scandal, this formula was used to impute collective ownership.[69] At the other extreme, Darlington's civic authorities were evidently eager to celebrate just how far the town's memorial was genuinely the product of a communal effort by having engraved on the pedestal of its figurative monument the fact that it 'was erected by 5,576 subscribers'.[70] What was implicit in these inscriptions was made explicit by Lord Cawdor at the dedication ceremony for Pembrokeshire's memorial. He told those assembled that just as the war had been a collective enterprise, in which 'men of every rank and class gave their lives ungrudgingly', so the Celtic cross they had just seen unveiled belonged to all for 'it had been contributed to by all classes throughout the county'.[71]

Reinforcing claims of collective ownership were the lists of the names of the fallen that appeared on memorials. No longer were these rolls of honour dominated by an aristocratic officer corps but, instead, all who had served, irrespective of rank, were honoured. This democratisation of naming provided a further link between the memory site and the community which it served. The insistence of the members of the Suffolk regiment and county memorial committee at their very first meeting that each of the four memory sites in

---

[67] BLA, L/c/Cha3, Bedfordshire Lieutenancy, Notice of Public Meeting, 10 July 1902; letter from Duke of Bedford to honorary secretary of Bedfordshire county memorial committee, 27 November 1902.

[68] Jones, 'The Yorkshire County Memorial', p. 66. Despite the memorial committee's attempt to encourage subscriptions from all classes through the imposition of a financial cap, only 231 people contributed to the scheme. This for a memorial with 1,490 names of the fallen inscribed on it. *Yorkshire Evening Post*, 3 August 1908.

[69] See pp. 24–25 above.

[70] Gildea, *For Remembrance*, p. 49.

[71] PRO, HDX/94/1, *Booklet on the Pembrokeshire South African War Memorial*, 1908, p. 4.

Ipswich, Bury St Edmunds, Cambridge and Ely must include the names of the fallen was replicated across the country.[72] Without exception, rolls of honour formed an integral part of civic memorialisation schemes. Indeed, the importance which civic leaders attached to naming can be seen in the meticulous steps taken by memorial committees to guarantee the accurate and comprehensive compilation of lists of the fallen. In Halifax, the bereaved were required to send in documentation from the War Office to support any request for the inclusion of a loved one on the borough's roll of honour.[73] More typical was the approach adopted in Buckinghamshire where the memorial committee utilised a range of local agencies, from parish councils to the headquarters of the county's regiments, to verify the list of fallen for inclusion on the county monument on the summit of Coombe Hill, near Wendover.[74]

However, problems could arise when messages about ownership implicit in public subscriptions lists were not matched by inclusion on rolls of honour. The *Islington Daily Gazette* carried letters from subscribers aggrieved that a lost loved one was deemed ineligible for the memorial. One man wrote stating his doubts over the comprehensiveness of the official roll of honour, while a publican who raised £13 through events on his premises was extremely upset that his son was ruled a resident of Stoke Newington and therefore could not be added to the memorial.[75] On the eve of the unveiling the editorial of the local newspaper came back to this source of local strife and noted that some 'feel aggrieved that those whose names might have been recorded on the plinth have been overlooked', but defended the final decisions adding, 'the committee, however, have done their utmost to embrace the names of all who are justly entitled to the designation Islingtonians for the purposes of the Memorial'.[76] In Ilford a similar debate broke out as to whether men who were not resident in the borough but had served with units associated with it should be included, which was finally decided in favour of local residents only.[77] Although the members of the Bedfordshire county memorial committee arrived at an equally narrow definition of community, they singularly failed to make this clear to the county's residents. Having resolved at the first committee meeting that by Bedfordshire men they meant 'men serving in the Bedfordshire regiments (regular army, militia and volunteers), the yeomanry, and all other Bedfordshire men serving in HM forces', it was left until the day after the unveiling for the local paper to elucidate the parameters more precisely. The roll of honour

[72] *Bury Free Press*, 12 November 1904.
[73] *Halifax Courier*, 28 June 1902.
[74] *Slough Observer*, 9 July 1904.
[75] *Islington Daily Gazette*, 19 May 1904.
[76] *Islington Daily Gazette*, 14 July 1905.
[77] *Ilford Recorder*, 17 February 1905; Ilford Local History Library, Ilford Urban District Council, minutes, 1904–05, p. 103.

was shorter than originally anticipated, the readers of the *Bedfordshire Times and Independent* were informed, because, 'the terms of the resolution [at the first public meeting] admitted natives of Bedfordshire who served as soldiers in the war, and also others who fought in Bedfordshire contingents, but not soldiers who were merely associated with the county by residence at some time or other'.[78] Unsurprisingly, this clarification came too late in the day to appease everyone. Mr. E. F. Bell complained in the following week's paper that his nephew, Trooper J. D. K. Bell, an old boy of Bedford Grammar School, had been left off the memorial despite two of his peers being included. This was, Bell argued, 'to offer an affront and to do an injustice to those who have been passed over, and to cause pain to many to whom pain is no stranger'.[79]

Underscoring such complaints were the practical difficulties many memorial committees faced in delineating precisely the boundaries of community. This was particularly the case for county memorial schemes, where the inclusion of county regiments on what were generally regarded as civic sites often blurred the criteria for inclusion.[80] The insistence by Frank Green, the honorary secretary of the Yorkshire county memorial committee, that he was guided by attestation papers when adjudicating on eligibility for the roll of honour did not prevent a flurry of letters in the local press pointing out omissions. This is hardly surprising considering Green failed to state whether he was referring to the attesters' stated place of birth, residence or both.[81]

Occasionally, even those in charge of the projects seemed unsure of the exact definition of the community they were serving. At the inaugural meeting for the Kent county memorial in Maidstone town hall in June 1902, Major Cornwallis firmly placed the scheme within the confines of a clearly defined locality when he stated that the object of the project was to raise a 'memorial to the soldiers from the county who have fallen'. The Earl of Stanhope, in apparently supporting Cornwallis, managed, however, to muddy the waters by injecting a note of regional competition into proceedings. There were, he said, currently '3,203 Kentish men in South Africa' and although 'many of them might feel that the Royal West Kent regiment would be the first to command their interest, it would be impossible to leave out the other side of the county'.[82] Although Cornwallis's proposal was unanimously adopted by the meeting, a

---

[78] *Bedfordshire Times and Independent*, 3 June 1904.

[79] *Bedfordshire Times and Independent*, 10 June 1904.

[80] Typical was the formula used by the Leicestershire county memorial committee who resolved to erect a memorial to 'the fallen of the Leicestershire Regiment and Leicestershire men in other regiments'. LRRO, DE171, Leicestershire South African War Memorial Committee, minutes, 12 January 1903.

[81] Jones, 'The Yorkshire County Memorial', pp. 70–73.

[82] *Queen's Own Gazette*, Vol. XX, No. 6 (June 1902), p. 1759. Stanhope's use of 'Kentish' was in itself somewhat divisive. Traditionally, those born west of the River Medway were deemed to be 'Kentish men' while those from the east were 'Men of Kent'.

subsequent amendment that any surplus funds should be 'invested for the benefit of the county regiments' further confused matters.[83] With the scheme now split between a memory site based on residence and a practical fund centred on regimental affiliation, the precise constituency for the committee's work seemed less clear than ever. Despite public appeals for subscriptions stating that the memorial was to the memory of men from the county, the commemorative plaque which was unveiled in Rochester Cathedral in 1903 lists only the county regiments.[84] A similar sense of imprecision can be found in the construction of the county memorial in Newcastle. Originally known as the Northumberland War Memorial, the inscription on the monument cites only 'the men of the Northumbrian regiments' with a further layer of iconographical confusion thrown in with the addition of the motto of just one regiment, the Royal Northumberland Fusiliers.[85]

These debates and uncertainties reveal competing concepts of identity and belonging. Controlling officials did not always make their objectives clear and where complaints did arise, they invariably had their roots in conflicting ideas about ownership. The guardians of the schemes wanted to ensure the honour of their districts by including only those strictly eligible, while others argued for a slightly looser, but nonetheless still passionately felt, definition of community and belonging. Both sides in the disputes saw the issue of inclusion as a matter of great pride and honour. In particular, for the bereaved, to have a lost relative subsumed within what George Mosse has termed the 'cult of the fallen' was to have him endowed with heroic qualities and to have his death transformed from what might otherwise have seemed a tragic and senseless waste into a meaningful and legitimate sacrifice.[86]

As well as retaining responsibility for establishing the boundaries of community, the vast majority of memorial committees also controlled the precise form of the memorial. In almost every instance the committees were the only body to examine different proposals and they usually made a choice without placing a shortlist or range of options before their constituencies. Even on the very rare occasion when a vote was taken, this hardly amounted to a genuine public consultation. In the small East Perthshire town of Alyth, the subscribers to the memorial were invited to a meeting in the town hall to choose the final design from the memorial committee's shortlist of four proposals. However, the combination of a timeslot on a weekday afternoon and a prior announcement that the memorial would be some form of obelisk ensured that

---

[83] *Queen's Own Gazette*, Vol. XX, No. 6 (June 1902), p. 1759.
[84] Royal East Kent Regiment, *The Dragon*, March 1904, p. 12.
[85] Paul Usherwood, Jeremy Beach and Catherine Morris, *Public Sculpture of North-East England* (Liverpool: Liverpool University Press, 2000), pp. 129–131.
[86] George Mosse, *Fallen Soldiers: Reshaping the Memory of the World Wars* (Oxford: Oxford University Press, 1990), Ch 5.

only seventeen people attended, the majority of whom were already members of the committee.[87]

Nearly all committees opted for some form of aesthetic, plastic memorial. In sharp contrast to the protracted debates that punctuated the work of memorial committees in the aftermath of the First World War, this decision to eschew the utilitarian seems to have met with little opposition.[88] Occasionally the local press contained letters from servicemen or their dependants questioning the wisdom of spending money on monuments when families were still suffering. The following to the editor of the *Yorkshire Weekly Herald* from the wife of a volunteer was typical:

> There would have been much more honour in getting back the work they had lost through volunteering for South Africa than writing their names up in the drill hall … We are having to go through the mill. But what can we do? We are obliged to be content with a little sooner than be out of work altogether.[89]

Such complaints were, however, relatively rare, especially when viewed in the context of the depressed state of the British economy in the years immediately following the end of the war, and they certainly did not result in any serious soul-searching by the civic dignitaries charged with organising memorial schemes.[90] This can, in part, be explained by the general public's sense of disconnection with the logistics of memorial construction. Public interest in events in South Africa had waned in the last months of the conflict during the protracted guerrilla endgame and although the final casualty figures were higher than initially anticipated, the country was spared the universal grieving that engulfed it in the aftermath of the First World War. Yet, the potential for dissent did still exist. At a public meeting to discuss Salford's commemorative plans, Sir James Lees Knowles, local Conservative MP and chairman of the Lancashire Fusiliers Compassionate Fund, defended the decision to opt for a figurative monument by pointing out that the men had been insured with the Prudential and as a result £240 had already been disbursed to support the families of the fallen.[91] Elsewhere, as was the case in Tonbridge and Folkestone, criticism was deflected by combining memorial construction with a relief fund.

Another significant difference from Great War commemoration was the lack of comment about grief, mourning and the fate of the dead. Further, again

---

[87]   *Dundee Courier and Argus*, 15 October 1900; 8 November 1900
[88]   For the debate over utilitarian schemes in Scotland see Spiers, *The Scottish Soldier and Empire*, pp. 205–206 and for England see King, *Memorials of the Great War*, pp. 75–79.
[89]   *Yorkshire Weekly Herald*, 5 March 1904; Jones, 'The Yorkshire County Memorial', p. 68
[90]   For more on the state of the economy in this period see Martin Pugh, *State and Society: A Social and Political History of Britain since 1870* (London: Hodder, 1994), pp. 122–134.
[91]   *Salford Chronicle*, 20 September 1902

in sharp contrast to the Great War, it was rare for the ultimate symbol of Christian sacrifice, the cross, to be an overt or main element in the scheme.[92] More often civic pride was the dominant theme. Typical was the borough of Islington which opted for an impressive piece of statuary. As has been seen, there was dissent from some quarters over form, but the majority of the committee held firm for an aesthetic, plastic memorial. Designs were invited, but from relatively unknown or emerging artists in order to contain costs; however, no decision was taken throughout the whole of 1904. It was not until May 1905 that a contract was formally signed with Bertram Mackennal, a sculptor who was rapidly cementing his reputation, for a figure of Glory holding a figurine of Victory in her right hand and a laurel wreath in her left.[93] The committee did not, therefore, opt for anything overtly funereal or connected with grief: the dominant iconographic message was the glory won for the borough by the sacrifice of its inhabitants. The editorial in the *Islington Daily Gazette* revealed the borough's wish to display its importance and aesthetic taste: 'The Memorial will, we think, be voted by all who see it a fitting tribute by the largest and most important borough in the metropolis to its townsmen who fell fighting for Queen and Country'.[94] The aesthetic significance of the memorial was once again stressed at the unveiling ceremony with the *Islington Daily Gazette* describing fully its every last detail.[95]

Just occasionally, monumental iconography did focus on peace and bereavement. George Wade's memorial to the fallen of Norfolk, unveiled by Lieutenant-General A. S. Wynne on 17 November 1904, depicted the 'angel of peace, alighting on a globe and shattering its sword'.[96] In a similar vein, idealised female figures representing peace also dominated Albert Toft's monument to the men of Birmingham in Canon Hill Park and Joseph Crosland McClure's memorial in honour of the fallen of Leicestershire in Leicester. Indeed, the 'sad and solemn' aspect of Toft's memorial was reinforced with the inclusion of a bronze bas-relief on the pedestal containing representations of 'Grief' and 'Sympathy', while flanking McClure's central sculpture were two groups of figures which, 'abandoned to despair', were 'intended to recall the

---

[92] A notable exception is the Celtic cross of the Pembrokeshire county memorial in Haverfordwest. A possible explanation for this may be the fact that heading the list of the fallen was captain William Edwardes 5th Baron Kensington, whose father had been the Lord Lieutenant of the county until 1896.

[93] *Islington Daily Gazette*, 17 May 1905. For details on Mackennal's career see *British Sculpture, 1850–1914* (London: Fine Arts Society, 1968), p. 28.

[94] *Islington Daily Gazette*, 17 May 1905

[95] *Islington Daily Gazette*, 17 July 1905. Doubtless the committee would have been happy with Gleichen's later judgement: 'a particularly charming bronze figure of Glory'. E. Gleichen, *London's Open-Air Statuary* (London: Longmans, Green and Co., 1928), p. 194.

[96] *Norwich Mercury*, 19 November 1904.

horrors of war'.[97] Yet, even in Birmingham and Leicester, the sombre nature of the memorials' iconography hardly captured the true mood of the schemes. Both memorials were unveiled amid celebratory scenes. In Birmingham, the 'enthusiastic' crowd which greeted the arrival of Sir John French with a 'salvo of cheering' required seventy policemen and the erection of crush barriers to control it, while Municipal Square in Leicester was 'gay with flags' for the dedication of McClure's statue.[98]

The genesis of the Leicestershire memorial further reveals that the final design was hardly representative of the committee's original intentions. Indeed, members of the Leicestershire memorial committee had only adopted McClure's proposal as a last resort after protracted and costly negotiations with their original choice of sculptor, Alfred Gilbert, had ended in failure. As early as May 1903, the committee, under the chairmanship of Lord Rutland, the Lord Lieutenant of the County, had appeared to have painlessly fulfilled their remit to commemorate Leicestershire's war dead. They had secured the services of Gilbert, chosen the form, an allegorical figure of Victory atop a bronze pedestal, and raised the estimated total costs of £1,140. However, the first hint that all might not be well came at the next committee meeting in January 1904. In a letter to Alderman Freer, the mayor of Leicester and honorary secretary of the committee, Gilbert requested that, contrary to the original agreement, the second instalment of the contract price should be paid directly to his bank in Bruges rather than to the Compagnie Generale des Bronzes, the company tasked with casting the memorial. Initially reluctant to alter the terms of an agreement entered into on behalf of a large body of subscribers, the committee eventually acceded to Gilbert's persistent pleas to be allowed to do his own founding on the understanding that the memorial would be ready by September 1904. Ominously, the September deadline passed with no sign of the statue and, even more worryingly, no word from Gilbert. There then followed a round of increasingly desperate committee meetings. Attempts to secure precise progress reports were met by ever more farcical delaying tactics from Gilbert, culminating, in November 1905, with a report from the sculptor announcing that a dispute over non-payment of rent for his studio in Bruges had resulted in a court order to seize the plaster cast model of the Leicestershire statue. Astonishingly, the committee, despite revelations in the press about other unfulfilled contracts, decided to stick with Gilbert and agreed to his request to commence work on a new memorial, this time a figure of a medieval knight.[99] However, notwithstanding frequent progress reports from one

---

[97]   *Birmingham Daily Mail*, 23 June 1906; Gildea, *For Remembrance*, p. 217; *Leicester Daily Post*, 26 June 1909.

[98]   *Birmingham Daily Post*, 25 June 1906; *Leicester Daily Post*, 2 July 1909.

[99]   In 1905 Julia Frankau had employed Gilbert to design a memorial to her late husband. The following year, with the deadline missed, she publicly denounced Gilbert in the magazine,

of Granby's acquaintances who lived in Bruges and the offer of a £100 bonus should a new November 1906 deadline be met, the new scheme was no more successful. Finally, in January 1908, over five years after the first public meeting, the committee admitted defeat and abandoned the contract with Gilbert. The £905 already paid in fees was written off, a second round of funding through private appeal to the principal subscribers quickly raised £1,039 and Joseph Crosland McClure of Leicester Art School was engaged to replace Gilbert. With completion on time and at cost now the sole goal, the committee gave McClure a free hand over design. His decision to replace the terminal lions of his original proposal with allegorical figures of peace, war, grief and sympathy was unquestioningly accepted at a committee meeting in August 1908 so long as it 'would not increase cost'.[100] By the time of the unveiling ceremony in July 1909, memories of the war in South Africa had receded to such an extent that McClure's iconography could be detached from the recent past. An anonymous art critic writing for the *Leicester Daily Post* felt the significance of McClure's work lay not in any commentary on the conflict with the Boers but rather in the universal truths it exposed:

> It would have been easy for Leicester to have acquired a commonplace monument, hung about with festoons of laurel wreaths and Martini rifles, and exploiting all the obvious ideas which can be so cheaply got together by assembling the materials and instruments of warfare. The khaki-clad soldier is by no means a contemptible attribute of a war memorial, especially when such a memorial is erected in his honour; and there are worse ways of paying him respect than by setting up his counterfeit presentment in bronze. But from the artistic point of view this literal and personal way of furnishing forth a monument has the demerit of lacking originality, even if the other demerit of cheapness of idea be not admitted. It has been said that all great art is impersonal, and the statement can be supported by sufficient number of references to really great achievements. In any event, it seems probable that a memorial which endeavours to be a fine emblem of the thoughts and emotions inspired by all warfare will live longer and have more abiding interest than one which commemorates with exacting particularity any single war. Whilst events fall in time into that limbo from which historians strive to reclaim them, and a battle becomes a thing labelled with a date, the struggles of humanity will inevitably produce war of one kind or another till the end of time, and its dreadful handmaidens, 'leashed in like hounds, will crouch for employment.'[101]

The Truth. R. Dorment, *Sir Alfred Gilbert* (London: Weidenfeld and Nicolson, 1986), p. 45
[100]   LRRO, DE171, The Leicestershire South African War Memorial Committee, minutes, 1903–1909. Terry Cavanagh, *Public Sculpture of Leicestershire and Rutland* (Liverpool: Liverpool University Press, 2000), pp. 157–165.
[101]   *Leicester Daily Post*, 2 July 1909.

The sombre motifs of Toft and McClure's work at Birmingham and Leicester respectively were, therefore, the exception rather than the rule. As the *Leicester Daily Post*'s anonymous art critic indicated, much more common were depictions of soldiers, frequently in action, where the emphasis was on a combination of heroism and realism. For the editor of the *Bury and Norwich Post*, A. G. Walker's Suffolk regiment and county memorial, which portrayed 'a wounded soldier raising himself from a large rock, and grasping his Lee Mitford rifle as though anxious for another shot at the enemy', was 'singularly appropriate'.[102] In Salford, Sir James Lees Knowles's desire that the town's monument should be of 'historical interest' was realised in George Frampton's triumphalist statue of a Lancashire Fusilier caught in the moment of victory, waving his busby in the air.[103] Llanelli's figurative statue of a bare-headed soldier with rifle at the ready in anticipation of an enemy attack was considered by the local newspaper to be of particular worth because 'it was modelled from a North County guardsman – a magnificently built young fellow – who went through the South African War. He was shot in the neck at Belmont, the bullet coming out near his left shoulder'.[104] The civic dignitaries who comprised Warrington's memorial committee also opted for a figurative representation of the soldier-hero in action. Their decision to have the town's memorial modelled on the last moments of Lieutenant-Colonel William McCarthy-O'Leary, who had commanded the local volunteers and died at the battle of Pieter's Hill on 18 February 1900, not only rooted the site firmly in the locality but also, as the editor of the *Warrington Guardian* noted, presented future citizens with an unambiguous lesson. The figure of O'Leary, the paper's readers were informed, caught 'at the moment when victory was about to crown the efforts of many arduous weeks … in what was perhaps the proudest moment of his life, … pointed the way to duty as clearly as anything ever did in this imperfect world'.[105]

As we have already seen, even when death or grief was a memorial's dominant iconographic message, this could be counteracted by the tone set on the day of its unveiling. Notwithstanding the sober nature of Alfred Drury's design, the dedication of the statue of O'Leary in Warrington was treated as a 'general holiday'.[106] In Ipswich, despite the fact that the solemnity of Albert Toft's sculpture of a mourning soldier in honour of 'the Suffolk soldiers who lost their lives in the South African War' was reinforced by the town council's decision that the unveiling ceremony 'was not an occasion for the elaborate display of flags and bunting', the 'immense crowd' that gathered to witness

102 H. R. Barker, *West Suffolk Illustrated* (Bury St Edmunds: F. G. Pawsey, 1907), p. 81; SRO, GB554/23/1, Supplement to the *Bury and Norwich Post*, 22 November 1904.
103 *Salford Chronicle*, 20 September 1902.
104 *Llanelli Mercury*, 31 August 1908.
105 *Warrington Guardian*, 23 February 1907.
106 *Warrington Observer*, 23 February 1907.

proceedings seemed intent on treating the day as a civic fête.[107] Noting that those assembled to greet the arrival of General French, the victor of Elandslaagte, and other officiating dignitaries soon 'began to wear an appearance of considerable animation', the local paper disapprovingly reported that the 'hubbub that was continually going on' had, in its opinion, undermined the dignity of the event.[108] A similar scenario unfolded at the unveiling of the county's sister memorial in Bury St Edmunds. Although the *Bury and Norwich Post* was certain that 'citizens will have taken due regard to the words of the mayor at the last council meeting when he pointed out that the proceedings were scarcely of a festive nature, and that the paramount feeling of the day would be regret that so many had fallen',[109] the coverage of the unveiling in the *Bury Free Press* suggested otherwise. Reporting that the appearance of Lord Methuen 'was greeted with applause which increased until the volume seemed to fill the Cornhill Square', the paper observed that the 'densely packed crowd' appeared to be in 'holiday mood'.[110] There was equal excitement in Nuneaton for the unveiling of A. E. Rost's bronze figure of a 'soldier at the ready'. With 'flags and bannerettes' bedecking the streets and the police straining to keep the crowds under control, the town was fully en fête. At the centre of this public clamour was Sir Redvers Buller. Invited to perform the unveiling honours, Buller found himself repeatedly 'mobbed by crowds anxious to shake his hand'.[111] Indeed, for many local inhabitants, the dedication of a remembrance site to their community's fallen seems to have played a poor second to the thrill of receiving a visit from a figure of national prominence. The *Dover Express* neatly caught the sense of breathless excitement that greeted Field Marshal Lord Roberts on his arrival to unveil the port's memorial in 1912: 'every eye was strained to catch a glimpse of the hero of a hundred fights. It would, indeed, have been a strong-hearted Briton who did not experience a thrill of emotion at that moment'.[112] The same appeared to hold true for Llanelli. Despite, as will be shown later, the editor of the local paper's disapproval of the war he was still prepared to concede that Roberts's visit for the unveiling of William Doyle-Jones's statue of a guardsman was 'the occasion of a great display of popular enthusiasm'.[113] The presence of Sir John French and Sir Redvers Buller at unveiling ceremonies in Folkestone and Tonbridge respectively received similar coverage.

---

[107]   Gildea, *For Remembrance*, p. 191; *East Anglian Daily Times*, 1 October 1906. The mourning soldier, head bowed and rifle reversed, was to become a staple of commemorative sculpture after the Great War. There is a particularly fine example, again by Toft, in the London borough of Streatham. See Borg, *War Memorials*, pp. 109–110.

[108]   *East Anglian Daily Times*, 1 October 1906.

[109]   *Bury and Norwich Post*, 8 November 1904.

[110]   *Bury Free Press*, 12 November 1904.

[111]   *Midland Counties Tribune*, 22 November 1904.

[112]   *Dover Express*, 25 April 1912.

[113]   *Llanelli Mercury*, 31 August 1905.

That unveiling ceremonies were viewed as grand spectacles rather than solemn rites is hardly surprising. Not only did they, more often than not, present the public with the chance to glimpse a national celebrity but they were also, frequently, carefully choreographed military pageants, redolent with all the pomp and circumstance that civilian audiences invariably found irresistible. Although the schemes in Dover and Tonbridge were, nominally, civic ones, the arrangements at the unveilings were dominated by the military authorities. In St Mary's Church, Dover, Field Marshal Lord Roberts's arrival was greeted by a general salute from the massed ranks of the locally billeted Kings Own Royal Lancaster Regiment, while 'the entrance to the church was lined with officers from the regiment and the aisles with sergeants'.[114] The presence of all the local volunteer battalions and the yeomanry in the precincts of Tonbridge castle for the unveiling of the memorial to the men of the borough who died in the war ensured that, in the words of the local paper, 'the grounds presented a truly military spectacle'.[115] Outside Kent, the same held true. The decision by the Bedfordshire county war memorial committee to fix the date for its unveiling ceremony 'in order that advantage might be taken of the fact that both the militia and yeomanry were in training' seems to have paid off, with the editor of the local paper enthusing that the presence of the Imperial Yeomanry 'with their lances held erect and pennants gaily fluttering in the breeze' ensured the occasion was truly 'a spectacle'.[116] The following description of the unveiling of Rochdale's memorial provides some insight into where the balance lay between civic reflection and military pageant:

> The yeomanry and the volunteers, in their brilliant scarlet, lent a much needed bit of colour to the other-wise sombre appearance of the gathering. The volunteers occupied positions to the right of the army veterans, the volunteer band divided the Fusiliers from the members of the Duke of Lancaster's Own Imperial Yeomanry who formed up immediately to the left of the speaker's platform near the tower, and the firing-party, drawn from the yeomanry were in line with the platform, making up an effective and impressive spectacle.[117]

What was implicit in the scale of the military arrangements for Rochdale's dedication ceremony was made explicit by the town's mayor, Alderman Jones, when he opened proceedings. Explaining the 'object of the gathering' to the assembled crowd, he 'remarked that to some whose relatives were being commemorated the day would be a sad one, to others not intimately connected with them it would be a day of rejoicing'.[118] With only forty-one names

---

114 *Dover Express*, 19 April 1912.
115 *Tonbridge Free Press*, 24 June 1904.
116 *Bedfordshire Times and Independent*, 3 June 1904.
117 *Rochdale Observer*, 6 June 1907.
118 *Rochdale Observer*, 6 June 1907.

appearing on the list of the fallen out of a population of over 165,000 it was clear which emotion Jones felt would be in the ascendancy. Both the rarity of Christian iconography on memorials and the general absence of overt grieving at unveiling ceremonies imply that the dead were often commemorated on a level beyond that of the immediate family and its needs.

By recalling the fallen as a collective rather than as individuals, ceremonies could be used to stress wider points about communities. In the process, the focus on the dead could be lost. This was most clearly seen in the unveiling of the Islington war memorial. The local newspaper's coverage of the event records speech after speech stressing the glory of Islington and the beauty of its memorial. Civic pride was very much the tenor of the day and the dead were almost incidental to the occasion.[119] For self-made businessman and mayor of Halifax, Josiah Wade, the actions of the living at the unveiling ceremony assumed greater importance than the names of the dead on the memorial. Keen to dispel any prejudices that might surround commerce, he told those gathered that by turning out in such 'strong force' they had shown that, 'even in a manufacturing town absorbed in making pounds, shillings and pence, they could devote a day to love of town, king and country. He was voicing the opinion of the inhabitants when he said they were a loyal people to the king, to his army and to his navy'.[120] Latent patriotism was also the leitmotif of Lord Barnard's address to the citizens of Darlington at the unveiling of the borough's aggressively militaristic statue of an advancing British soldier. Although theirs was 'primarily a trading and industrial district', the packed crowd inside the grounds of St Cuthbert's parish church were urged not to forget that 'there existed a military spirit which only required the occasion to bring it forth'.[121]

Local pride was frequently merged with the dual concepts of duty and sacrifice to infuse memorials with wider significance. In a florid opening to his coverage of the unveiling of the Suffolk county memorial in Bury St Edmunds, the editor of the *Bury Free Press* seamlessly linked past and present to underline the region's long tradition in the service of king and country:

> The memorial harks back to those stirring times in our local history when, to the roll of the drum, the inspiring music of the bands of their respective regiments and echoing and re-echoing cheers, these brave lads, realising the necessity of responding to their country's call, left our shores to fulfil the battle-cry of that far-famed East Anglian – Nelson – 'England expects that every man this day will do his duty'.

[119] *Islington Daily Gazette,* 17 November 1905.
[120] *Halifax Courier,* 12 November 1904.
[121] *Darlington and Stockton Times,* 12 August 1905.

The function of the site was clear; it was 'to remind our children's children of the pluck and heroism which characterised their forefathers'.[122]

Calls to emulate the fallen were features of unveiling addresses throughout the country. Canon Bartram, at the unveiling of the Dover civic memorial in St Mary's Church, taking as his text 'their name liveth for evermore' from Ecclesiastics XLIV, urged Dovorians to view the commemorative tablet as 'a reminder and example of courage and patriotism'.[123] His choice of text and lesson were, of course, to be the staples of remembrance services in the aftermath of the Great War. However, in contrast to the Great War, the South African War was not seen as the war to end all wars; the relatively short casualty lists and remoteness of the battlegrounds ensured that it had no such public resonance. Thus, central to speeches about the need to carry the spirit of the fallen forward into future generations was the warning that the conflict in South Africa was unlikely to be the last time that such self-sacrifice would be required. The vicar of Huddersfield made this explicit at the unveiling, in May 1905, of the memorial to the men of the district who fell in the war. In his dedication address he told the assembled crowd:

> Some day war may break out again for us. Some day the call may come for men to risk their all for the honour and defence of the fatherland, for the safety of wives and children, and then men will come forward cheerfully to do their duty. They will know what is expected of them, they will rise to their responsibilities, they will prove themselves not unworthy of such noble kinship. England will have brave sons because your sons were brave … this memorial is to stand here as a rebuke to softness. It is to tell us and all men that it is a sin and a shame to sit at ease when God and man call us to service, and that every man must be ready to give up time and money, and, if need be, health and life itself, if thereby he may win the honour and happiness of having served his generation according to the will of God.[124]

However, such fatalistic acceptance of a militaristic future met with some resistance. The town's Liberal MP, Sir James Woodhouse, who had toed the Campbell-Bannerman party line of muted support for the war, urged the citizens of Huddersfield to draw a more pacific lesson from the memorial they had just seen unveiled:

> War was a terrible thing for both sides and all classes of people – those who lived in the great halls no more than in the small cottages knew the feeling that arose when their loved ones were in danger. And it was for that reason that war brought home to us how great are the blessings of peace.

---

[122]   *Bury Free Press*, 11 November 1904.
[123]   *Dover Express*, 26 April 1912.
[124]   *Huddersfield Chronicle*, 27 May 1905.

We honoured those who had fallen in the war, but hoped that it would be long time before ever such another occasion was necessary as that which they commemorated that day.[125]

This sentiment was echoed in the *Huddersfield Examiner*, a paper which had been trenchantly anti-war throughout the conflict. Commending Woodhouse's speech, the editor indicated to his readers that a sea-change in public attitudes now meant that patriotic duty was no longer the sole preserve of the military:

> The signs of the times indicate that the wave of militarism has spent its force, that patriotism is recognised in those efforts which bring a country to the foremost place in science, in literature, in arts, in commerce, and the pursuits of peace. It requires very little urging now that to live for one's country is as necessary as to die for it is noble, though it is the latter thought which is principally suggested by the events of last Saturday.[126]

Frequently, messages about duty, service and sacrifice were fused with reminders about the value of Empire. At the unveiling of the civic roll of honour in Folkestone, Sir John French, who had commanded the 1st Cavalry Brigade in South Africa, was keen to cite the war as evidence of the enduring strength and popularity of Britain's imperial family. Although willing to accept that the war had revealed some fissures in the imperial sub-structure, he was, nonetheless, insistent that:

> One of the most noteworthy features connected with the recent war was the knowledge we had come to possess of the great fund of patriotic feeling which permeated the British Empire. Remembering what a world-wide Empire ours was, and of what different elements it was composed, he did not think the sacrifices in connection with the war were too great if such sacrifices could show us we all were bound together in one bond of fellowship.[127]

With the ethics of imperialism coming under increasing scrutiny councillor S. Brown, the mayor of Tonbridge and chairman of the town's memorial committee, was anxious that the inhabitants of Tonbridge should keep at the forefront of their minds the core values of the Empire. In his address at the unveiling ceremony in the castle grounds, he reminded them that, 'this was a great Empire, under the flag of which no man was a slave, and which carried with it peace and wealth of commerce'.[128] Indeed, the willingness of members

---

[125] *Huddersfield Chronicle*, 27 May 1905.
[126] *Huddersfield Examiner*, 20 May 1905. For a full account of the genesis of the Huddersfield Boer War memorial see Anne C. Brook, 'God, Grief and Community: Commemoration of the Great War in Huddersfield c. 1914–1929', unpublished PhD thesis (Leeds University, 2009).
[127] *Folkestone Express*, 23 April 1904.
[128] *Tonbridge Free Press*, 24 June 1904.

of the Tonbridge memorial committee to confront the contested memory of the conflict head-on can be seen in the choice of the recently dismissed Sir Redvers Buller as officiating dignitary. In offering a vote of thanks after the unveiling, Charles Fitch Kemp, the president of Tonbridge Central Conservative Association, dismissed public criticisms of Buller's military record by asserting that, 'Sir Redvers had been a gallant soldier and above all he had proved himself to be one of the kindest and best of generals'.[129] As a further endorsement of Buller's standing, a bereaved mother and three war veterans were then 'given the honour of shaking hands with the General'.[130] Equally aware of the divisive potential of imperial politics, the chairman of Wigan's memorial scheme, councillor S. Fyans, called for a unified front at the unveiling of Goscombe John's heroic statue of an advancing infantryman. 'The monument would', he told those gathered in Mesnes Park, 'serve as an incentive to duty; no matter what a man's political creed might be, his duty was to uphold the Empire'.[131]

Indeed, the contentious nature of the debates that surrounded both the motivation for, and conduct of, the war in South Africa meant that officiating dignitaries were particularly keen that the messages contained in their addresses should be seen as relevant to all sections of society. Sir F. S. Powell, the Conservative MP for Wigan, picked up on Fyans's call for cross-party collaboration by insisting in his unveiling address that he was there to represent 'all classes, all orders and all sorts of men'. To underline further the apolitical nature of the occasion, and to avoid the possibility of alienating any element of his audience, he quickly separated the men being commemorated from the wider context of the conflict:

> It had been more than any other army a sober army ... There had been criticisms on the conduct of the campaign but those criticisms had dealt with general officers and those in high command, but so far as he knew the only remarks made on the conduct of ordinary soldiers had been comments of admiration and commendation.[132]

The memory of the war was then to be found not in the heroics or victories of generals but rather in the more politically neutral virtues of the rank and file. In Ipswich, General Sir John French was equally keen to deflect any possible dissension and, in the process, rescue the reputation of Suffolk's fallen from the potentially damning verdict of history by extolling the qualities of the ordinary

---

[129] *Tonbridge Free Press*, 24 June 1904.
[130] *Tonbridge Free Press*, 24 June 1904. The decision to invite Buller to unveil the memorial must have owed a lot to the presence of John Le Fleming on the memorial committee. Le Fleming had been a tutor at the army crammer attended by Buller and his son had served under Buller in South Africa.
[131] *Wigan Examiner*, 6 February 1903.
[132] *Wigan Examiner*, 6 February 1903.

soldier. Pointing out that the majority of those named on Albert Toft's statue of a mourning soldier had died in 'a splendid but unsuccessful attempt' to take Suffolk Hill during the battle of Colesberg on the night of 5–6 January 1900, he explained to those gathered in the Cornhill just why such events should be viewed as sacred:

> It is not always because these encounters have been absolutely successful: it is not always because the immediate object had been obtained: it is because the men engaged have shown they are true soldiers of their country – because they have fought to the death, fought like men.[133]

At the unveiling of the Bedfordshire county memorial, Lady Cowper, deputising for her sick husband, again eulogised the spirit of the fighting men but this time within more narrowly defined parameters. Stating that the khaki-clad statue of an infantryman was representative of the ordinary British soldier, she asserted that, 'moreover, it was the type of those who had not made that splendid profession their own, but who, when there was a stress and some help was needed, came forward ... standing shoulder to shoulder with their fellows in the fight'.[134] This sentiment was echoed by councillor Fyans in Wigan for whom the town's memorial 'would, in some way, be a monument to bravery, particularly of the auxiliary forces'.[135] Such attempts to locate the memory of the war within the rank and file of the armed forces point towards the growth in public regard for the ordinary soldier and the development of closer ties between the civilian and military worlds in Edwardian Britain.[136]

Again and again public figures attempted to draw a veil over past divisions by refocusing remembrance on abstract virtues. Typical was colonel Kemp's exhortation at the unveiling of the commemorative plaque outside Rochdale town hall for the citizens of the borough to set aside their differences. Thanking General Fry for officiating, he concluded his address by observing that, 'Whatever might be the opinion as to any war, whether it was right or wrong, just or unjust, it was the duty of all those who were able to do what they could to bring it to a successful end. The men and women we are honouring saw what their duty was, and they did it'.[137] Efforts to depoliticise the commemoration of the war were particularly important at a time when the scandal over the importation of indentured Chinese labour to work in the mines of South Africa

---

[133] *East Anglian Daily News*, 1 October 1906. For Suffolks at Colesberg see Conan Doyle, *The Great Boer War*, pp. 236–238.
[134] *Bedfordshire Times and Independent*, 3 June 1904.
[135] *Wigan Examiner*, 6 February 1902.
[136] See Timothy Bowman and Mark Connelly, *The Edwardian Army: Recruiting, Training, and Deploying the British Army, 1902–1914* (Oxford: Oxford University Press, 2012), pp. 183–215.
[137] *Rochdale Observer*, 6 June 1907; See also *East Anglian Daily Times*, 1 October 1906; *Wigan Examiner*, 6 February 1902; *Queen's Own Gazette*, Vol. XX, No. 6 (June 1902), p. 1760.

had resurrected accusations that the war had been fought solely to advance the interests of the capitalist 'Randlords'. Such political sidestepping was attempted by the editor of the *Llanelli Mercury*. He sought to win over those opposed to the council's plan for a ceremonial unveiling of the town's war memorial by removing the ritual from the context of the war's contentious origins:

> There are those, we are aware, who look upon the whole occasion as a hateful thing. They see in the memorial nothing more than a vulgar appeal to the fighting instincts of the people, and have no desire to perpetuate the memory of men who sacrificed their lives in the national cause. Surely, however, this is not what is involved? The memorial had its inception, not in the spirit of militarism, but in that instinct of respect for the dead, which is inherent in the human breast. The war in which these men were engaged was no doubt precipitated by the avarice and greed of unscrupulous capitalists, but what did the soldiers know of this. The conflict was none of their making … Whatever we may think of the causes of that sanguinary conflict, or the diplomacy which preceded it, there can be but one opinion of the men who, when the call came, were ready to sacrifice themselves for their country.[138]

Not all attempts to appease opposition were, however, successful. Although, as already noted, the inscription on Darlington's memorial boasted of over 5,000 subscribers, seventy of the town's sizeable Quaker community boycotted the unveiling ceremony by attending a Peace Association prayer meeting arranged for the same time at the Friends' Meeting House.[139] Of the opinion that religious contemplation rather than civic celebration was more in harmony with the feelings of the relatives and friends of the fallen, the gathering's opprobrium was reserved in particular for the municipal authorities' choice of 'a memorial representing a soldier in fighting form'. This would, it was claimed in a press release signed by the meeting's chairman and president of the local Peace Association, Mr J. B. Friend, be 'likely to encourage defiant and revengeful feelings and [was] calculated to appeal to the lower and more savage instincts in our nature'.[140]

Yet the rhetoric of dedication addresses and the memorialisation process as a whole were not entirely depoliticised. Although dignitaries were generally keen to sidestep old questions about the morality of the war, they were, nonetheless, often happy to exploit the commemoration of the war to make political points about the state of Britain's armed forces. At the unveiling of the Suffolk county memorial in Bury St Edmunds in November 1904, Lord Methuen seized on the army's 'friendly relations with civilian life' to call for increased investment in the

---

[138]   *Llanelli Mercury*, 31 October 1905.
[139]   *Darlington and Stockton Times*, 12 August 1905; *Northern Echo*, 7 August 1905; Usherwood, Beach and Morris, *Public Sculpture of North-East England*, pp. 236–237.
[140]   *Yorkshire Evening Post*, 5 August 1905; *Darlington and Stockton Times*, 12 August 1905.

army. Those gathered were told that if they wished to ensure the country was in a 'state of readiness', they 'must stand the call on their pocket and be prepared to stand some discomfort in their daily lives'.[141] For many, an overriding concern was the issue of conscription. Unease over the performance of auxiliary troops in South Africa combined with wider misgivings about national efficiency had resulted in a vigorous and influential movement, spearheaded by the National Service League, dedicated to the introduction of compulsory military service. At a public meeting in September 1902, Salford's MP, Mr J. Groves, was quick to claim the town's remembrance project for the anti-conscription lobby. Endorsing the mayor's plans for a figurative monument, he expressed the hope that the lesson of the memorial 'might be in favour of volunteering to save us from conscription'.[142] The following week's edition of the *Salford Chronicle* threw its full weight behind Groves's stance. Urging all citizens to support the scheme wholeheartedly, the paper's editor directed his readers towards what he felt was the true lesson of the war by encouraging them to cast their minds back to the rush to volunteer in the wake of Black Week:

> These volunteer companies marked a new era in the history of the army. A movement, the importance of which cannot be too highly extolled, and the inception of which was in the ranks of the Lancashire Fusiliers, has shown the nation the possibilities of a vast economical fighting force. The extension of the volunteer system contains a germ of a system that might, by good administration and a little generosity, be fostered and strengthened, and it would at once provide a solution for that dread bugbear conscription.[143]

At the forefront of the campaign for national service was Field Marshal Lord Roberts, who had assumed the presidency of the National Service League in December 1905.[144] In great demand as a guest of honour at unveiling ceremonies, he took full advantage of the flurry of invitations that came his way after his retirement in 1904 to tour the country propagating the cause of military reform. In York he warned the assembled crowd that the country would remain in the 'van of civilisation' only if it had an army 'trained to be able to take its place in the defence of this great empire'.[145] For the townspeople of Llanelli the message was more explicit; if they were to 'make war impossible',

[141] SRO, GB554/23/1, Supplement to the *Bury and Norwich Post*, 22 November 1904.
[142] *Salford Chronicle*, 20 September 1902.
[143] *Salford Chronicle*, 20 September 1902.
[144] For more on the campaigning of the National Service League see R. J. Q. Adams, 'The National Service League and Mandatory Service in Edwardian England', *Armed Forces and Society*, 12: 1 (October 1985), pp. 53–74; Matthew Hendley, '"Help Us Secure a Strong, Healthy, Prosperous and Peaceful Britain": The Social Arguments of the Campaign for Compulsory Service in Britain, 1899–1914', *Canadian Journal of History*, 30: 2 (August, 1995), pp. 261–288.
[145] Quoted in King, *Memorials of the Great War*, p. 213.

then they would need to tap the 'great potential reserve in the entire manhood of the country'.[146] Coming at a time when the future of the volunteer movement seemed under threat from Hugh Arnold-Foster's attempts to reduce the military budget, this apparent call for compulsory service hit a raw nerve with the editor of the *Llanelli Mercury*:

> Does the Field Marshal propose to introduce conscription into the country? … Lord Roberts may rest assured that Britain will never be defended by the conscript, for we believe that the volunteer will do all that is necessary in that direction. The treatment meted out by the present government to the volunteer force is nothing short of a scandal, and if Lord Roberts would use his great influence to secure more liberal recognition from the War Office of our 'citizen army' he would be doing a great service to the Empire.[147]

Even those who opposed the introduction of conscription felt that the experience of South Africa had revealed serious shortcomings at the heart of British society. Sir Ian Hamilton, fresh from his experience as a military observer during the Russo-Japanese War, used the occasion of the unveiling of Birmingham's civic war memorial to contrast unfavourably the value systems of the Occident and the Orient.[148] In Japan, he told those assembled, life is regarded 'as a bubble compared with the national honour' whereas 'Western civilisation laid more and more stress on the value of life until even the most feeble and flickering manifestation is guarded from natural extinction'.[149] Britain's increasing social 'degeneracy', as Hamilton called it, was also the theme of Sir Redvers Buller's address at the dedication of the memorial plaque in East Ham town hall in July 1904. All citizens, Buller insisted, must be prepared 'to defend home and hearth … as the fight for existence was becoming harder'.[150] For both men, the solution to Britain's declining martial appetite lay in the introduction of compulsory drill.

The civic commemoration of the South African War was, therefore, partly an extension of and partly a break with previous commemorative customs. The memorial forms were remarkably consistent with Victorian funerary practice, as were their iconographic messages, reinforced during unveiling ceremonies, which were always conformist and reassuring. As noted, messages and symbols aimed squarely at those grieving were rare and often the dead were used by the wider communities to which they belonged to make a range of other statements.

---

[146] *Llanelli Mercury*, 31 August 1905.

[147] *Llanelli Mercury*, 31 August 1905. See Edward M. Spiers, *The Army and Society, 1815–1914* (London: Longman, 1980), pp. 253–256 for more on Arnold-Foster's plans for the volunteer forces.

[148] Hamilton formally set out his objections to conscription in a 1910 pamphlet, *Compulsory Service: A Study of the Question in the Light of Experience* (London: John Murray, 1910).

[149] *Birmingham Daily Mail*, 25 June 1906.

[150] *East Ham Echo*, 22 July 1904.

However, although control was almost without fail retained by self-selecting civic elites, the memorialisation process did show signs of democratisation. Officiating dignitaries were keen to stress the cross-class nature of their work and this manifested itself in the insistence that memory sites should honour all who served not just those from more privileged backgrounds. Despite this, not all memorial schemes were accepted with universal approval and dissent was expressed. As in the aftermath of the Great War, certain pre-requisites for a successful war memorial scheme emerged: leadership had to be firm and clear, the fund-raising target needed to be set early and, crucially, it had to be realistic and within the means of the community and the form of the memorial had to be advertised quickly and effectively. Some communities, most notably Islington and Dover, failed to do this and their civic pride took a knock in the protracted gestation which followed. The commemoration of the war in South Africa in civic communities was, then, a transitional moment, marking the beginnings of a shift from the paternalism of the nineteenth century to the collectivism of the twentieth. The next chapter will focus on the ways in which the army remembered its fallen of 1899–1902 to explore how much this sense of transition can be extended to the military sphere.

Chapter 2

Pro Patria Mori:
Remembering the Regiment

THE South African War was an important moment of transition in the nature and perception of the British army. A central element in this process of change was the growth of mass literacy. Almost every British soldier had at least basic literacy skills and could write about their experiences in letters to loved ones back home. Frequently such accounts were disseminated to a wider public through local newspapers, works journals and school magazines. The soldiers were also accompanied by journalists, artists, illustrators and cinematographers. Modern technology was then used to give a public educated in popular patriotism and imperialism an on-going diet of stories and information.[1] At the same time, the ranks of the army were swollen by a large number of volunteers, particularly from the British middle classes. This gave the army, albeit for a very short space of time, a demographic much more akin to its parent population.[2] These trends helped the army to transform the image of the Tommy from Wellington's 'scum of the earth' to Kipling's salt of the earth. This chapter will explore the extent to which this shift in perception was reflected in, and even exploited by, the military authorities as they embarked on the time-honoured tradition of raising monuments to their fallen. It will explore how the, often uneasy, relationship between regulars and volunteers impacted on the memorialisation process and, thus, provide an alternative window on the debates that surrounded the structure and function of the nation's military forces on the eve of the Great War.

At regimental level the formation of an organising committee to oversee the memorialisation process was a relatively straight-forward matter. In the majority of cases, retired officers took the lead in conjunction with a smattering of serving officers. In London the Royal Artillery scheme commenced with a meeting at the Royal United Service Institute in November 1902. Former

---

[1]   See Gooch (ed.), *The Boer War*, pp. 187–244.
[2]   See M. D. Blanch, 'British Society and the War', in Peter Warwick (ed.), *The South African War*, pp. 186–209.

commander-in-chief of the British army and cousin of Queen Victoria, the Duke of Cambridge chaired the meeting and oversaw the creation of a committee. Retired Major-General Sir George Marshall, who had commanded the Royal Artillery during the conflict, was appointed as chairman and was joined by two other major-generals and four retired colonels; three ex-officio posts were created for the Director of Artillery, the Inspector-General of Artillery and the Assistant Adjutant General at the War Office.[3] Lord Roberts, the commander-in-chief in South Africa who masterminded the fall of the Boer capitals, also played an active role on the committee. Colonel A. Sprot, the recently retired commanding officer of the 6th Dragoon Guards (the Carabiniers), took the position of chair of the regimental committee assisted by a small group of other retired officers. He had to play a particularly active role as the regiment moved to India soon after the war and so was a long way from the centre of events.[4] The idea to erect a memorial to the Royal Marines resulted in a poll of all officers on the active list to propose names for a memorial committee under the chairmanship of retired marine, Lieutenant-General Sir Arthur French.[5] The historic and prestigious City of London volunteer unit, the Honourable Artillery Company, took direction on its war memorial from its governing body, the Court, under its chair, Lieutenant-Colonel the Earl Denbigh, which then created a Roll of Honour committee.[6] Although the Royal Engineers chose, in the words of Major A. T. Moore, the honorary secretary of the committee, to adopt 'a course which has been consecrated by long-usage in all non-official matters' and elect its committee at a general meeting of the corps on 6 June 1903, the outcome, nonetheless, firmly reflected the existing command structure.[7] Lieutenant-General Sir Robert Grant, Inspector-General of Fortifications until 1898 and senior serving officer, was voted in as president with the rest of the committee comprising two major-generals and two colonels.[8]

Occasionally civic authorities were included in the process, although where this was the case the schemes invariably originated within the confines of the military. The King's Liverpool regiment, having launched a fund in the late 1880s for a memorial to the fallen of the Afghan and Burma campaigns,

[3] *The Times*, 9 July 1910.
[4] The National Archives (TNA) WORK 20/57 Carabiniers' Memorial, 1905–1906. Letter from Sprot to Office of Works, 6 February 1906.
[5] *The Globe and Laurel. The Journal of the Royal Marine Light Infantry*, Vol. II, No. 62 (December 1900), p. 139.
[6] Honourable Artillery Company Archive (HACA), Court Minutes, Vol. JJ, 1899–1905, 19 January, 30 March 1903. (Many thanks are due to Justine Taylor, Archivist to the Honourable Artillery Company, for making the records available for inspection.)
[7] Royal Engineers Museum (REM), RO270, Royal Engineers War Memorial Committee Book, Corps meeting minutes, 6 June 1903
[8] However, as will be seen later, this committee was only formed after a lengthy and relatively protracted dispute.

agreed to widen the scope of the scheme in the wake of the South African War and allow the city's mayor, Sir Charles Petrie, along with a number of other leading citizens to serve on the memorial committee.[9] The Royal Sussex Regiment established a memorial committee at the start of 1901 in response to a series of letters 'from the officers commanding the battalions' and only after it was resolved that the scheme should take the form of a 'Cottage Home' was it felt necessary to cast the financial net wide through the inclusion of leading civic notables.[10] The East Kent Regiment's (The Buffs) scheme was initiated at a meeting held at Howe Barracks in Canterbury on 9 May 1903. Chaired by the Lord Lieutenant of the county, Earl Stanhope, who was supported by the colonel of the regiment, General Sir Julius Raines, acting in the capacity of vice president, the committee was, with one exception, made up of the senior officers of the regiment. The only civilian member of the committee was the deputy mayor of Canterbury, Alderman W. Mason, and this was simply a matter of form as the proposed site for the memorial was on municipal land.[11] Indeed, the extent to which Mason's membership was meant to be no more than a courtesy became abundantly clear when a decision had to be reached as to the memorial's exact positioning. Despite the assertion in the local press that the site had been chosen through 'negotiation between the city council and the military authorities', an examination of the council minutes tells a very different story.[12] A meeting of the parks sub-committee of Canterbury city council on 10 February 1904, chaired by the mayor, recommended that the memorial should be erected on the south side of the Dane John Gardens to avoid it 'being dwarfed by the city walls'.[13] However, the following week a full session of the council rejected the sub-committee's recommendation on the grounds that 'the military authorities saw objections' and the memorial was built in the shadow of the walls.[14]

Regimental control over the memorialisation process can also be seen in the financing of the schemes. Committee members were all too aware of the proprietorial sub-text of subscription lists and so were keen to limit contributions to those who fell within the boundaries of their communities. For the military,

---

[9]   For much of the war, the local press had been calling for Liverpool's civic authorities to become involved in the King's Regiment's commemorative plans. As early as November 1900, the *Liverpool Mercury* had published a letter insisting that the city council should mark the return of 'our Imperial Volunteers' with 'some permanent recognition, some memorial worthy of the event'. *Liverpool Mercury*, 23 November 1900.

[10]   West Sussex Record Office (WSRO), RSR/MS/11/6 Royal Sussex Memorial Fund, minutes, 24 April 1902, p. 4.

[11]   *Kentish Gazette and Canterbury Press*, 9 May 1903.

[12]   *Kentish Gazette and Canterbury Press*, 4 June 1904.

[13]   Canterbury Cathedral Archives (CCA), CC/AC23, Parks Committee, minutes, 10 February 1904.

[14]   CCA, CC/AC/23/1, Canterbury City Council, minutes, 17 February 1904.

this could raise the delicate issue of how to deal with requests from bereaved relatives who wished to contribute to regimental memorials. When the mother of one of the fallen of the Royal Engineers sent in a donation of £20 towards the Corps' memorial scheme it required a full meeting of the committee to 'authorise that the money could be accepted on this occasion'.[15] A similar compromise was reached by the memorial committee of The Buffs, East Kent Regiment. An announcement in the local paper stated that, although it had been unanimously decided not to open subscriptions to the general public, Hammond and Company in Canterbury and Cox and Company in London would still receive donations 'in deference to the requests of relatives and friends of those who gave their lives for Queen, King and Country'.[16] The Queen's Own Royal West Kent Regiment chose to make no exceptions to the rule that the process should be kept in-house and donations for the regimental memorial in All Saints' Church, Maidstone, were restricted to past and present members of the regiment.[17] Similarly, although the Duke of Cambridge was fully aware of the desire of relatives to make a contribution to the Royal Artillery memorial, he was nonetheless adamant 'that subscriptions should be confined exclusively to members of the regiment'.[18] By insisting that contributions should come from the regiment alone, Cambridge cut the men from their families and made the dead the possession of the army.

Even the inclusion of non-military personnel on the organising committee did not automatically lead to an acceptance of civilian financial help. The memorial committee for the Queen's Royal West Surrey regiment was chaired by a civilian, Viscount Midleton, the Lord Lieutenant of the County, and contained both the mayor of Guildford and the vicar of Holy Trinity Church, but still chose to restrict subscriptions to past and present members of the regiment only.[19] On the relatively rare occasion when a regimental scheme was opened up to civilian financing, the primary ownership of the memorial was still made abundantly clear. The inscription on the commemorative tablet to the 10th Royal Hussars in All Saints' Church, Aldershot, states that the memorial was erected by 'Officers, Warrant Officers, Non-com Officers and men of the Regiment past and present and a few near relatives and friends'.[20] The Cheshire regiment and the Lancashire Fusiliers were equally keen to downplay the importance of civilian donations. The honorary secretary of the Cheshire regiment's memorial committee pointed out to the editor of the *Chester Chronicle* that while 'all ranks serving in the Cheshire regiment' had subscribed to the

15 REM, RO270, Royal Engineers War Memorial Committee, minutes, 11 February 1903.
16 *Kentish Gazette and Canterbury Press*, 9 May 1903.
17 Chaplin, *The Queen's Own Royal West Kent Regiment 1881–1914*, p. 111.
18 *The Times*, 9 July 1910.
19 Surrey History Centre (SHC), QRWS/1/8/2/22, unveiling programme, no date.
20 Gildea, *For Remembrance*, p. 73.

regiment's memorial, this had been supplemented by only 'some friends in the county'.[21] At the unveiling of the Lancashire Fusiliers' memorial in Bury on 18 March 1905, Lieutenant-Colonel Sir Lees Knowles, chairman of the memorial committee and commanding officer of the 3rd volunteer battalion, was quick to make a similar distinction between civilian and military contributions. He opened his dedication address by informing those gathered for the ceremony that although 'the townspeople of Bury' had made some financial contribution, the scheme had been funded 'principally by Fusiliers'.[22] Colonel Donne of the Royal Sussex regiment felt equally obliged to set the financial record straight at the unveiling of the Royal Sussex memorial in Brighton. He noted that of the £1,400 collected, 'the three Battalions of the Royal Sussex Regiment had subscribed £803 towards the erection of the monument'.[23] By marginalising the financial input of the wider community the military authorities were carefully detaching the fallen from their civilian roots and were signalling their right to be viewed as their memory sites' sole owners.

For the military, restricting subscriptions to those who fell within the boundaries of their self-contained communities was, by and large, a luxury it could well afford. Although regimental and corps committees generally made a point of proclaiming that donations were entirely voluntary, the organisational structure of the army meant that sufficient indirect pressure could be applied to the pool of potential subscribers that initial targets could be both ambitious and attainable.[24] All of the regiments studied for this survey published lists of subscribers in the regimental magazines, with officers being individually named and the rank and file listed by company.[25] These lists served the dual function of, on the one hand, celebrating those who had fulfilled their obligations and, on the other, encouraging the remainder to match their efforts. Such encouragement could, of course, take on an official tenor. In November 1903, the Royal Engineers' memorial committee, in one last push to reach their target of £2,800, sent a letter to all the district commanders containing a list of 'officers who are known not to have subscribed or to have notified their intention not to do so' with the instruction that they should 'ascertain whether they will subscribe'.[26] Fund-raising for the Royal Marines was also not without its difficulties. Marines tended to contribute together from the ships on which

---

21 *Chester Chronicle*, 6 August 1908.
22 The Fusilier Museum (TFM), *The Lancashire Fusiliers' Annual*, 1905, p. 3.
23 *Brighton Herald*, 5 November 1904.
24 REM, RO270, Royal Engineers Memorial Committee, minutes, 7 November 1902.
25 Royal Engineers, *RE Journal*; Royal West Kent Regiment, *Queen's Own Gazette*, Royal East Kent Regiment, *The Dragon*.
26 REM, RO270, Royal Engineers War Memorial Committee, minutes, 11 November 1903. Although this final drive did have some effect with over £110 being collected in the following month, there was still a shortfall by the time of the memorial's unveiling which resulted in two of the bas-reliefs not being added until a later date.

they were serving and it was noted in February 1901 that only thirty-seven ships had subscribed thus far. Three months later eighty-six had contributed, but thirty capital ships, on which the largest numbers of marines served, were still absent from the subscriptions lists.[27] The committee was prepared to concede that perhaps some of the problem was in the lack of information. It was noted that 'some of the circulars may not have reached their destination; that in many cases the appeal has been accidentally overlooked and forgotten; or that would-be subscribers are desirous of more information before sending their contributions'.[28] In August 1901 the committee came close to a 'naming and shaming' move of its former officers, as it stated that of 300 officers on the retired list only 120 had subscribed to the scheme. To remedy this situation the committee was going to send each of them a fresh letter of appeal.[29] The efforts of the committee paid off with the full amount in hand before the unveiling ceremony.[30]

Where shortfalls in fund-raising did occur this was often, in part, the result of the memorial committee's failure to provide concrete detail on the form. As will be discussed later, both the Royal Marines and the Royal Sussex regiment engaged in protracted debates about the relative merits of utilitarian versus plastic memorials. Consequently both launched their fund-raising campaigns before the nature of their memory sites, let alone their precise form, had been decided.[31] For the Royal Sussex this meant that their original intention of raising subscriptions through the issuing of a discreet circular, on the grounds that the committee did 'not want to bother people or worry them in any way', was soon abandoned in favour of a more vigorous campaign involving charity balls, amateur dramatics, concerts and cinema showings.[32] This more pro-active approach proved successful and by the time of the monument's unveiling in

---

[27] *Globe and Laurel*, Vol. VIII, No. 64 (February 1901), p. 21; Vol. VIII, No. 67 (May 1901), p. 52.
[28] *Globe and Laurel*, Vol. VIII, No. 66 (April 1901), pp. 38–39.
[29] *Globe and Laurel*, Vol. VIII, No. 70 (August 1901), p. 87.
[30] *Globe and Laurel*, Vol. IX, No. 86 (December 1902), p. 136.
[31] *Globe and Laurel*, Vol. VIII, No. 64 (February 1901), p. 21; WSRO, RSR/MS/11/6, Royal Sussex Memorial Fund, minutes, 24 April 1902, p. 7.
[32] WSRO, RSR/MS/11/6, Royal Sussex Memorial Fund, minutes, 24 August 1902, p. 30; Royal Sussex Memorial Fund, subscriptions list, 31 October 1903. Another possible explanation for the difficulties the Royal Sussex faced was put forward by one potential donor. In declining to serve on the memorial committee, William Grantham suggested that donor fatigue may have an adverse effect on the scheme's success. He noted that, 'only a few weeks ago Lady Idina Brassey and other ladies in Sussex were asking me to subscribe in memory of officers and men who had fallen, to Cape Town Cathedral Fund, following on the heels of that was an application by the Lord Lieutenant for more funds for the Volunteer equipment fund, which I tried to get support for as chairman of my parish council, but could get hardly any to give besides myself, and then we want a good deal more money for our Soldiers and Families Fund in our district and on top of all this you bring out this

1905, a deficit of £700 only a year before had been turned into a surplus of £1,112.[33]

As well as keeping a tight rein on fund-raising, most regimental war memorial committees also controlled the precise form of the memorial. In almost every instance the committees were the only body to examine different proposals and they usually made a choice without placing a shortlist or range of options before their constituencies. Even in those schemes where the wider community had been invited to contribute financially, it was not uncommon for decisions over form to be restricted to a small clique of senior officers. Three colonels of the Manchester regiment took the lead in selecting a design for the monument in St Anne's Square and in Canterbury it was left to the commanding officer of The Buffs to provide precise instructions as to the form of the regimental memorial in the Dane John Gardens.[34] The Royal Marines' memorial committee was an exception, as the committee members consulted every branch of the corps through representatives before resolving 'that the memorial should be in the form of a monument, to be erected in some open space in London'.[35] However, in opting for a formal, plastic memorial, the Royal Marines fell in line with the decision reached by the overwhelming majority of committees.

Remarkably little dissent or disagreement was caused by this lack of consultation. However, where there was debate it was frequently sparked by the issue of the practical utility of the chosen designs. A member of the Honourable Artillery Company asked whether the regiment would do more good by sponsoring a hospital bed as a memorial.[36] The Manchester regiment had originally proposed that a soldiers' club should form part of their plan, although the idea was dropped on the grounds of cost.[37] Despite the seeming acceptance of the Royal Marines' scheme, it did not stop some officers from asking whether an educational fund for the orphans of NCOs should be established, and it was noted that repeat subscribers to the fund often asked for part of their donation to be diverted to other Royal Marine charities.[38] The suggestion to fund the education of NCOs' orphans is particularly revealing of a late Victorian/Edwardian mindset for it shows a desire to encourage the respectable and self-improving element within the other ranks.

---

subscription list'. WSRO, RSR/MS/11/6, William Grantham to the honorary secretary of the Royal Sussex Memorial Fund, 23 March 1901.

[33] WSRO, RSR/MS/11/6, Statement of accounts; 31 July 1904; Statement of Accounts 30 September 1905.

[34] CCA, CC/BB149, Canterbury City Council, minutes, 13 April 1923; *Manchester Guardian*, 10 October 1907.

[35] *Globe and Laurel*, December 1900, p. 163.

[36] HACA, Court Minutes, 19 January 1903.

[37] *Manchester Guardian*, 10 October 1907.

[38] *Globe and Laurel*, Vol. VIII, No. 63 (January 1901), p. 9; No. 66 (April 1901), pp. 38–39.

The decision by the committee of the Royal Sussex regiment's memorial fund to establish a cottage home 'for deserving soldiers of the regiment (including regulars, yeomanry, militia and volunteers) with or without their families, in memory of the officers, non-commissioned officers and men who have fallen during the South African War' was also typical of the philanthropic drive of charitable society in this period.[39] The initial impetus for the Royal Sussex's scheme had been provided by Mrs Papillon, a leading light of Sussex polite society, who had offered to donate the £245 she had collected as part of the Prince Christian Victor fund for cottage homes should the regiment adopt a home as its memorial.[40] However, notwithstanding the ease with which the resolution was passed at the memorial committee's first meeting in April 1902, when the proposal for a cottage home was made public it was greeted by some influential dissenting voices from within the regiment. At the forefront of this opposition was the regiment's commanding officer, Lieutenant-Colonel Donne. Still on active service, he wrote to the honorary secretary of the memorial committee expressing concern that such a utilitarian scheme would not only be unworthy of the regiment but would also be too limited in scope as it 'would stand in the way of a great memorial TO ALL THE SUSSEX CORPS who have shared in the Campaign'.[41] On the regiment's return to England in mid-August 1902, Donne was duly elected to the memorial committee and his twin concerns about prestige and inclusiveness were dealt with when it was resolved at the very next meeting of the committee to abandon the cottage home in favour of 'a memorial which shall be worthy of Sussex and the brave men of whose devotion to their country it is to be a lasting commemoration' and a benefit fund 'to assist as large a number of men as possible'.[42] Colonel E. C. Browne of the Royal Scots Fusiliers shared Donne's misgivings about utilitarian schemes, although his concern lay more with the didactic function of commemoration. Responding to the criticism that the regiment would have done better to have spent the memorial funds on practical schemes to ameliorate the sufferings of former soldiers, Browne argued that figurative monuments:

---

[39] WSRO, RSR/MS/11/6, Royal Sussex Memorial Fund, minutes, 24 April 1902. For more on the philanthropic response of British society to the Boer War see Andrew Thompson, 'Publicity, Philanthropy and Commemoration', in Omissi and Thompson (eds), *The Impact of the South African War*, pp. 106–113.

[40] Prince Christian Victor, the grandson of Queen Victoria, died of enteric on 29 October 1900 while serving in South Africa. See Pakenham, *The Boer War*, pp. 458–459. The fund was established at the end of 1900 under the presidency of Field Marshal Frederick Roberts with Sir Redvers Buller acting as chairman.

[41] WSRO, RSR/MS/11/6, Lt-Colonel Donne to Colonel Kilgour, 8 March 1902 (capitalisation in the original).

[42] WSRO, RSR/MS/11/6, Royal Sussex Memorial Fund, minutes, 12 January 1903.

educated and enriched the minds of youth, engendering a spirit of veneration for, and a desire to emulate, noble deeds and personal sacrifices undergone by their countrymen in times of stress and danger. Thus, the dead in the service of their country were made alive again on the canvas of the painter, in the marble and bronze of the sculptor.[43]

However, monumental commemoration was not entirely unproblematic. Concern over the impact that the dominant iconographic message of the Royal Engineers' commemorative project might have on regimental prestige resulted in the corps' ambitious scheme at their headquarters in Chatham becoming embroiled in controversy. The first hint that all was not well with the corps' memorialisation process was to come from a retired colonel, E. Lloyd. In a letter to the memorial committee, he expressed his concern that decisions had been taken without the convening of a general meeting of the officers, the traditional forum for such matters.[44] In fact, the committee could have been forgiven for assuming that such an informal channel for validation need not have applied in this case, for the scheme had been instigated by no less a person than Lord Kitchener. In May 1902, Kitchener had written to the commandant of the Royal Engineers at Chatham, Sir T. Fraser, with the offer of 'four bronze statues of Boers and four bas-reliefs for use in a war memorial to the fallen'. For good measure he had enclosed a detailed sketch of the proposal.[45] Unsurprisingly, Fraser had been quick to accept the offer and a memorial committee meeting in October 1902, chaired by Sir Richard Harrison, the Inspector General of Fortifications, had unanimously agreed to press ahead with the plan.[46] Although Colonel Lloyd's protest, which had been prompted by an article outlining the scheme in the regimental magazine, was soon followed by others, the committee 'decided to inform the correspondents that they intended to continue with the memorial nonetheless'.[47] It was only when Field Marshal Sir John Simmons, former Inspector-General of Fortifications from 1875–1880 and governor of Malta until his retirement in 1888, added his name to the list of complainants that the committee eventually caved in and resolved 'to defer any further action until a General Meeting of the Corps can be held'.[48] Predictably, the first resolution the general meeting passed was to elect an entirely new committee.

Yet, though procedural irregularities undoubtedly antagonised many retired officers, at the root of the Royal Engineers' dispute lay much graver concerns over the form that the corps' memory site should take. As Alex King has

---

[43]   Quoted in Spiers, *The Scottish Soldier and Empire*, p. 205.
[44]   REM, RO270, Royal Engineers' War Memorial Committee, letter from Colonel E. Lloyd to the memorial committee, 7 November 1902.
[45]   REM, RO270, letter from Kitchener to Sir T. Fraser, 21 May 1902.
[46]   REM, RO270, Royal Engineers War Memorial Committee, minutes, 24 October 1902.
[47]   REM, RO270, Royal Engineers War Memorial Committee, minutes, 21 November 1902.
[48]   REM, RO270, Royal Engineers War Memorial Committee, minutes, 19 December 1902.

shown in his survey of commemoration in the aftermath of the First World War, choice of design was considered to be all-important in an age when it was generally believed that iconographical symbolism was fixed.[49] The Boer statues and bas-reliefs at the centre of the Royal Engineers' scheme had originally been intended as the focal points for a monument in honour of Paul Kruger, the former president of the Transvaal. The pieces had been embargoed at the outbreak of war and eventually donated to Kitchener who, as we have seen above, subsequently offered them to the Royal Engineers' memorial committee. Such unpropitious origins must have rung some alarm bells even with the original memorial committee members and, indeed, they seem to have been not entirely unaware of the sensitive nature of Kitchener's gift. Although, in general, they viewed the pieces as 'impersonal' and 'works of art', they, nevertheless, decided that a bas-relief depicting the peace conference at McNeill's Farm after the battle of Majuba Hill was a step too far and should be replaced by a 'plaque recording Lord Kitchener's gift of the bronzes'.[50] That this nod towards conciliation would prove to be far less than was going to be necessary to stem the tide of criticism that the committee would eventually face over the inclusion of such contentious images is hardly surprising, but that it should ever have been considered sufficient does provide us with a fascinating insight into the contested meaning of the war in Britain at the conclusion of hostilities.

Anti-Boer feeling, which was an inevitable consequence of the brutality of war for British combatants and which had been fuelled domestically by the 'yellow press', sat uneasily with the assimilation of the Boer Republics into a federated British South Africa by the Treaty of Vereeniging.[51] Although nearly all those present at the general meeting of the Royal Engineers on 6 June 1903 were in agreement that the original plans of the memorial committee to include the Boer statues and bas-reliefs on the corps' memory site should be abandoned, there were still heated exchanges when it came to providing a rationale for this stance. Major M. Hildebrand, a retired Royal Engineers officer, clearly articulated the view that consideration of Boer sensibilities had to take precedence when it came to commemorating the war. In a letter sent to the editor of the Royal Engineers' journal and read out at the meeting, he made plain the repercussions that pressing ahead with the original plan would have:

> Having lately been in the Transvaal, I learned that the idea [of using the statues and bas-reliefs on the Royal Engineers' monument] had become known to the Boers, to whom, I was assured, it would give immense annoyance

[49] Alex King, *Memorials of the Great War in Britain*, pp. 11–15.
[50] REM, RO270, Royal Engineers War Memorial Committee, minutes, 24 October 1902. The battle of Majuba Hill, 27 February 1881, was a decisive defeat for the British in the First Boer War. See Ian Castle, *Majuba 1881: The Hill of Destiny* (Colchester: Osprey, 1996).
[51] See Bill Nasson, *The South African War 1899–1902* (London: Arnold, 1999), pp. 227–233.

and pain. My informant, who broached the subject with me asked if it were true, which he did not until then believe, had exceptional opportunities of learning the Boer sentiments, though himself a supporter of the new order of things. He said to make such use of what had been intended for Mr. Kruger's statue would cause the keenest feeling of resentment amongst our new fellow subjects.[52]

Major-General Sir Elliott Wood, who had served as engineer-in-chief during the war and was a member of the original memorial committee, was quick to voice his support for this line of reasoning. Having been responsible for drawing up the original sketch-plan of Kitchener's scheme, he was clearly keen to distance himself from what had turned out to be a contentious and manifestly unpopular proposal.[53] The choice of design was, he insisted, 'a very important question … for it might become more than a corps matter; it might go beyond this and affect the army and perhaps the country generally, if we were to give offence to our new fellow subjects'.[54] For two retired senior officers, however, the memory of the human cost of the recent fighting was still too fresh for consideration of such political niceties to take priority. Arguing that it was first important 'to clear up our own views before we consider those of other people', Lieutenant-General Sir Robert Grant, Inspector General of Fortifications from 1891 to 1898, urged those assembled to 'remember that it was through what we hold to be [the Boers'] mistaken views and their mistaken actions that we lost the officers and men to whom we wish to erect the memorial'.[55] General Sir James Browne, a former Colonel Commandant of the corps, was prepared to go one step further when apportioning blame. In a letter read out at the meeting on his behalf, he maintained that to use such 'undesirable images would be a monument to bad taste, never to be effaced', for the statues 'were made to honour Mr. Kruger, the man above all others in this world responsible for the deaths of those we wish to honour'.[56]

An interesting argument to bolster further the case against the original proposal was presented by Sir Thomas Gallway, who had succeeded Sir Richard Harrison as Inspector General of Fortifications earlier that year. Insisting that the minutes should record his 'strong protest' against Kitchener's scheme on

---

[52] REM, RO2070, letter from Major Hildebrand to Royal Engineers War Memorial Committee, undated.
[53] REM, RO270, Royal Engineers Memorial Committee, minutes, 6 June 1903. Later in the same meeting, Wood explicitly disassociated himself from ownership of the sketch by insisting that, 'The sketch was not … in any sense my sketch, except that I embodied the ideas of Lord Kitchener in that sketch'. REM, RO270, Royal Engineers Memorial Committee, minutes, 6 June 1903.
[54] REM, RO270, Royal Engineers Memorial Committee, minutes, 6 June 1903.
[55] REM, RO270, Royal Engineers Memorial Committee, minutes, 6 June 1903.
[56] REM, RO270, Royal Engineers Memorial Committee, minutes, 6 June 1903.

2 Royal Engineers' Memorial, Brompton Barracks, Chatham.

the grounds that the statues 'represent an armed enemy', Gallway raised the moral stakes by arguing that, before any decision could be reached, the meeting must first 'consider the feelings of the relatives of our gallant dead'.[57] Major J. Winn, a member of the original war memorial committee, although differing on the nature of the views held by the bereaved, was still equally adamant that they merited special consideration. His attitude had, he said, 'hardened' against using the statues as the result of a letter he had recently received from the father of one of the fallen:

> I am thinking of a man who in a letter said he thought that, if the Boers would consider it to be a bad thing for the figures to be used, it ought not to be done. Knowing that man lost a son in the war, I feel more strongly that his views should carry weight on the subject.[58]

In advancing their own viewpoints by privileging the opinions of a group which fell outside the bounds of the military community, both Winn and Gallway

---

[57]   REM, RO270, Royal Engineers Memorial Committee, minutes, 6 June 1903. The was a tactic that would be deployed with greater regularity in the more heated and protracted debates over commemorative form in the aftermath of the First World War. See Donaldson, *Ritual and Remembrance*, p. 72.
[58]   REM, RO270, Royal Engineers Memorial Committee, minutes, 6 June 1903.

were, inadvertently, raising wider questions surrounding the ownership of the memorial. Only four months earlier members of the organising committee had made abundantly clear, by the grudging manner in which they had accepted an unsolicited contribution to the memorial fund from a bereaved mother, that the construction of a memory site should be a matter for the corps alone.[59] However, aware that such an exclusive approach could not be sustained if a climate developed where iconographical symbolism and, by extension, the very meaning of the war were contested, the meeting unanimously resolved to elect a new committee with instructions to start the process afresh. The threat of any further dissent was subsequently averted by devolving the question of form to the professional care of an established architect, Ingress Bell.[60] His decision to opt for a triumphal arch, to mirror the Crimean Arch erected at the corps' headquarters in Brompton in the 1860s, was reassuringly uncontroversial and the project proceeded to completion without further hitches.[61]

Such debates highlight the extent to which, for the military, remembrance was underpinned by regimental prestige. Location as well as form could be crucial. Having made commitments to extravagant memorials, it became important that the positioning of memory sites drew the public attention their scale demanded. The Royal Marines' memorial committee originally requested a site in front of the Royal Exchange. A highly significant location passed by many thousands each day was regarded as fitting for the corps with its long history and deep connections with the City of London. The corps' journal referred to it as 'a spot which has been rightly called the "Centre of the Universe"'.[62] When the City authorities announced that a place could not be guaranteed, the committee turned to another prestige site, requesting Trafalgar Square or a site near the Admiralty as the memorial 'will to a great extent be of national interest', and enlisted the assistance of the Prince of Wales to help secure it. The Office of Works duly obliged by allotting a space on the corner of St James's Park and the Mall facing the newly planned Admiralty Arch, which itself formed part of the Queen Victoria memorial project.[63] A highly prestigious site linking the

---

[59] See p. 50 above.

[60] Ingress Bell had previously worked as a surveyor for the War Office and was a partner of Aston Webb, the then president of the Royal Institute of British Architects. See A. Stuart Grey, *Edwardian Architecture: A Biographical Dictionary* (London: Duckworth, 1985), pp. 46–47

[61] The political significance of the Boer statues was once again brought into high relief in the aftermath of the First World War. In December 1920, General Smuts, the Prime Minister of South Africa, approached Alfred Milner, the Secretary of State for the Colonies, requesting their return. Milner duly obliged for, in his words, 'political reasons ... as an act of goodwill'. REM, *The Sapper*, Vol. 26, No. 307 (February 1921), p. 99.

[62] *Globe and Laurel*, Vol. VIII, No. 69 (July 1901), p. 76.

[63] TNA WORK 20/55 Royal Marines' memorial. Letter from Major-General A. French to Office of Works, 31 October 1901; Office of Works to French, 25 November 1901; *Globe*

Royal Marines to the monarch's formal London home and the Royal Navy, the service which formed its home, was thus achieved. The memorial committee had no doubts about the impact such a prestigious site would make:

> The position is an excellent one, within a few yards of what, in a few years, when the Victoria Memorial scheme is accomplished, will be a much used thoroughfare. There are no buildings within sixty yards or so, therefore there will be nothing to dwarf the Monument, which will then be seen at its best advantage.[64]

The Royal Artillery also petitioned for a site equalling its perceived importance and was granted a site facing Carlton House Terrace on the Mall.[65] Having achieved this enormously significant site, the war memorial committee found themselves required to submit all plans to Lord Esher who was chairing the Queen Victoria memorial scheme which included the refashioning of the Mall. As will be seen, this was not always an easy relationship and led to much intrusion into the Royal Artillery scheme. By contrast, the Carabiniers were forced to accept a much less visible location. Allocated a position on the corner of Chelsea Gardens on the approach to Chelsea Bridge, the site lacked real presence. In his 1928 survey of London statuary, Edward Gleichen rather tartly states that the Carabiniers' memorial was placed there because the Office of Works could think of nowhere else.[66] The Manchester regiment also had to settle for a relatively modest site. Anxious to secure a prominent position in St Albert's Square opposite the town hall, the war memorial committee approached the council about removing the statue to Bishop Fraser to make room for the regiment's monument. However, with the town council concerned that the 'war memorial would be out of keeping with the other statues in the square', the regiment had to accept the offer of a secondary site in less prestigious St Anne's Square.[67]

Even where plans were on a more modest scale, location was still an important consideration. Although the Honourable Artillery Company limited its memorial plans to a bronze tablet for its headquarters, it also took the decision to erect a small marble tablet in its church of St Botolph, Bishopsgate. The second memorial gave the Company's sacrifice public presence in a way a memorial sited in the headquarters, and inaccessible to the general public, could

---

and Laurel, Vol. VIII, No. 74 (December 1901), p. 137.

[64]   *Globe and Laurel*, Vol. IX, No. 86 (December 1902), p. 136.

[65]   TNA WORK 20/59 Royal Artillery memorial, Office of Works memorandum, 12 December 1905.

[66]   Gleichen, *London's Open-Air Statuary*, p. xl; See also file TNA WORK 20/57 Carabiniers' Memorial.

[67]   *Manchester Guardian*, 10 October 1907.

3 Carabiniers' Memorial, Chelsea Embankment.

not.[68] This was supplemented still further by financial support for an official history of the Honourable Artillery Company during the war compiled by two of its members, Basil Williams and Erskine Childers, published by Smith, Elder and Co. in 1903.[69] A large number of regiments chose a cathedral location as the most obvious way of providing a local presence.[70] This simultaneously served to reinforce regional ties and underscore regimental tradition. The King's Royal Rifle Corps chose to erect a plaque in Winchester Cathedral because it was the regiment's 'Valhalla'. It was, according to the regimental magazine, in a cathedral 'that every young rifleman begins his career as a soldier and learns to be proud of his regiment'.[71]

---

[68] HACA Court Minutes, 19 January, 30 March 1903; *City Press*, 8 June, 20 July 1904.

[69] HACA Court Minutes, 21 March, 11 April 1904.

[70] Meurig Jones, in his survey of Boer War memorials, has estimated that nearly 40 per cent of regimental memorials are located in cathedrals. M. Jones, 'A Survey of Memorials to the Second Anglo-Boer War in the United Kingdom and Eire', *Journal of the Africana Society* (1999), reproduced on the Anglo-Boer War Memorials Project website, http://members.aol.com/abwmp/briefing.htm (accessed 20 June 2012).

[71] Jones, 'A Survey of Memorials to the Second Anglo-Boer War'.

4 Coldstream Guards'
memorial, St Paul's Cathedral.

Themes of tradition and continuity frequently underpinned the iconographical symbolism of regimental memorials. For the Coldstream Guards the weight of regimental history was the leitmotif of its memorial tablet. Designed by the celebrated sculptor, William Goscombe John, the engraved tablet imparts a message of tradition, heroism and sacrifice. The foreground of the panel consists of two soldiers on the veldt; one wounded, the other in the act of providing solace. In the middle distance are the famous kopjes of South Africa, while the sky contains the ethereal presence of former Coldstreamers including General Monck, who raised the original force, figures from the Peninsula War, Waterloo and the Crimean campaign. This host, looking down approvingly on their modern counterparts, signals that the honourable traditions of the regiment have been maintained.[72] John employed a similar symbolic artifice for the memorial to the King's Liverpool regiment in St John's Gardens, Liverpool. Flanking the central statue of Britannia are two soldiers standing at ease: one in the uniform of 1685, the year of the regiment's enrolment,

---

[72]   See Gildea, *For Remembrance*, p. 129.

the other in the field-service uniform of the South African War. At the rear of the monument, linking past and present, is the figure of a drummer-boy from the battle of Dettingen in 1743. In the act of beating the call to arms he reinforces the message that, throughout its glorious history, the regiment has answered its country's call.[73] John was not the only sculptor to employ this technique. Thomas Rudge's commemorative frieze to the Cheshire regiment in the south transept of Chester Cathedral bookends the central panel listing the names of the fallen with two niches in which stand a soldier from 1689, the date the Duke of Norfolk first raised the regiment, and a bugler from 1902.[74] A more common way of stressing regimental tradition was to have inscribed on memorials references to previous battle honours. The figure of a soldier commemorating the fallen of the Lancashire Fusiliers sports a primrose hackle in his busby and a red rose on his tunic; the former a reminder of the colour of the regiment's original facings, the latter a reference to the roses worn by the men during the battle of Minden in 1759.[75] The Suffolk regiment adopted a more direct approach. Recalling the most famous episode in the regiment's history, the word 'Gibraltar' was given pride of place on the memorial plaque in St Mary's Church, Bury St Edmunds.[76]

For the committees of the Royal Marines and Royal Artillery, the key issue of impressing the importance of their worth and role was expressed in their desire to erect memorials of the finest quality making a significant aesthetic statement in the process. Artistic value was regarded as a prime signifier of a memorial's value. Given a site in the Mall, the Royal Artillery committee was extremely keen to provide a memorial grand in drama and aesthetic quality and approached an established sculptor, W. R. Colton, to commence work on designs.[77] The site allocated to the Royal Artillery drew in King Edward VII, as it would form an integral part of the Mall widening and Victoria memorial scheme, on which he was consulted at every stage by the project's chair, Lord Esher. As will be discussed later, Esher was initially worried about the inclusion and positioning of the roll of honour on the memorial, eventually insisting that

---

[73] Terry Cavanagh, *Public Sculpture of Liverpool* (Liverpool: Liverpool University Press, 1997), pp. 177–179.

[74] *Chester Chronicle*, 6 August 1904. Goscombe John continued to employ this iconographic device in the aftermath of the First World War. See his monument to the Royal Welch Fusiliers at Wrexham.

[75] TFM, *The Lancashire Fusiliers' Annual*, 1907, p. 4.

[76] The Suffolk regiment had held out for four years against a Spanish blockade of Gibraltar in the late eighteenth century. As a result the regiment took as its own the coat of arms of Gibraltar. Lieutenant-Colonel E. A. H. Webb, *History of the 12th (Suffolk Regiment)* (London: Spottiswoode and Co., 1914), pp. 1899–1901.

[77] For details on Colton's career see *British Sculpture, 1850–1914*, p. 28.

it should be relegated to a less prominent location.[78] Colton duly amended his plans, but this did not resolve the matter. Sir Shomberg McDonnell, the Secretary to the Office of Works, was concerned by the sketches of the horse, representing the spirit of war, due to crown the memorial. He wrote to Colton outlining his belief that the King would not approve the current designs: 'In fact without wishing to urge upon you the design of a conventional horse it is quite certain that only a perfect horse is likely to meet His Majesty's approval'.[79] Colton was content to oblige and confirmed the changes he had made to bring the designs into line with the requests.[80] However, the final design of the memorial was still not set. In December 1906, Colton requested permission to exhibit a model of the memorial at the Royal Academy with a notice that the design had been approved by the King. McDonnell agreed to the exhibition of the model, but refused permission to advertise the King's approval, as it had not yet been formally agreed.[81] Somewhat amazingly, the issue made no progress over the next three years. The precise reasons for this delay are obscure, but were probably caused by Colton's commitments to other projects. A model was ready for exhibition in 1909, but still caused disquiet. By this time, McDonnell's patience with Colton was severely stretched and he was using Thomas Brock of the Royal Academy as an intermediary to influence Colton's designs. In one letter to Brock, McDonnell took the opportunity to vent his frustrations:

> Mr Colton, for some reason of his own which he endeavoured to describe, but which I confess I am not quite able to fathom, has placed the right wing of the figure at a curious angle: the effect is to make the wing droop over the neck of the horse, and to give the impression that Peace has sustained a wound in that member, and is unable to keep it at the same angle as the left wing.
>
> I feel that this must be remedied, and the two wings placed at the same angle: otherwise the symmetry of the monument will, I think, be seriously impaired, and it may possibly appear a little absurd, which would be unfortunate in the highest degree.[82]

This time, Colton seems to have taken everything to heart and produced a fresh model. McDonnell travelled to Colton's studios near High Wycombe to examine

---

[78] TNA WORK 20/59 Royal Artillery memorial. Secretary of Office of Works [Sir Shomberg McDonnell] to Lord Knollys [Royal Private Secretary], 9 December 1905.
[79] TNA WORK 20/59 Royal Artillery memorial. Letter from McDonnell to Colton, 16 July 1906.
[80] TNA WORK 20/59 Royal Artillery memorial. Letter from Colton to McDonnell, 16 November 1906.
[81] TNA WORK 20/59 Royal Artillery memorial. Letters between McDonnell and Colton, 15, 17 December 1906.
[82] TNA WORK 20/59 Royal Artillery memorial. Letter from McDonnell to Thomas Brock, 9 May 1909.

5 Royal Artillery memorial, The Mall.

it and found 'the result extremely good', as he told Esher by letter. However, he still had a problem with the angle of Peace's left wing. The intention was that it should cover the horse conveying the impression that Peace had tamed War. 'This idea may be excellent, but the result is grotesque: it gives the impression that somebody has shot at the angel and tipped it in the wing'. McDonnell confirmed that Colton 'is a charming man, and his work is delightful; but he is rather inclined to be obstinate about it'; he therefore requested Esher to visit Colton personally in order to press the case.[83] By the autumn the amendments had been made and the memorial was finally given royal consent.[84]

Having completed fund-raising in 1906, explaining the delay to both the regiment and the general public was extremely difficult and embarrassing. Lord Roberts, honorary chair of the Royal Artillery memorial committee, had been anxious to exhibit full designs of the memorial to contributors in 1906, but had not been able to do so.[85] When the memorial was finally unveiled in July 1910, *The Times* noted that the delay in completion was due to debates over

[83] TNA WORK 20/59 Royal Artillery memorial. Letter from McDonnell to Esher, 10 June 1909.

[84] TNA WORK 20/59 Royal Artillery memorial. Letter from Colton to McDonnell, 30 September 1909.

[85] TNA WORK 20/59 Royal Artillery memorial. Memorandum by McDonnell, 25 April 1906.

siting. The source of this information is unclear, but it was a tactful excuse to cover the catalogue of revisions.[86] Rather sadly, the memorial was not then considered an unqualified success. F. W. Speight of the Society for the Protection of Ancient Buildings complained that the memorial had not been centred on the Duke of York's steps on the opposite side of the Mall meaning that it looked unbalanced to anyone descending the steps.[87] Another correspondent to *The Times* drew attention to the fact that the names were placed too low down, and overheard two spectators at the unveiling 'disputing as to whether the wings on the monument belonged to the "horse or the lady." I shared their doubts'.[88] Two more complaints were then received on the position of the names. Both correspondents implied that the hapless Colton was to blame, when in fact he had originally proposed a much more prominent siting of the name panels.[89] The convoluted gestation of the Royal Artillery memorial reveals the tensions inherent in a public memorial. Because of its location, it was expected to conform to a different aesthetic from that originally desired by its instigators. However, the Royal Artillery committee was never prepared to forego the prestigious site in order to regain closer control of its form and function.

The Royal Marines were also keen that the corps' exulted standing should be reflected in the aesthetic quality of any proposed memorial. As with the Royal Artillery, an established sculptor, Adrian Jones, a former cavalry officer, was commissioned to undertake the work.[90] The committee was quick to stress the reputation of Jones and the favourable reaction to his ideas from experts, stating in the corps' journal: 'An eminent sculptor has volunteered his service and advice to the Committee, and has furnished a design of a monument which has been criticised in most favourable terms by the leading artists of the day'.[91] However, aesthetic values could clash with the desired narrative, for on inspection of the full design the committee had certain reservations: 'while all admired the artistic effect of the design as a work of art, it was not considered suitable to the purpose in view, being not sufficiently true to fact and there being no direct allusion to China, or principle achievements which have brought fresh honour to the Corps both in South Africa and China'.[92] The committee decided to request amendments asking Jones to include figures of two marines,

---

[86]   *The Times*, 9 July 1910.
[87]   *The Times*, 21 July 1910.
[88]   *The Times*, 23 July 1910.
[89]   *The Times*, 26 July, 2 August 1910.
[90]   Adrian Jones had a distinguished career as a war memorial sculptor, especially of cavalry subjects. He also designed the Carabiniers' memorial. For details of Jones's career see Selwyn Hodson-Pressinger, *Captain Adrian Jones, 1845–1938. Military and Equine Works* (London: Sandilands Press, 2004) and Selwyn Hodson-Pressinger, *Adrian Jones, 1845–1938, British Sculptor and Artist* (London: Sandilands Press, 1997).
[91]   *Globe and Laurel*, Vol. VIII, No. 69 (July 1901), p. 76.
[92]   *Globe and Laurel*, Vol. VIII, No. 70 (August 1901), p. 87.

6 Royal Marines' memorial, The Mall.

one 'wounded lying down on or falling to the ground, the other standing over, or by him, firing or at the "Charge" bayonet fixed'.[93] Jones duly supplied the required drama, which was much admired by the committee. The twin themes of the quality of the memorial and its drama were then reinforced once again during the unveiling ceremony. General Sir Arthur French told the crowd that Jones had 'provided the Corps with what has been described by critics well versed in art as one of the best Monuments in London', and he concluded:

> All who see the memorial will recognize how well the two marines have done their work … One has just received a severe wound, and has fallen. His comrade is standing over the prostate body, raising rifle to shoulder in the grim determination to defend and avenge. The scene, simple as it is in accompanying detail, is one of singular realism, and the sculpture will be regarded as an important addition to the finest public memorials of the Metropolis.[94]

---

93 *Globe and Laurel*, August 1901, p. 87.
94 *Globe and Laurel*, Vol. X, No. 91 (May 1903), p. 51.

Such 'singular realism' was a characteristic of regimental memorials that was frequently pinpointed as being of particular importance. The editor of the local paper in Chatham, noting that the redesigned bas-reliefs on the Royal Engineers' memorial depicted scenes of the corps' work in South Africa, informed his readers that, 'All these have an historical value inasmuch as they are based upon photographs of the actual incidents'.[95] The citizens of Canterbury were urged by their local paper to visit The Buffs' figurative monument in the Dane John Gardens as it would allow them to gain 'a clear impression of the costume worn in South Africa'.[96] The readers of the *Scotsman* were told that the battle scene depicted on the bas-relief of William Birnie Rhind's Black Watch memorial in Edinburgh had been 'purposely modelled to hand down to the future the uniform and accoutrements worn in the Boer War'. The paper's editor was certain that such an insight into military life would 'no doubt prove of considerable interest to the public'.[97] To underscore a monument's verisimilitude, it was sometimes stressed that figures had been modelled on serving soldiers. The *Manchester Guardian* pointed out that William Hamo Thorneycroft's memorial to the Manchester regiment in St Ann's Square could be 'fairly described as a study from life, for it was suggested by an incident of the fighting in which the Manchesters took part at Caesar's Camp near Ladysmith and Mr Thorneycroft had two of the Manchesters – two who survived the terrible slaughter – to pose for him as models'.[98] Both the Lancashire Fusiliers and the Royal Scots Greys went one step further and named the soldiers on whom their memorials were modelled.[99] This focus on realism, the insistence on precision and accuracy in figurative representations, does point towards a growing fascination with all things military in late Victorian/Edwardian society.[100]

For memorial committees, realistic commemorative sculpture had the advantage of not only engaging the public's interest but also emphasising both the ennobling qualities of military service in general and the worth of individual

---

[95] *Chatham News*, 29 July 1905.
[96] *Kentish Gazette and Canterbury Press*, 4 June 1904.
[97] *Scotsman*, 25 May 1908.
[98] *Manchester Guardian*, 27 October 1908.
[99] There remains some confusion over the true identity of the model for the Scots Greys' memorial. The day after the unveiling, the *Glasgow Herald* named 'Frank Dodd, the father of the current regimental secretary' as the subject but this was subsequently challenged by the *Edinburgh Evening News*, which opted for Robert Alexander, the *Weekly Scotsman*, Johnny Hadden Banffshire, and the regiment's own in-house journal, *Eagle and Carbine*, Sergeant-Major Anthony James Hinnigan. The debate continues to this day on the website, edinphoto.org.uk. *Glasgow Herald,* 17 November 1906; *Edinburgh Evening News,* 30 April 1947; *Weekly Scotsman*, 22 June 1967; *Eagle and Carbine*, Vol. 16 (May 1987).
[100] A similar trend towards authenticity can be found in battle paintings of this period. See J. Hichberger, *Images of the Army: The Military in British Art, 1815–1914* (Manchester: Manchester University Press, 1988), pp. 114–118. For more on the growing popularity of the army in this period see Bowman and Connelly, *The Edwardian Army*, pp. 177–180.

regiments in particular. The latter could be accentuated if the statuary referred to a specific incident. As shown above, the Manchesters' memorial in which a soldier with bayonet fixed is seen defending a wounded comrade who is offering him his last cartridge was drawn from the regiment's heroic defence of Caesar's Camp in January 1900. Described by the *Manchester Guardian* as being 'at once dignified, impressive and rich with virile beauty', Sir George White, the hero of Ladysmith, was sure that the monument would act as 'an imperishable memory ... to the steadfastness of devotion of the Manchester regiment'.[101] The Royal Sussex's memorial in the King's Road, Brighton, recalled the regiment's role in the fall of Johannesburg in May 1900. A press release issued by the memorial committee on the eve of the unveiling ceremony explained that the monument was 'surmounted by a figure of a bugler of the regiment sounding the charge at Doornkop, where the 1st Battalion charged and cleared the Boer entrenchments'.[102] To ensure that the full significance of this iconographic reference was appreciated, Colonel Donne, who had commanded the 1st battalion during the war, reminded those gathered for the unveiling of the memorial in November 1905 that 'this was the very ground on which Jameson's forces had surrendered'.[103]

The most prolific exponent of the commemorative battle scene was, undoubtedly, the Scottish sculptor, William Birnie Rhind. Elected an academician of the Royal Scottish Academy in 1905, Birnie Rhind worked for the majority of his career in Edinburgh and was commissioned by a series of regimental memorial committees in the aftermath of the South African War, most notably the Highland Light Infantry in Glasgow, the Royal Scots Guards and the Black Watch in Edinburgh and the Argyll and Sutherland Highlanders in Alloa. The typical product of these commissions, all of which were figurative, was the Highland Light Infantry memorial in Kelvingrove Park, Glasgow. Unveiled on 28 September 1906, the monument, which takes the form of an anxiously alert infantryman clambering over a rocky outcrop, was described by the regimental journal as a 'vigorous representation of a soldier engaged in scouting duty' designed to convey 'a vivid impression of the strenuousness

---

[101]   *Manchester Guardian*, 27 October 1908; letter from Sir George White to the honorary secretary of the Manchester regiment memorial committee quoted in *The War Memorial at Manchester* (Portsmouth: Gale and Polden, 1908). Manchester Regiment Archives, MR3/18/11.

[102]   *Penny Illustrated Paper and Illustrated Times*, 5 November 1904.

[103]   *Brighton Herald*, 5 November 1904. Leander Starr Jameson's attempt to instigate an Uitlander uprising in the Transvaal had come to an inglorious end on 2 January 1896 when his force was captured by the Boers at Doornkop. See Chris Ash, *The If Man: Leander Starr Jameson, the inspiration for Kipling's Masterpiece* (Solihull: Helion and Company, 2012), pp. 246–251.

and heroism of active military service'.[104] An interesting deviation from this pattern of heroic realism was the Royal Scots Greys' memorial on Princes Street in Edinburgh. Depicting a mounted trooper in review order uniform as if on parade, the monument was notable for the absence of any action scene. For Michael Bury such an omission was deliberate, stemming from the memorial committee's desire to erect a memory site in which iconographical symbols would act 'as visual reminders of the heroic traditions of the regiment through history, rather than of its performance in the South African campaigns in particular'.[105] The context of the memorial's unveiling would certainly seem to support Bury's view. With the construction of the memorial coinciding with the cost-cutting proposals of the Liberal Secretary of State for War, J. B. S. Haldane, to remove the regiment from its Piershill barracks in Edinburgh and exclude mounted troops from the Scottish command, for many the memorial came to be viewed as symbolic of not just the regiment's but the nation's martial traditions. In its coverage of the unveiling ceremony on 16 November 1906, the *Glasgow Herald* clearly conveyed just how deep the outpouring of national sentiment that surrounded the memorial was:

> The newest statue in Princes Street is very instructive. It is of a trooper on horseback. Who is he? Why, he is the last of our Scots Greys. He is the only one left to us of our famous regiment, so long quartered in Edinburgh, and the pride of Scotland. Who has not heard of the Scots Greys at Waterloo? It was at Waterloo that Sergeant-Major Ewart took the eagle from three Frenchmen. It was the conduct of the Greys at Waterloo that won the regiment the right to bear its emblem, an eagle, and the word 'Waterloo'. But the story that sets every true Scot's blood tingling is the story of how, late in the day, the Scots Greys charged to the cry of 'Scotland for Ever' ... Here, in Princes Street, stands the memorial to those of the Scots Greys who fell in South Africa. It was unveiled on a cold, wet November day in 1906 by Lord Rosebery, who made one of his most inspired speeches – a speech whose impression will not easily be forgotten by those who heard. 'Flesh of our flesh', he said, 'bone of our bone, Scotland for Ever'. The Scots Greys have left us. There stands the silent mounted trooper in Princes Street – 'Lest we forget'.[106]

Unveiling ceremonies were invariably used to reinforce iconographic messages and provide memory sites with meaning. Unsurprisingly, for the military these occasions were seized on as prime opportunities to impress upon those present that regiments had lived up to their traditions and inheritance. General French

---

[104] Royal Highland Fusiliers Museum (RHFM), *Highland Light Infantry Chronicle*, December 1906, pp. 129–134.
[105] Michael Bury, 'The Royal Scots Greys Monument', *Eagle and Carbine*, 16 (May 1986), p. 150.
[106] *Glasgow Herald*, 17 November 1906.

reminded those at the unveiling of the Royal Marines' memorial of their pride in their fallen comrades who had added 'their names to the already glorious roll of fame of our Corps', which brought forth cheers from the crowd.[107] When Lieutenant-General Sir John Fryer spoke at the Carabiniers' memorial, he noted that the regiment had been raised in 1685, had served ten sovereigns and before the South African War had participated in the Afghan campaign of 1879: the dead had upheld the 'old character of the Carabiniers'.[108] The same connection between past and present was made by Lord Roberts in Chester Cathedral at the unveiling of the Cheshires' commemorative frieze. Having recounted the history of the regiment at Dettingen, Gibraltar, Quebec, Mecanec and in India, he concluded by asserting that in South Africa 'all ranks had upheld this glorious tradition'.[109]

Both General Sir Ian Hamilton and Viscount Midleton, the Lord Lieutenant of Surrey, presiding at the unveiling ceremonies of the Manchester regiment and the Queen's Royal West Surreys respectively, found in the battlefields of South Africa new chapters to add to the regiments' glorious histories. Refashioning the war into a traditional heroic narrative, Hamilton opened his address with a stirring account of the Manchesters' performance under his command at Elandslaagte in October 1899:

> Never was a fairer stand-up fight than Elandslaagte. Not a thought amongst the Boers of giving way, not a notion amongst the British of hanging back. Each side determined, resolute, fired with desperate intent. Manchester lads – boys who had never before heard the vicious whistle of a bullet – advanced boldly across the open veldt. I remember the Manchesters fixing bayonets and then pipes playing and drums beating; the irresistible rush on to and over the guns; the white flag raised; the premature 'Hurrahs'; the Boers – powerful men in their prime, aristocrats, landowners – surprised, astonished to find themselves routed; the last of them rallying, refusing defeat – no surrender; scorning death, ignoring the white flag. I remember the Manchesters advancing again with a yell and again that wild cry of 'Majuba, Remember Majuba' ringing out over the darkening veldt proclaiming victory and the honour of the army retrieved.[110]

Drawing inspiration from Thorneycroft's memorial, he then concluded with an equally rousing description of the regiment's defence of Ladysmith at Caesar's Camp in January 1900:

> There were no shirkers; malingering was unknown. From 2:30 in the morning until five thirty in the afternoon on the 6th of January those ragged, starving

---

[107]   *Globe and Laurel*, Vol. X, No. 91 (May 1903), p. 51.
[108]   *The Times*, 25 June 1906.
[109]   *Chester Chronicle*, 6 June 1904.
[110]   *Manchester Guardian*, 27 October 1908.

boys kept back the enemy from the vitals of the town. Never did the Manchesters win greater glory.[111]

In Guildford, Midleton also turned to the set piece battles of the war's early stages for evidence that a proud record of martial prowess had been upheld, although this time it was in defeat not victory that such proof was to be found. Citing the unlikely example of Colenso, he argued that the Surreys' conduct had been 'so conspicuous for its courage, its coolness, its steadiness and its reliability that it justified my remark that the history of the regiment has been largely a replica of the history of England'.[112]

For the Sharpshooters, active service in South Africa was seen to have established rather than extended regimental tradition. Lieutenant-General Robert Baden-Powell, the hero of Mafeking, insisted, when unveiling the regiment's memorial in St Martin's-in-the-Fields, London, that the regiment should no longer consider itself to be a junior partner in the army:

> The Sharpshooters had had as a regiment but a short life, but in the four years of their existence they had made a history for themselves such as any other regiment might be proud of by the self-sacrifice and devotion to duty they showed when in South Africa.[113]

At the unveiling of the Lancashire Fusiliers' memorial in Bury, Sir Lees Knowles, colonel of the 3rd volunteer battalion and chairman of the memorial committee, linked regimental tradition with the immutable qualities that underpinned military service and in the process took the opportunity to extol the virtues of army life in general:

> 'While a man is able to do his duty it is infamous to retire'. These are the words of General Wolfe. This regiment was commanded by Wolfe, it was commanded by Wellington, and it was mentioned by General Buller, who, in South Africa, declared that the Lancashire Fusiliers had 'magnificently maintained the best traditions of the British Army'. May this memorial, unveiled this day by the Lord Lieutenant of the county, enthuse each one of us with the spirit of self-sacrifice, obedience, patience, endurance, fortitude – fearing God and honouring the King – to keep and to maintain the brilliant traditions of an excellent and honourable past. (Cheers)[114]

---

[111]   *Manchester Guardian*, 27 October 1908.
[112]   SHC, QRWS/1/8/2/22; *Queen's Royal West Surrey Regiment Unveiling Souvenir* (Guildford: Surrey Advertiser and County Times, 1904). For an account of the Surreys at Colenso see Byron Farwell, *The Great Anglo-Boer War* (New York: Harper and Row, 1976), pp. 127–138.
[113]   *Historical Record of the 3rd County of London (Sharpshooters) Imperial Yeomanry, 1900–1905* (London: no imprint, 1905), pp. 67–68.
[114]   *Salford Reporter*, 25 March 1905.

Such focus on the intrinsic moral worth of the army as an institution was a major theme of many unveiling ceremonies. The Reverend F. L'Estrange Fawcett told the congregation of St Mary's Church, Bury St Edmunds, assembled for the unveiling of the Suffolk regiment's memorial plaque that it was 'the pride of all Englishmen to remember acts of grace or heroism or unselfishness on the part of any of their fellowmen' but that this was especially the case when 'those deeds were done at the call of duty, in obedience to the word of command, with unswerving fidelity'.[115] Colonel F. E. Mulcahy hoped that those who stopped to drink from the water fountain in the Army Ordnance Corps memorial would reflect on the memorial and its message of 'duty well done … that they may thereby be inspired with feelings of loyalty and devotion to Sovereign and country'.[116] Similarly, the Royal Fusiliers' memorial was to act 'as a bright example to those who came after – a bright example of devotion, loyalty and patriotism to the young men of the country'.[117] Pride at those who had fallen doing their duty was also the theme of the Duke of Connaught's address during the Honourable Artillery Company ceremony.[118]

Central to any claim about the personal integrity and moral fibre of those who had fought was the inclusion of the ordinary soldier. This was made explicit by Sir Lees Knowles when he reminded the citizens of Bury that, 'Today in this simple model of a soldier we glorify the rank and file of the British army.'[119] No longer was the function of a regimental memorial simply to glorify the service of an individual general or the aristocratic officer corps, but instead it was to celebrate the sacrifice of all who had fought. This shift was most apparent in the naming of the fallen where equal prominence was given to all who served, regardless of rank. Indeed, one of the few memorials not to include a full roll of honour was the Coldstream Guards' memorial in St Paul's cathedral, which was confined to officers only. However, even a socially exclusive Guards regiment felt the need to offset this omission. The *Household Brigade Magazine* explained that 'it had been found impossible to record the names of the 207 non-commissioned officers and men on the memorial in St Paul's Cathedral owing to the limited amount of space available, but all the names will be inscribed in the Guards' Chapel and in the Cape Town Cathedral'.[120]

The Royal Artillery scheme provides further evidence of just how embedded in the work of memorialisation the full listing of names had become. As we have already seen with the allocation of a prime site on the Mall, the memorial

---

[115] SRO, GB554/W/13–16, *Journal of the 2nd Battalion XIIth Regiment*, No. 162 (1 November 1903), p. 216.
[116] *The Times*, 8 December 1905.
[117] *City Press*, 18 January 1908.
[118] *The Times*, 18 July 1904.
[119] *Salford Reporter*, 25 March 1905.
[120] *Household Brigade Magazine*, Vol. VII (1905), p. 542.

committee of the Royal Artillery found itself subjected to a significant amount of outside interference, not least from Lord Esher, who had been tasked with overseeing the Victoria memorial project. Esher's aesthetic tastes were immediately disturbed by the preliminary designs he received from the Royal Artillery and in the process he cut to the heart of the memorial's function. Recognising the importance of every member of the regiment and revealing an understanding of the equality of sacrifice, the Royal Artillery committee wanted to include panels giving the full roll of honour. For Esher the name panels were abhorrent. He wrote to the Secretary of the Office of Works: 'one thing is absolutely hideous, which is the idea of inscribing *the long list of names* on the memorial … It would be turning St James' Park into Kensal Green'.[121] Esher clearly believed the listing of names was inappropriate in this public space and was instead the preserve of a cemetery – hence the reference to one of London's great Victorian necropoli, Kensal Green. However, finding himself isolated by adopting this position, with even the King offering broad support for the plan, Esher backed down and gave his permission for the panels to be placed at the bottom of the memorial. Although such a half-hearted concession shows that Esher still believed that it was inappropriate to allow the roll of honour to dominate the memorial, it does, nonetheless, highlight the strength of support there was for a full record to be included.[122]

In honouring the courage and sacrifice of the ordinary soldier, unveiling ceremonies could also be used to promote regimental connections with and standing in the local community. General French reminded the audience gathered for the Royal Marines' ceremony of the corps' roots in the London trained bands; while Major-General Sir George Barton presented a potted history of the Royal Fusiliers when unveiling its memorial and referred to the regiment's long-standing association with the City of London.[123] In Brighton, Colonel Donne, having recounted for those assembled for the dedication of the Royal Sussex memorial the 'gallant deeds' of the regiment, was quick to 'draw attention to the fact that it was composed almost entirely of Sussex men'.[124] The same pattern held true for Scotland. Having witnessed the unveiling of an Ionic cross to the memory of the fallen of the Seaforth Highlanders, the people of Ross-shire were told by Provost Macrae that they should be proud of their 'county' soldiers, while Lord Lovat insisted that the memorial the townsfolk of Beauly had just seen unveiled should remind them that the Lovat Scouts were 'a movement in which Highlanders alone were occupied. It was the development

---

[121]   TNA WORK 20/59 Royal Artillery memorial. Letter from Lord Esher 9 November 1905 (emphasis in the original). See also his letter of 13 November 1905.
[122]   TNA WORK 20/59 Royal Artillery memorial. Secretary of Office of Works [Sir Shomberg McDonnell] to Lord Knollys [Royal Private Secretary], 9 December 1905.
[123]   *Globe and Laurel*, Vol. X, No. 91 (May 1903), p. 51; *City Press*, 18 January 1908.
[124]   *Brighton Herald*, 5 November 1904.

of a particular form of duty for which Highlanders were specially adapted, and the men and officers were entirely Highland'.[125]

Unsurprisingly, volunteers were particularly keen to lay stress on their local connections. Having, with the exception of the City Imperial Volunteers and the Imperial Yeomanry, been amalgamated with the regular army on deployment in South Africa, volunteers battalions were often eager to reassert their individual identity by having their active service commemorated separately at an intimate, community level. The 3rd, 6th and 7th volunteer battalions of the Manchester regiment all chose to erect commemorative plaques in their former drill halls. Both the 2nd volunteer battalion of The Buffs, East Kent Regiment and the 2nd volunteer battalion of the Queen's Own, Royal West Kent Regiment, although included on regimental memorials in Canterbury, Rochester and Maidstone, also opted to dedicate memorial tablets in the parish churches of their base towns.[126] This desire to go ahead with commemorative sites, in which inclusion was so narrowly restricted, not only highlights the parochialism that underpinned the volunteer movement at the turn of the twentieth century but also hints at some of the tensions that existed between the regular and reservist forces.[127] With over 30,000 volunteers having served in South Africa, it is perhaps unsurprising that their performance should have become the subject for close scrutiny by both the press and Whitehall.[128] Although the public, in general, applauded the volunteers' patriotism, their professionalism was viewed in a much more critical light by government experts. St John Brodrick, the Secretary of State for War between 1900 and 1903, made little attempt to mask the grave concerns which he felt the volunteers' performance in the war had raised regarding their ability to fulfil their primary function of home defence. In early 1903 such expressions of doubt were given official form with the appointment of the Norfolk Commission to look into the organisation and terms of service of the militia and volunteer forces. Inevitably the Commission interpreted its remit in a relatively elastic manner and its focus fell on the performance of the volunteers on active service.[129] Such a highly charged atmosphere could make volunteer battalions all the more determined to celebrate publicly their

---

[125] *Ross-shire Journal*, 12 August 1904; *Inverness Courier*, 22 December 1905; both quoted in Spiers, *The Scottish Soldier and Empire*, p. 206.
[126] The 2nd volunteer battalion of The Buffs' memorial was erected in St Dunstan's parish church, Cranbrook; the Royal West Kent's equivalent can be found in St Alfege's parish church, Greenwich.
[127] Bennett, *Absent-Minded Beggars*, p. 31
[128] Ian F. W. Beckett, *Riflemen Form: A Study of the Rifle Volunteer Movement, 1859–1908* (Aldershot: The Ogilby Trust, 1982), pp. 225–234.
[129] Stephen Miller, *Volunteers on the Veld: Britain's Citizen-Soldiers and the South African War, 1899–1902* (Oklahoma: Oklahoma University Press, 2007), pp. 166–180; Hugh Cunningham, *The Volunteer Force: A Social and Political History, 1859–1908* (London: Croom Helm, 1975), pp. 127–135.

individual contributions to the war effort. At a fund-raising dinner held by the memorial committee of the 2nd volunteer battalion of the Queen's Own, Royal West Kents in May 1903, the battalion's commander, Colonel Satterthwaite, clearly viewed the committee's memorialisation project as a way to counter public criticism. Although he was confident that the war would be 'the means of bringing the volunteer battalions in closer touch with their comrades of the line', he was, nonetheless, insistent that, 'as the volunteer force had been, and still was, the subject of much abuse … in the half-penny press', it was essential that the proposed memorial 'should be something more worthy than a tablet'.[130] In fact, restricted funds meant that Satterthwaite was to be disappointed and a simple commemorative plaque to the fallen of the 2nd volunteer battalion was unveiled in St Alfege's parish church, Greenwich the following year.

Despite the negative press surrounding the military contribution volunteers made to victory in South Africa, local volunteer forces remained points of community interest and were frequently seized on as the foci for civic pride. General Sir Owen Tudor Burne opened proceedings at the unveiling of the Lancashire Fusiliers' memorial by noting that 'the county of Lancashire had been the first to offer to the country the aid of Volunteer active service companies', while the congregation in St Giles's Cathedral, Edinburgh, for the Royal Scots' dedication service were told by Lord Rosebery, the Lord Lieutenant of Mid-Lothian, that they should take pride in the fact that, 'this regiment of Royal Scots, the regiment most closely identified with Mid-Lothian, was the only one of which it could be said that all its reservists had come to the colours, or been fully accounted for'.[131] In a similar vein, although the readers of the *Manchester Evening News* were told that they should feel a sense of deep satisfaction that Manchester had sent nearly 5,000 men to the war, it was 'the 12 officers and 465 men from the volunteer battalions' who were singled out for special mention.[132]

Yet, such local pride was not simply confined to the exploits of volunteers. In his dedication address before unveiling the Lancashire Fusiliers' memorial in Market Square, Bury, Lord Derby, the Lord Lieutenant of the county, focused on the significance the regiment as a whole had for the status of the town: 'We feel that it is an honour to be the home of the regiment, and we hope that this connection between the Lancashire Fusiliers and the town of Bury will remain … as a source of honour to the town'.[133] He then proceeded to provide an explanation for the strength of the bonds that connected the civic and military worlds:

130   *Queen's Own Gazette*, Vol. XXI, No. 6 (June 1903), p. 1858.
131   *Salford Reporter*, 25 March 1905; *The Thistle*, Vol. 1, No. 1 (10 March 1904), p. 13.
132   *Manchester Evening News*, 26 October 1908.
133   TFM, *The Lancashire Fusiliers' Annual*, 1905, p. 8.

There were those who thought some years ago, when the scheme was established for bringing the depots of battalions and localising them in different counties, that no connection would grow up between regiment and county. I would ask those who were of that opinion to look round and see those vast crowds in all directions as far as the eye could reach, all anxious to come and see an occasion which was one of honour to the regiment with which they were connected.[134]

Although Derby, who had served as War Secretary between 1878 and 1880, was, in part, vindicating his own support for the localisation of the army and the subsequent territorialisation of volunteers, he was, nevertheless, not alone in drawing civic pride from the war record of a localised regiment.[135] The editor of the *Kentish Gazette*, notwithstanding the regimental nature of The Buffs' memorial in Canterbury, felt sure that the 'men who had died had not only raised a monument to themselves but also to the patriotism and military efficiency of East Kent'.[136] Councillor Mitchell, on accepting custody of the Highland Light Infantry memorial in Kelvingrove Park, was certain that Glaswegians would be especially proud to possess such 'a work of art' because 'it spoke of the bravery of the officers and men of a regiment which had been so long associated with Glasgow'.[137] Sir Thomas Thornhill Shann, mayor of Manchester from 1903 to 1905, used the unveiling of the Manchester regiment memorial as an opportunity to rebrand the city as a seat of loyalty and respectability. The memorial would, he said, 'serve to show that in this city of Manchester, however much we are all immersed in the fierce strife of commerce and industry, we are by no means insensible to the claims of patriotism, and that we are ready, as ever our forefathers, to come forward in the hour of need to our country's aid'.[138]

This fusion of military and civic pride could mean that the focus on the dead became lost at unveiling ceremonies. The following description from the *Brighton Herald* of the unveiling of the Royal Sussex regiment's memorial in Regency Square clearly captures the combination of military spectacle and civilian pageant that suffused the day:

With all the pomp and circumstance attending a military ceremony in the sunshine, the monument erected opposite the West Pier, Brighton, to the memory of soldiers of the Royal Sussex Regiment who fell in the South African War, was unveiled on Saturday by the Marquis of Abergavenny. For

---

134 TFM, *The Lancashire Fusiliers' Annual*, 1905, p. 8.
135 For more on the reforms to the regular and volunteer forces see Beckett, *Riflemen Form*, pp. 129–138 and Spiers, *The Army and Society*, pp. 177–206.
136 *Kentish Gazette and Canterbury Press*, 4 June 1904.
137 RHFM, *Highland Light Infantry Chronicle*, December 1906, p. 133.
138 *Manchester Guardian*, 27 October 1908.

the time being Regency Square, at the foot of which the statue stands, was fairly under a military occupation. The roadways about the square resounded with the tramp of marching men; on the wide square of green, men in red and men in khaki manoeuvred; excited officers – why do officers always get excited? – were dashing about on horseback; bugles sounded, drums beat; and in the bright sunshine everything made a brave show. The balconies and windows in the square – many decorated – had their groups of spectators, and away from the privileged enclosures, themselves filled with a fashionable throng, stretched enormous crowds of the general sightseers. One would have to go back to Coronation times to remember a similar crowd in Brighton.[139]

The addition of a visit by an important public figure to officiate at an unveiling merely added to the excitement of the occasion. On the day of the dedication service for the Cheshire regiment's memorial in Chester an 'animated' crowd lined the route to the cathedral ready to greet the appearance of Lord Roberts 'with loud cheering, waving of handkerchiefs and clapping'.[140] The 'thousands of sightseers' who poured into an 'en-fete' Bury to witness the Lancashire Fusiliers' ceremony cheered not only the arrival of Lord Derby but also the moment the memorial was unveiled.[141] In the Medway towns of Rochester, Gillingham and Chatham, the determination of the local populace to use the King's attendance at the unveiling of the Royal Engineers' memorial as an excuse to turn the day into a patriotic carnival was vividly captured by the *Chatham News*: 'Flags! Flags! Flags! Flags here, flags there, flags everywhere – nothing but flags of all colours, all sizes and all descriptions, the whole combining to make a bright display'.[142]

Yet, on this occasion, the event failed to match the expectations and efforts of the public. Determined that the ceremony should remain exclusively a military one, the parade ground in Brompton Barracks where the victory arch was situated remained firmly closed to civilians. Indeed, for the organisers of the day not even the demands of the national press were to be allowed to detract from the military splendour of the occasion. *The Times'* royal correspondent was unable to provide an account of the King's unveiling address because, as he deferentially explained in his report of the event, 'It had been felt, rightly perhaps, that the presence of anybody in plain clothes would have spoilt the brilliant effect of the military picture'.[143] The assertion of such exclusive rights over the ownership of the memory of the fallen did not, however, sit easily with the editor of the *Chatham News*. Although full of admiration for the precision

139   *Brighton Herald*, 5 November 1904.
140   *Chester Chronicle*, 6 August 1904.
141   *Salford Reporter*, 25 March 1905.
142   *Chatham News*, 29 July 1905.
143   *The Times*, 27 July 1905.

of the Royal Engineer's organisation and the panache of the military spectacle, he felt obliged to conclude his coverage of the unveiling on a note of discord:

> In one respect only could there have been an improvement suggested. One would liked to have seen a further recognition, on the part of the military authorities, of the fact that it was a civic as well as a military function, for if the event of the day was a tribute paid to military faithfulness and valour, it was paid by civilians no less than by their comrades.[144]

Occasionally passing references were made to the sense of sorrow that underscored the unveiling of regimental memory sites, although these were rarely allowed to detract from the dominant celebratory mood. The Manchester regiments' official souvenir programme noted that it was only with the sounding of the last post at the conclusion of proceedings that, 'the vast mob around and in St. Ann's Square, the crowds in and on buildings, seemed to realise what the function meant, that it was in a sense a funeral service'.[145] The equivalent publication for the Queen's Royal West Surrey regiment was similarly sure that pride not grief was the leitmotif at the dedication of its memorial in St Mary's Church, Guildford. Acknowledging that the service was 'solemn and impressive', it went on to argue that, 'it was not mournful for though the regiment sustained heavy loses ... the emotions which were uppermost in the minds of those present were more akin to the feeling of ultimate triumph'.[146]

The South African War had certainly raised the public profile of the army. Although administrators in Whitehall and senior commanders on operations were subjected to stinging criticism, especially in the disastrous early stages of the war, the rank and file, by contrast, received almost universal praise. This new found admiration for the professional soldier was, of course, augmented by the public's admiration for the patriotism of the tens of thousands of volunteers that flocked to the colours from late 1899 onwards. In the aftermath of the fighting, the military authorities looked to capitalise on the wider community's fascination with khaki through a wave of commemorative activity. Memorials to the fallen, more often than not figurative and realistic in design, served to promote regimental prestige through the veneration of the personal qualities and heroism of the ordinary fighting man. Yet, if the war in South Africa in general, and the volunteer movement in particular, helped to make the civilian population more receptive to such didacticism, they also resulted in fresh tensions surrounding the control and nature of military commemoration. By connecting the service of respectable citizens to the professional army, the war

---

[144] *Chatham News*, 29 July 1905.
[145] Manchester Regiment Archives, MR3/18/11, *The War Memorial at Manchester*.
[146] SHC, QRWS/1/8/2/22; *Queen's Royal West Surrey Regiment Unveiling Souvenir* (Guildford: Surrey Advertiser and County Times, 1904), p. 2.

and, by extension, its memorialisation became focal points for civic pride. Thus, although the military authorities retained, for the most part, firm control of the commemorative process, they, nonetheless, found themselves under increasing pressure from the expectations of outside agencies and the weight of civilian sensibilities.

Chapter 3

Vitai Lampada:
Remembering the War in Schools

*A*T the forefront of the communal commemoration of the South African War in Britain were educational institutions and in particular the great public schools. James Gildea, in his beautifully produced 1911 gazetteer of memorials, listed eighty-one schools that constructed memory sites in honour of old boys who died in the South African War.[1] That such a large number of schools chose to commemorate the sacrifices of their alumni in this way should come as no surprise when one considers the guiding principles at the heart of a late Victorian and Edwardian education. As J. A. Mangan has noted, with an ethos underpinned by the twin imperatives of manliness and service guaranteeing a steady flow of enthusiastic school-leavers into the officer corps of the British army, the primary function of the public school system at this time was largely restricted to the production of 'warrior-patriots'.[2] Certainly the empirical data seems to confirm this conclusion. Edward Spiers has calculated that 62 per cent of regular army officers who served in the conflict against the Boers came from public school backgrounds.[3] Indeed, according to a survey undertaken during the war, this stranglehold can be narrowed down even further, with 41 per cent of officers coming from just ten schools and 11 per cent from Eton College alone.[4] The inevitable corollary of this was that it was the great public schools which were hit the hardest by the mounting casualty lists coming out of South Africa. Unsurprisingly, given

---

[1]   Gildea, *For Remembrance*, p. xiv.
[2]   J. A. Mangan, *The Games Ethic and Imperialism* (Harmondsworth: Viking, 1986).
[3]   Edward M. Spiers, *The Late Victorian Army, 1868–1902* (Manchester: Manchester University Press, 1992), p. 97.
[4]   A. H. H. MacLean, 'Public Schools and the War in South Africa', quoted in W. J. Reader, *At Duty's Call: A Study in Obsolete Patriotism* (Manchester: Manchester University Press, 1991), p. 91.

its service record, Eton College suffered the most with 129 old boys dying as a result of disease or enemy action in the course of the war.[5]

Although some state schools erected memorials (Gildea lists five from his total of eighty-one), this chapter will focus on the public schools. Not only were these schools dominant in the officers' mess, but, as Geoffrey Best has noted, they also enjoyed something of a cultural hegemony in the civil world as well.[6] Citing as evidence the popularity of public school fiction in state elementary and secondary schools, Best has argued that there was a widespread acceptance in the non-public school world of the elite's cultural ideals and that these ideals 'filtered downwards and outwards until they permeated the whole of society'.[7] Furthermore, it was the great public schools which had both the resources to construct elaborate memorials and the influence to attract men of standing to unveil them. As a result it was on the commemorative activity of the public schools that regional and, occasionally, national attention fell and it was through these schools' memory sites that concerns about the national shortcomings which the South African War had revealed were to be addressed and debated.

This chapter will then explore the construction of public school war memorials from their genesis, with the establishment of memorial committees, through financing and debates over form to the rituals of unveiling and dedication. In so doing light will not only be shed on how war memory could be shaped and packaged to serve the purposes of individual communities but also how ideas of self-representation through memorialisation interacted with issues of national identity. The war in South Africa had revealed serious fissures in the British imperial family and, as Bill Nasson has noted, had prompted a reassessment of the motherland's imperial role and her relationship with the Empire.[8] As such the conflict served to test the very principles on which the public school system rested. A half-century of small colonial wars had provided the public school pupil with an on-going diet of soldier-heroes prepared to sacrifice all in the service of King and country.[9] This apotheosis of the imperial warrior was itself firmly rooted in the cult of medievalism that permeated high culture in Victorian and early Edwardian Britain. Central to this cult were

---

[5]   Gildea, *For Remembrance*, p. xiv. Eton's total was nearly double that of the next school, Wellington College, which lost sixty-five old boys in the war.

[6]   Geoffrey Best, 'Militarism in the Victorian Public School', in Brian Simon and Ian Bradley (eds), *The Victorian Public School: Studies in the Development of an Educational Institution* (Dublin: Gill and MacMillan, 1975), pp. 123–146.

[7]   Best, 'Militarism in the Victorian Public School', p. 130.

[8]   Bill Nasson, *The Boer War: The Struggle for South Africa* (Cape Town: Tafelberg, 2010), pp. 13–19.

[9]   J. A. Mangan, 'Images of Empire in the Late Victorian Public School', *Journal of Educational Administration and History*, 12: 1 (1980), pp. 31–39.

romantic images of chivalry and idealistic concepts of gentlemanly conduct.[10] Thus, as Peter Parker has argued in his wide-ranging cultural study of the British public school in the era of the First World War, by the time the Peace of Vereeniging had brought to an end Kitchener's brutal counter-insurgency campaign against the Boers, the elite's chivalric code, predicated as it was on notions of honour and duty and celebrated through the lionisation of 'heroic deeds in the cause of Empire', found itself under threat from a war where both honour and nobility seemed to have been so signally absent.[11] The following case studies will, therefore, consider how the various agencies involved in the memorialisation process interacted to ensure that the commemoration of the war in South Africa tied in with the public schools' templates of war remembrance.

Discussions about commemorative schemes were frequently initiated by old boys through the letters' columns of school magazines and it was, almost without exception, the old boys' associations which took on the responsibility of overseeing the commemorative process. At Wellington College, originally founded to educate the orphans of army officers, the constitution of the Old Wellingtonian Society specifically stated that one of its 'chief functions [was] the erection of memorials to Old Wellingtonians who had fallen in action'.[12] After a preliminary meeting in November 1900, it was decided that all Old Wellingtonians should be canvassed for their views as to the form the memorial should take. Although, at a third meeting of the Society's executive committee in October 1901, it was unanimously agreed that the memorial should be a commemorative plaque in the chapel, this decision was not ratified until the school's most illustrious military alumnus, Sir Ian Hamilton, had given the final seal of approval.[13]

Elsewhere, old boys' associations, without the constitutional power enjoyed by the Old Wellingtonian Society, simply took it upon themselves to assume control of the memorialisation process. A meeting of the Old Wykehamist Society in December 1900 chaired by the Earl of Selborne, the First Lord of the Admiralty, resolved to invite 'all who have been educated at Winchester College to attend Old Hall, Lincoln's Inn, to discuss the erection of a monument in memory of Old Wykehamists who have lost their lives in the

---

[10]   For more on chivalry and the cult of medievalism see Marc Girouard, *The Return to Camelot: Chivalry and the English Gentleman* (New Haven and London: Yale University Press, 1981).

[11]   Peter Parker, *The Old Lie: The Great War and the Public-School Ethos* (London: Hambledon Continuum, 1987), p. 104.

[12]   Patrick Mileham, *Wellington College: The First 150 Years* (London: Third Millennium Publishing, 2008); Wellington College Archive (WCA), *Wellingtonian*, Vol. XVII, No. 1 (December 1901), p. 2.

[13]   The Honorary Secretary of the Old Wellingtonian Society was tasked with contacting Hamilton to check that the scheme 'would, in his opinion, commend itself to Old Wellingtonians in the army'. WCA, *Wellingtonian*, Vol. XVII, No. 1 (December 1901), p. 3.

war in South Africa'.[14] At the Lincoln's Inn meeting in April 1901 both a general and an executive committee were unanimously elected and these two bodies subsequently oversaw the process to completion. Similar procedures were followed at Dulwich College, St Paul's School, Charterhouse School and Harrow School.[15] At the first general meeting of Old Cheltonians, called to discuss Cheltenham College's memorial plans in June 1901, not one member of the teaching staff was in attendance. It was left to the principal of the college, the Reverend Reginald Waterfield, to assure the old boys at a subsequent meeting that, 'whatever was done by them would find loyal support at Cheltenham'.[16] Indeed, so ingrained was the assumption that it fell within the remit of the old boys' network to direct any activity regarding the 'memory' of their alma mater that any attempt by an institution to circumvent this process could lead to serious dissension. As will be shown later, a meeting in December 1900 between the headmaster of Eton, Dr Edmond Warre, and his five heads of house at which it was provisionally decided to construct a memorial building in memory of former pupils who had died in the war was to cause serious ructions within the ranks of Old Etonians and lead to a heated exchange of letters in the national press.[17]

The alacrity with which former pupils seized control of school memorial-isation schemes not only highlights the rapid development and growing importance of old boys' associations in the last quarter of the nineteenth century, but also reveals something of the imprint that the public school system left on those who passed through it.[18] The alumni clearly felt a great pride in their old schools and saw it as their duty to protect and perpetuate what they thought to be their institutions' core values. Sir Richard Jebb, Regius Professor of Greek at Cambridge and Old Carthusian, was in no doubt just how important schooldays were in shaping the life and work of adulthood. He told the assembled staff and pupils of Charterhouse, at the unveiling of the memorial plaque in the school cloisters in July 1903, that:

> Attachment to one's old school is not merely a matter of sentiment; a sentiment
> indeed there is, a strong and healthy one; but there is much more. There is

[14]   Winchester College Archive (WinCA), *Wykehamist*, No. 376 (December 1900), p. 238.
[15]   Dulwich College Archive (DCA), *Alleynian*, Vol. XXIX, No. 211 (June 1901), p. 163; Michael F. J. McDonnell, *A History of St. Paul's School* (London: Chapman and Hall, 1909), p. 445; Charterhouse School Archive (CSA), *Carthusian*, Vol. VIII, No. 253 (October 1900), p. 9; Harrow School Archive (HSA), *Harrovian*, Vol. XIV, No. 8 (16 November 1901), p. 6.
[16]   Cheltenham College Archive, *Cheltonian*, June 1901, p. 189
[17]   Eton College Archive (ECA), Misc/EMF/1, 'Eton Officers Memorial 1902', committee meeting minutes, 7 December 1900.
[18]   For more on the expansion and importance of the old boys' associations see J. R. de S. Honey, 'Tom Brown's Universe: The Nature and Limits of the Victorian Public School Community', in Simon and Bradley (eds), *The Victorian Public School*, pp. 20–21.

the knowledge that the school world and all that we learned in it – not only, perhaps not chiefly, from books – went far towards moulding our characters. Our school is a country within a fatherland.[19]

Such feelings of pride and institutional loyalty were rooted in the firm belief that the character forming properties of a public school education were unrivalled and should serve as a model for others to follow. At the initial meeting of Old Wykehamists in the Inner Temple in December 1900, E. T. Cook seconded the motion that a memorial should be erected to honour the memory of their fallen peers by asserting that, 'of the training grounds for patriotism none were so powerful as that of the public schools'. It was, he continued, therefore the responsibility of 'public schools to lead the way to foster and to encourage thoughts of public duty and public service'. Positive that where Winchester led others followed, Cook concluded by somewhat condescendingly noting just how far-reaching the college's example was: 'the Wykehamist spirit has even spread in a quarter that was little to be expected. Even the workhouse schoolboys had a splendid record in this war'.[20]

Indeed, so keen were schools to acclaim this record of public service and celebrate the ethos that underpinned it that commemorative plans were frequently initiated long before the war had ended. News of the capture of Bloemfontein in March 1900 and Pretoria in June of the same year, followed by the formal annexation of the Boer Republics three months later, was sufficient to rouse a number of old boys' associations to action. By October 1900 the Old Carthusian Society had not only decided on the form the Charterhouse memorial should take but had also had it approved by the school's governing body.[21] Wellington, Winchester and Eton were quick to follow, with all three forming memorial committees before the year was out.[22]

Unsurprisingly, the strong sense of ownership that former pupils had over the image and identity of their old schools could lead to ill-feeling when it was felt that the 'memory' of the institution was being unfairly appropriated by one sectional interest group. The establishment, in December 1900, by the board

---

[19] CSA 83/3/2, Sir Richard Jebb's unveiling address, 4 July 1903.
[20] WinCA, *Wykehamist*, No. 377 (20 December 1900), p. 247.
[21] CSA, *Carthusian*, Vol. VIII, No. 253 (October 1900), p. 9.
[22] WCA, *Wellingtonian*, Vol. XVII, No. 1 (December 1900), p. 3; WinCA, *Wykehamist*, No. 377 (20 December 1900), p. 245; ECA, Misc/EMF/1, 'Eton Officers Memorial 1902', committee meeting minutes, 7 December 1900. The members of the memorial committees at Wellington and Eton were, however, a little more circumspect than their counterparts at Charterhouse. Perhaps recognising that the victories of the spring and summer of 1900 did not necessarily mean the war was won, both decided to postpone any further action. The Eton committee didn't meet again until 1902 and at Wellington it was decided that, 'it would be better to wait until the spring, when there was some chance of the war being over, before settling on the actual form that the memorial should take'. WCA, *Wellington Year Book 1900*, p. 4.

of governors of Eton College of a provisional memorial committee comprising of only the headmaster and five senior masters, and this committee's decision to press for a commemorative building, was to cause serious unrest within the ranks of Old Etonians. Although a carefully selected panel of old boys ratified the committee's decision in February 1902, this nod to democratisation was not enough to silence dissent when the scheme was publicised in advance of a general meeting of all Old Etonians three months later. First to voice his concern in a bad-tempered letter to *The Times* was Ian Malcolm, Conservative MP for Stowmarket and Old Etonian. Aware that the governing body and headmaster were keen to tackle overcrowding in the school through an extensive rebuilding project, Malcolm was convinced there had been a calculated effort to hijack the whole commemorative process:

> From the newspapers, we outsiders learn that [a memorial building] is the scheme adopted by 'the committee'. We are not, however, informed who are the committee; who elected them; or to whom they are responsible. The usual procedure seems, doubtless for some good if obscure reason, to have been reversed. No general meeting of Etonians has sanctioned the formation of a committee to discuss the comparative merits of various schemes and to draw up a report. In this case somebody seems to have selected a committee; somebody has driven a scheme through; and somebody at last calls a general meeting to ratify the findings of this select committee.[23]

The theme was taken up four days later by a Commons colleague of Malcolm, the MP for Gainsborough, Seymour Ormsby-Gore. Once again choosing the letters' columns of *The Times* as a forum for public dissent, Ormsby-Gore reiterated Malcolm's belief that an attempt had been made to authorise the memorial scheme by covert means. But this time he was prepared to go one step further by naming those at the heart of the putative conspiracy:

> It strongly smacks of the Eton masters. Why Eton masters should have the controlling voice in this matter I cannot understand, especially when such a monument as suggested would be conducive of mere benefit to them than to the rest of Etonians, past and present.[24]

No doubt motivated by concern about the reputation of the school generally, and the viability of the scheme specifically, such public dissent elicited an immediate response from the headmaster, Dr Warre. A circular reviewing, in detail, the gestation of the remembrance project was hastily issued to all Old Etonians with the stated intention of 'countering the severe criticism that we have acted *ultra vires*'.[25] Two emergency sessions of the memorial committee

---

23   *The Times*, 15 May 1902.
24   *The Times*, 19 May 1902.
25   ECA, Misc/EMF8, 'Eton Memorial', 27 May 1902.

were then convened to ensure that a hastily arranged general meeting of Old Etonians at the Mansion House would be a model of stage-managed open consultation. Lord Rosebery, Liberal Prime Minister from 1894–1895, Bishop Welldon, the bishop of Calcutta and a former headmaster of Harrow, Alfred Lyttleton, international cricketer and soon to be Secretary of State for the Colonies, St John Brodrick, the Secretary of State for War, and Field Marshal Lord Roberts, commander-in-chief of the British army during the taking of the Boer capitals, were all dragooned into proposing or seconding motions in support of the memorial buildings. With the blessing of such famous alumni the anticipated opposition, unsurprisingly, failed to materialise and the resolution that the memorial 'should take the form of a building worthy of the school' was unanimously passed.[26]

The tensions surrounding Eton's commemorative plans, and the method by which the ensuing conflict was resolved, both throw into high relief the centrality of the role played by old boys' associations in school remembrance projects and highlight the strength of the bonds that tied former pupils to their schooldays and the institutions that they believed had played such a significant part in shaping their adult lives. At the heart of this deep sense of attachment was pride. In advocating the benefits of a memorial hall to Old Etonians at the Mansion House meeting in June 1902, both Lord Rosebery and Bishop Welldon resurrected for their adult audience the childhood passions of interschool rivalries. Welldon provocatively pointed out that Harrow, where he had been headmaster for thirteen years, had a 'fine memorial hall' that played 'a very considerable part in school life', while Rosebery warned of the impact continued dissent would have in the eyes of their rivals by noting that, 'two Winchester men he knew had assumed an air of casual superiority and said, "We have settled our memorial without any meetings at the Mansion House and without any discussions in the papers"'.[27]

Predictably, the loyalty and pride of former students was seized on by members of school memorial committees to galvanise fund-raising. At Mansion House, Rosebery continued with his theme of interschool competition by urging Old Etonians to give generously to the now unanimously endorsed memorial hall so that they could 'remove from the charge against Eton that, as compared with other public schools, it does not do much in the way of contributing as the old pupils of other public schools have done'.[28] At the conclusion of the same meeting, Dr Warre struck a similar chord by invoking the impressive charitable record of arch-rivals, Harrow: 'I don't wish to suggest Eton should become an imitator of Harrow … except in the noble generosity that has moved

---

[26] ECA, *Eton College Chronicle*, No. 970 (14 June 1902), p. 106.
[27] ECA, *Eton College Chronicle*, p. 104.
[28] ECA, *Eton College Chronicle*, p. 105.

Old Harrovians to enlarge their school at a cost which would amply meet the whole contemplated expenditure of the Eton Memorial'.[29]

The need to be seen to have played one's part in maintaining the reputation of the old school is also evident in the frequency with which subscription lists appeared in the pages of school magazines and year books. All the schools studied for this survey published lists of subscribers with many institutions providing monthly or even weekly updates. These lists served the dual purpose of, on the one hand, celebrating those who had fulfilled their obligations to the school while, on the other, encouraging those who had yet to contribute to match their efforts. They also provide further evidence of the intense loyalty and affection that subscribers had for their old schools.

The Dulwich College records reveal nine people making at least two separate donations to the memorial fund and at least one making three.[30] Subscribers also signalled allegiance through the lavish amounts given. At Eton there were three contributions of £1,000 or more and two of £500, while at Charterhouse and Dulwich donations of £50 and £100 appear in the lists.[31]

Occasionally, memorial committees decided to impose a ceiling on donations. This was the case at Simon Langton Boys' School in Canterbury where old boys were requested to 'send a contribution not exceeding two shillings and six pence'.[32] The reason given was, in the words of the headmaster, Mr Mann, so 'that all might feel free to give and the memorial would equally belong to all'.[33] Such egalitarian measures to ensure the sanctity of collective ownership were, however, to remain a rarity until after the First World War.[34] Thus, although an upper limit was also imposed at Winchester College, the decision had nothing to do with the proprietorial subtext of subscription lists but was, instead, based solely on the exigencies of financial practicality. H. Bargreave Deane QC, in putting forward the idea of a cap in December 1900, assured the assembled old boys that, 'if they limited the amount to £5 every Old Wykehamist would feel he could join in and they should get a large sum'.[35] By way of contrast, the chairman of Cheltenham College's war memorial committee, Lord James of

---

[29]   ECA, *Eton College Chronicle*, p. 105.

[30]   DCA, *Alleynian*, 1901: July, p. 221; October, p. 319; 1902: February, pp. 8–9; April, p. 64; May, pp. 114–115.

[31]   ECA, Misc/EME/1, Eton Memorial Fund Balance Sheet, 25 March 1903; CSA, *Carthusian*, Vol. VIII, No. 253 (October 1900), p. 10; DCA, *Alleynian*, 1901: July, p. 221; October, p. 319; 1902: May, pp. 114–115; November, p. 339; 1903: June, pp. 159–160.

[32]   Simon Langton Boys' School Archives, *Langtonian*, Vol. II (December 1902), p. 106.

[33]   Simon Langton Boys' School Archives, *Langtonian*, Vol. II (December 1903), p. 2.

[34]   For more on the funding of memorial schemes in the wake of the Great War see C. Moriarty, 'Private Grief and Public Remembrance: British First World War Memorials', in M. Evans and K. Lunn (eds), *War and Memory in the Twentieth Century* (Oxford: Berg, 1997), pp. 125–142.

[35]   WinCA, *Wykehamist*, No. 377 (20 December 1900), p. 427.

Hereford, cited the pressures of fund-raising as the very reason the imposition of a limit on personal donations should be rejected. 'It was', he successfully persuaded his fellow committee members, 'never a good idea to shut out great wealth'.[36] James's reasoning seems to have been proved right. Within six months of the initial call for subscriptions being issued, Old Cheltonians had reached the committee's target of £1,975, whereas, by February 1903, five months after work on the Charterhouse's memorial cloister had begun, the College's fund was still £600 short of the required sum.[37]

In most of the schools surveyed, the combination of unchallenged leadership by a well-organised nucleus of old boys and unquestioning attachment from a clearly defined pool of wealthy prospective donors resulted in financial targets being achieved quickly and relatively effortlessly. The experience of the Harrow School memorial committee, which found its target of £600 exceeded within a few months of the call for subscriptions being issued, was by no means unusual.[38] The exceptions in this catalogue of financial success were Winchester and Eton. As we have seen, the Old Wykehamists directing the Winchester scheme had already limited the fund-raising potential of the College's enterprise by imposing an artificial constraint on the extent to which the not inconsiderable reserves of former pupils could be exploited. This financial miscalculation was compounded by the memorial committee's failure to provide clear leadership. The first two appeals for subscriptions, in February and July 1901, explicitly stated that neither the form of the memorial would be decided, nor an architect appointed, until the committee had received what it considered to be an adequate total.[39] In effect, Old Wykehamists were being asked to contribute towards a fund while being given no indication of the scheme's financial goal or its proposed form. Unsurprisingly, the two appeals did not elicit enthusiastic responses and it was not until February 1903, when a third call for subscriptions contained both an estimated total cost and a sketch of the approved design by the architect, Frank L. Pearson, that donations started to match expectations.[40]

By contrast, Eton's financial difficulties had nothing to do with administrative mismanagement but were simply the consequence of overly ambitious plans. Projected costs of £36,000 for a memorial hall and £5,000 for redecoration of the chapel meant Old Etonians were expected to foot a bill well in excess of ten

---

[36] Cheltenham College Archive, *Cheltonian*, September 1901, p. 190.

[37] WinCA, J10/5/1, Circular: Wykehamist South African War Memorial Fund, 20 February 1903; Cheltenham College Archive, *Cheltonian*, December 1902, p. 24.

[38] HSA, *Harrovian*, Vol. XVI, No. 7 (8 October 1903). The inclusion of both Lionel and Leopold Rothschild in the list of subscribers provides some explanation for the rapidity with which the school's relatively modest target was met.

[39] WinCA, J10/3, Circular: Wykehamist South African War Memorial Fund, February 1901; J10/4, July 1901.

[40] WinCA, J10/5/1, Circular: Wykehamist South African War Memorial Fund, 20 February 1903.

times that facing their counterparts at Harrow, Winchester or Charterhouse.[41] Indeed, as late as July 1908, the financial shortfall was so serious that members of the College's memorial committee, alone of all the schools investigated for this study, decided to extend the boundaries of community beyond the obvious definition of current and former students and masters by issuing a final appeal for contributions 'to all Old Etonians and friends of Eton'.[42] This appeared to do the trick and by the time Princess Alexandra of Beck laid the foundation stone four months later the total had been all but reached.

Eton's chequered fund-raising record was, in part, the result of differing interpretations of where the governing body's financial obligations ended. Many Old Etonians were initially reluctant to contribute towards a scheme which they felt was no more than an expansion of the academic premises and, as such, fell within the remit of the school's official budget.[43] Similar disquiet was voiced at Charterhouse where one Old Carthusian complained that 'funds being diverted to the building of a new wing for the chapel is unconstitutional because school funds ought to pay for any necessary additions to school buildings'.[44] In both instances the controlling authorities were keen to curb further criticism by explaining that the costs of substantial elements of the projects were being met by official means. The governing body at Charterhouse used the editorial column of the school magazine to point out that they were assuming responsibility for the costs of alterations to the Choir Vestry while the honorary secretary of Eton's memorial committee made clear, when appealing for subscriptions, that the purchase of the site for the memorial hall had been defrayed from the School Improvement Fund.[45]

However, such wrangling over financial practicalities masked deeper concerns about the true function of commemoration. When Lord Selborne told Old Wykehamists, at the inaugural meeting to discuss Winchester's remembrance plans, that a memorial should serve a tripartite role by being 'worthy of the fallen, helpful to the school and a real example to future generations', he was

---

[41] The total costs for Charterhouse, Harrow and Winchester were £4,000, £3,000 and £2,500 respectively. Although the total cost of the Charterhouse scheme was, in fact, £6,500, £2,500 came directly from school funds as the work to improve the existing chapel was not considered part of the memorial.

[42] *The Times*, 9 July 1908.

[43] *The Times*, 15 May 1902; 17 May 1902; 19 May 1902.

[44] CSA, *Carthusian*, Vol. VIII, No. 256 (February 1901), p. 48. Indeed, the author of this letter developed his theme to make a wider political point about the government's abnegation of its financial duties during the war. The funding of the extension of the chapel through voluntary subscriptions was, he said, as objectionable as 'the way private enterprise has been allowed to pay for some of the troops which have been sent out to South Africa'. CSA, *Carthusian*, Vol. VIII, No. 256 (February 1901), p. 48.

[45] CSA, *Carthusian*, Vol. VIII, No. 260 (July 1901), p. 93; ECA, Misc/EMF/8, 'Eton Memorial', 27 May 1902.

inadvertently highlighting an internal tension that was to trouble many school memorialisation schemes.[46] The adoption of practical schemes to improve educational provision was relatively common at institutions where it was felt the wealth of the alumni could support such ambitions, libraries and halls being especially popular choices. For many, however, such utilitarianism undermined the sanctity of commemoration. It was feared that not only might the cause for which a memorial had been constructed fade over time but that the very memory of the fallen could, in the interim, be besmirched by the profane nature of everyday usage. Ian Malcolm, the inveterate critic of Eton's remembrance project, best articulated this anxiety when he argued that, as the proposed memorial hall would be used for 'examinations or disciplinary purposes more frequently than for anything else', it would 'accumulate unpopular associations … and acquire a "short title" or nickname which may wholly falsify the intention of its pious founders '.[47] Keen to put the record straight before the crucial meeting of old boys at the Mansion House the following week, the editor of the school magazine was quick to refute such an accusation:

> It would be a noble and seemly monument to our bravest and best; and though
> it might, incidentally, be used for practical purposes, yet its raison d'etre
> should be to be connected with happy and festal associations; a place where
> on high days the masses of the great dead should look down, well-pleased,
> upon the happy joys and activities of the living.[48]

The members of Charterhouse's executive committee were equally anxious to forefront the sanctity of their schemes. Through the pages of the *Carthusian* they assured past and present pupils that the memorial cloisters were not simply an adjunct of the school's redevelopment plans. Pointing out that a commemorative relief had been added in August 1905, they insisted that there could now be 'no doubt about the purpose of the whole Memorial Cloister; namely to keep before the eyes and thoughts of Carthusians in times to come the memory of the many acts of self-sacrifice and unselfish service done for their country'.[49]

To obviate charges of profanity, a large number of memorial committees opted for the school chapel as the most appropriate location for their institution's commemorative site. Chapels not only benefited from the obvious associations with faith and reflection, but were, in the words Brian Simon and Ian Bradley, central to 'an integrated system of ideological control'.[50] Although the proportion of teaching staff in holy orders had declined rapidly in the third quarter of the nineteenth century, the link, at least in philosophical terms, between education

---

46   WinCA, *Wykehamist*, No. 377 (20 December 1900), p. 245.
47   *The Times*, 15 May 1902.
48   ECA, *Eton College Chronicle*, No. 968 (7 June 1902), p. 98.
49   CSA, *Carthusian*, Vol. IX, No. 298 (August 1905), p. 189.
50   Simon and Bradley, *The Victorian Public School*, p. 13.

and religion which had underpinned the Arnoldian vision of the public school still held firm at the start of the Edwardian era.[51] Christianity's central tenet of self-sacrifice, reinforced by its close association with the cult of chivalry, continued to serve as the leitmotif of a public school education. Moreover, despite the laicisation of public school teaching staff towards the end of the nineteenth century, the headmaster of Harrow, the Reverend R. E. C. Welldon, could, in 1898, still assert without fear of contradiction that, 'In every great public boarding-school, the chapel is the centre of school life'.[52]

The importance of Christian precepts of service and sacrifice was reflected in the insistence of memorial committees, where the decision had been made to opt for a utilitarian scheme, to supplement their plans with some form of memory site in the school's chapel. The editor of the *Eton College Chronicle*, while wholeheartedly endorsing his headmaster's campaign for a memorial hall was, nonetheless, adamant that some part of the scheme should be sited in the chapel as Eton was 'pre-eminently a religious foundation'.[53] In this he was pushing at an open door, with the executive committee's proposal that a roll of honour should be placed in the school chapel receiving universal approval from Old Etonians at the otherwise heated Mansion House meeting.[54]

In addition to being viewed by staff and old boys alike as repositories of school traditions and, hence, the natural home for memory sites, chapels had the added advantage of being the buildings in which whole school instruction most commonly took place. Lord Roberts was in no doubt about just how important the school chapel was in moulding the men under his command. He told those assembled for the laying of the foundation stone of Harrow School's commemorative transept in July 1902 that, 'whatever lessons of obedience and hard work may have been learned in the pupil room, whatever lessons of manliness, unselfishness and good fellowship may have been learned on the playing fields, it was within the walls of the chapel that the seeds were sown that had had the best and lasting results'.[55] In opposing the construction of a commemorative hall, Ian Malcolm adopted similar reasoning, arguing that Old Etonians had been able to face death cheerfully only because they had

---

[51] Michael Sanderson has noted that between 1870 and 1906 the proportion of staff at the leading public schools who were clergymen declined from 54 per cent to 13 per cent. Michael Sanderson, *Education and Economic Decline in Britain: 1870 to the 1990s* (Cambridge: Cambridge University Press, 1999), p. 42.

[52] Quoted in Bradley and Simon, *The Victorian Public School*, p. 13. Welldon's sentiment was echoed by the editor of the *Eton College Chronicle* who, in promoting the siting of a roll of honour in his school's chapel, similarly claimed that, 'the whole of Eton centres about the chapel'. ECA, *Eton College Chronicle*, No. 968 (7 June 1902), p. 96.

[53] ECA, *Eton College Chronicle*, No. 968 (7 June 1902), p. 96.

[54] ECA, *Eton College Chronicle*, No. 970 (14 June 1902), p. 106.

[55] HSA, *Harrovian*, Vol. XV, No. 6 (26 July 1902), p. 66.

been 'inspired in the college chapel by lessons of high chivalry and sacrifice'.[56] For those charged with overseeing the construction of memorials to the South African War, the chapel was, then, the obvious location for a remembrance site.[57] The didacticism of chapel sermons could be reinforced by the iconographical lessons of monumental sculpture.

Although, as will be discussed later, it was not uncommon for the contentious nature of the struggle against the Boers to be alluded to in unveiling addresses, monumental symbolism allowed for no such equivocation over the justness of the cause for which the fallen had sacrificed their lives. Biblical warriors figured regularly on commemorative plaques and stained glass windows. Tonbridge School, Bedford Grammar and Blundell's School in Tiverton all chose to feature George and the Dragon as the central motif for their memorial windows, while at Eastbourne College the message was the same although the personnel differed, St Michael taking the place of St George.[58] At Charterhouse, the memorial relief in the cloisters presented the war as a heroic narrative in which both the martial prowess and founding principles of the British Empire had been tested and passed fit. A bronze of the angel of victory holding a dying hero, flanked by four panels bearing the legends Mafeking, Ladysmith, Paardeberg and Pretoria, presented a carefully constructed vision of the fighting from gallant defence through glorious victory to ultimate triumph. Further iconographical embellishments placed this central statement in the wider context of the conflict. Topped by a depiction of St George slaying the dragon and buttressed by statues representing 'Clemency' and 'Loyalty' alongside the letters 'A' and 'C' for Australia and Canada, the symbolic meta-narrative reinforced for the pupils the image of motherland and colonies uniting to draw back into the fold a people whose selfish ambitions had threatened to undermine the collective harmony of the British imperial family. There was no place in this sanitised version of the past for either the political complexities thrown up by Boer claims to sovereignty or the military realities revealed in the embarrassing reverses of Black Week and the grim campaigning of the guerrilla endgame.[59]

Frequently, monumental imagery had more to do with a school's sense of identity than the memorialisation of the war in South Africa. The Arnoldian reformers of the second half of the nineteenth century were inspired by the belief that the primary function of the public school should, in the words of a former headmaster of Harrow, 'be the pupils' initiation into the high and

---

[56] *The Times*, 15 May 1902.
[57] In over 90 per cent of the schools listed by James Gildea in his gazetteer of memorials to the South African War, at least part, and in most cases all, of the memory site is housed in the school chapel. Gildea, *For Remembrance*.
[58] Gildea, *For Remembrance*, pp. 90, 3, 41, 212.
[59] CSA, *Carthusian*, Vol. IX, No. 298 (August 1905), p. 189.

ennobling idea of the Law'.[60] Central to such a lofty ideal was a classical education, with its stress on the subordination of individual will and ambition to public service and duty.[61] Westminster, St Paul's, Eton, Charterhouse and The Merchant Taylors' School, London, all used Latin quotations or verses in their memorials. Westminster erected a plaque and invited an old boy, Professor J. S. Philimore, a classicist, to compose the Latin inscription.[62] The use of former scholars was also seen in the St Paul's School memorial. A classical 'tempietto' was designed by one old boy, F. S. Chesterton, and judged by another, the architect Sir Edward Poynter. The memorial consisted of a ribbed copper dome supported by seven Tuscan columns with a frieze inscription in Latin.[63] Classical virtue was reinforced at Merchant Taylors' School and Eton College by the decision to record the names of the fallen in their Latinised form. At Winchester College the classical theme extended to the unveiling ceremony with the officiating dignitary, Lord Roberts, being greeted by the head prefect who made a lengthy opening address entirely in Latin.[64] By linking their memory sites to a classical heritage, these schools were making clear statements about their self-image and the sacrifices of their alumni. The fallen had upheld the ethos of their alma maters by dying in the service of their country. Such noble sentiments clearly signal that it was institutional pride rather than personal loss that lay at the heart of these memorials.

Even when allusions to the ancient world were eschewed, architects frequently symbolically located commemorative sites in moments of national glory. The memorial library at Dulwich College was designed by Edwin Hall, an Old Alleynian, in the style of an English Renaissance hall in red brick and Portland stone.[65] In form, Hall was playing with Tudor ideas thus reinforcing the period many Victorians and Edwardians took as a key moment in the transition of England into a great power.[66] Similarly, W. Protheroe, an Old Cheltonian, carefully connected the memory of the fallen of Cheltenham College with

---

[60]   E. M. Goulbourn, *The Book of Rugby School: Its History and Daily Life* (1856) quoted in Simon and Bradley (eds), *The Victorian Public School*, p. 14.

[61]   As evidence of the pivotal role Classics played in the school curriculum, in 1884 Eton College had twenty-eight classics masters but only six mathematicians and one historian. H. Bergoff, 'Public Schools and the Decline of the British Economy 1880–1914', *Past and Present*, 129: 1 (1990), p. 152.

[62]   Lawrence E. Tanner, *Westminster School: Its Buildings and their Associations* (London: Philip Allan and Co., 1923), p. 30.

[63]   McDonnell, *A History of St. Paul's School*, p. 445.

[64]   WinCA, *Wykehamist*, No. 396 (October 1902), p. 448. This clearly took Roberts a little by surprise who felt obliged, in his unveiling address, to admit to the boys that his Latin was 'somewhat rusty'. WinCA, *Wykehamist*, No. 396 (October 1902), p. 448.

[65]   DCA, *Alleynian*, Vol. XXXI, No. 228 (July 1903), pp. 224–225.

[66]   See Roy Strong, *And When Did You Last See Your Father: The Victorian Painter and British History* (London: Thames and Hudson, 1978), pp. 113–161.

7 St Paul's School memorial, London.

the military prowess of Edward I's England through the construction of an Eleanor Cross.[67]

Underpinning these aesthetic choices was a desire to celebrate the bonds of continuity which tied the past with the present. Memory sites were used both to extend and reinforce the traditions around which school life revolved. In his address at the dedication of the memorial transepts at Charterhouse in August 1903, Sir Richard Jebb was quick to reassure those present that the school's relocation to the Surrey countryside did not mean a break with the past. Pointing out that there was 'another Carthusian cloister in London', he stressed that 'this new cloister and today's ceremony show how completely the unity of Carthusian feeling has survived the change of abode'.[68] Indeed, when the proposal to erect a memorial cloister had been first presented in the school magazine, it was this very aspect which had been used to emphasise its

---

[67] For more on Eleanor Crosses see Borg, *War Memorials*, p. 9 and p. 95.

[68] CSA, 83/3/2, Sir Richard Jebb's unveiling address, 4 July 1903. Originally founded on the site of an old Carthusian monastery in Charterhouse Square, Smithfield, London, the school moved to its present day site in Godalming, Surrey, in 1872.

suitability. By noting that, 'in the cloister will be recorded the names of those who have fallen for their country in the past, and in it will also be placed the monuments now in the ante-chapel and those which will be erected in the future', the editor of *The Carthusian* had assured his readers that the cloister would 'become the home of Carthusian traditions'.[69]

It was at the unveiling of memorials that messages about identity, tradition and ethos were made explicit. To signal the day as one of institutional celebration, unveiling ceremonies were frequently planned to coincide with important days in the school calendar. Both Dulwich College and Harrow dedicated their commemorative buildings on Founder's Day, while Simon Langton Boys' School, Tonbridge, Cheltenham College and Charterhouse all opted for Speech Day. Attended by parents and old boys, these festivals provided governors and headmasters with the opportunity to promote the achievements of past and present pupils and to advertise their schools' worth to the wider community. Indeed, for the headmasters of Dulwich College and Simon Langton Boys' School, the very existence of a memory site was proof of the high regard that old boys had for their former homes. In his dedication address, Dulwich's head focused on the excellence of the school's new memorial library to draw out the esteem that Old Alleynians had for their alma mater while Mr Mann, the headmaster of Simon Langton, was equally certain that, 'the handsome memorial to the memory of those that fell and fought in the late war which has just been unveiled ... meant that the position of the school was safe for it showed the affection that old boys who had passed through still retained'.[70]

However, it was in the actions of the fallen, rather than the affections of the living, that officiating dignitaries attempted to validate institutional values. Old boys who had sacrificed their lives in South Africa were, rather like pupils who had gained regional or national sporting honours, frequently spoken of as if they had been acting on behalf of their former schools. To the pupils of Winchester College, assembled for the laying of the foundation stone of the memorial cloisters, the fallen were presented by Field Marshal Lord Roberts as 'soldier representatives of your great school'.[71] The compilers of the Eton College roll of honour adopted a similar line. In the introduction to a bound volume listing all Old Etonians who had served during the war, published by Spottiswoode and Co. in 1908, they asserted that the names would 'provide Eton with a permanent record ... of those who represented her in the war'.[72] Implicit in

---

[69] CSA, *Carthusian*, Vol. VIII, No. 253 (October 1900), p. 9.

[70] DCA, *Alleynian*, Vol. XXI, No. 228 (July 1903), pp. 224–225; Simon Langton Boys' School Archives, *Langtonian*, Vol. II (December 1903), p. 249.

[71] WinCA, *Wykehamist*, No. 396 (October 1902), p. 449.

[72] ECA, MISC/EMF/8, 'List of Etonians who served in the South Africa between October 11 1899 and May 31 1902'.

such claims to ownership was a belief in former pupils' devotion to their schools over and above all other forms of community. Educators, particularly those in the public school system, considered it their duty to provide their charges with moral as much as intellectual guidance and, as Geoffrey Best has pointed out, at the core of this value transference was loyalty.[73] For the pupil, the inculcation of this message was complemented by the intensity of communal life in a public school, with its esoteric rituals, language and culture. As a consequence, loyalty to school could, for many, come to match if not outweigh loyalty to country. It was in the classroom and on the playing field, in the 'experienced community' of the school rather than the 'imagined community' of the nation, that pupils and former pupils found the social and cultural reference points which gave meaning to their everyday lives.[74] This narrow definition of identity was intensified during the war as school magazines buttressed feelings of local patriotism by publishing reports about, and letters from, old boys serving at the front. For some, perhaps the majority, the school community came to serve as a surrogate family. Thus, Henry Montagu Butler, headmaster of Harrow from 1859 to 1885, could, without embarrassment, support the president of the Old Harrovians' resolution to construct a cloister in honour of former pupils who had died in the South African War by equating the intimate bonds of kinship with the allegiances that tied old boys to their former schools:

> The link of the Public School brotherhood is one which supported our school-fellows in days of trial, of danger, and of suffering. When men lay wounded out at night, or for long days together in the hospital, they instinctively thought of all the dear and tender home associations. But what I contend is that one other recollection helped to soothe the suffering as well as to inspire courage, the recollection of those happy days of what I may call the second home, the home where boyhood turns into manhood, the home where boyish friendships are cemented, the home symbolised by the Hill, the Church, the Chapel, the House, the Cricket Ground, the Football Field, the Racket Courts – all those various scenes of boyhood returning now at their best and dearest. Yes, I can imagine that many a Harrow man, stretched out on the bed of pain, found, among the sources which solaced him most, recollections of the happy time when the beloved friends of his boyhood were around him.[75]

Butler's imagery, and the assumption about the unswerving loyalty of former pupils that underpinned it, would undoubtedly have resonated with his audience of old boys.

---

[73]   Best, 'Militarism in the Victorian Public School', p. 145.
[74]   Jay Winter and Jean-Louis Robert (eds), *Capital Cities at War: Paris, London, Berlin 1914–1919* (Cambridge: Cambridge University Press, 1997), pp. 3–8.
[75]   HSA, *Harrovian*, Vol. XIV, No. 8 (16 November 1901), p. 100.

Having claimed the fallen as their own, it was not uncommon for officiating dignitaries to hold up the service record of former pupils as evidence of institutional worth. The headmaster of Simon Langton Boys' School in Canterbury, Mr Mann, was quick to make a connection between the war record of the old boys and the school's ethos. Having unveiled the memorial plaque to the thirty-one Old Langtonians who had served in the war, he told the assembled pupils that, 'This is, I think, a large number for a school of this size. We have never had a desire to uphold the warlike spirit, but we have most strongly inculcated patriotism and we think we are justified in feeling pride that so many of our old boys were ready to respond to their country's call'.[76] Indeed, for Mann, the memory site not only validated the schools' guiding principles but added another layer to the traditions that underpinned them. 'It would', he said, 'have its place among the honours' records of the school which are helping to make history for us'.[77] For Baden-Powell, honour had been brought to his old school not simply by the number of Old Cathusians who had served in the war but by the nature of that service. During a visit to lay the foundation stone of the memorial cloisters in September 1901, he informed the assembled school that:

> Of the 360 Old Boys, I think, no mean proportion, 80, have had honourable mention in despatches and 27 have laid down their lives at the call of duty. That is a record of which no public school in England would stand ashamed. We read the Roll of Honour with a just and grateful pride.[78]

Field Marshal Lord Roberts, attending Harrow in July 1902 to perform a similar ceremonial function, was equally sure that it was in death that true glory could be found. He was, he told the boys, certain that, 'the fact that a large proportion [of the 500 Old Harrovians who served in the war] should have fallen, one in ten, must make everyone connected with Harrow feel very proud'.[79] Indeed, Lord Selbourne took such reasoning to its logical conclusion. Having told an audience of Old Wykehamists, gathered to discuss the construction of the war memorial at Winchester, that the honour of the College had been upheld by the '250 Old Boys already engaged in South Africa', he went on to suggest that they should feel especially proud for, 'of that number no less than twenty-one had lost their lives, and what was more remarkable, of that twenty-one only two had died of disease, the other nineteen having been killed in action or died of wounds received in action'.[80] The implication was that, by dying at the hands of the enemy rather than succumbing to disease,

---

[76] Simon Langton Boys' School Archives, *Langtonian*, Vol. II (December 1903), p. 243.
[77] Simon Langton Boys' School Archives, *Langtonian*, Vol. II (December 1903), p. 243.
[78] CSA, *Carthusian*, Vol. VIII, No. 263 (November 1901), p. 140.
[79] HSA, *Harrovian*, Vol. XV, No. 6 (26 July 1902), p. 66.
[80] WinCA, *Wykehamist*, No. 377 (20 December 1900), p. 246.

fallen Wykehamists had brought greater glory to the school by combining loyalty with that other key public school virtue, manliness. For the Jesuit authorities at Stonyhurst College in Lancashire, it was not only the institution's military principles but also its religious ethos that had been reinforced by the sacrifice of its former pupils. The inscription on the memorial plaque to the six Old Stonyhurstians who fell in the war proclaims that their memory will: 'Further bring to mind a great Company of Old Stonyhurst Boys who in the same Campaign left for all time an example of Catholic loyalty, and of soldiery service worthy of the traditions of this College'.[81]

Pride rather than grief was, then, the overriding emotion at most school unveiling ceremonies. This was made explicit by the captain of Eton College. Addressing the King and Queen at the opening of the school's memorial hall and library in November 1908, he was anxious that the memory sites should be viewed as tributes to courage and duty rather than tokens of sorrow and mourning. The buildings would, he said, 'to us who are still members of the school … serve as a memorial, not so much of friends whom we ourselves have lost, as of gallant deeds of former Etonians in the hour of their country's need'.[82] This sentiment was echoed by the editor of Winchester School's magazine in his coverage of Baden-Powell's visit to lay the foundation stone of the memorial cloisters. Prepared to acknowledge that the ceremony would have evoked 'mixed feelings', he was, nonetheless, in no doubt about what must have been the dominant mood:

> But to all surely came one thought, prevailing even against pity, and sympathy, and regret, namely, that now, as of old, Winchester was justified of her children. That when England had called for men in her time of need, Winchester had given of her best, and that her best had proved themselves faithful, even unto death.[83]

Others used the unveiling of school memory sites to make wider points about the education of the nation's young men. Lord Spencer, the president of the Old Harrovians Association, used the sacrifice of the fallen as a validation of the education provided by not just his alma mater but by all public schools. Preaching, one can't help thinking, to the converted, he adumbrated for an audience of Old Harrovians gathered to discuss their former school's remembrance plans the advantages of having passed through such a distinctly British system:

> I believe that there is no other country in the world which can claim to have the institution and the organisation of Public Schools. The system of

---

[81]   Gildea, *For Remembrance*, p. 117.

[82]   ECA, *Eton College Chronicle*, No. 1251 (26 November 1908), p. 383.

[83]   WinCA, *Wykehamist*, No. 396 (October 1902), p. 448.

the Public Schools is peculiar to this country; it is one which we think has high excellence, we believe that not only does it ensure the teaching of high learning and good education, but more than any other system it tends to strengthen and improve the character of men. We speak as Harrovians, and we admire the system; though we may say it can be criticised, that it may have dangers about it and it may have its faults, yet we recognise that it is a very admirable system ... It creates and engenders high qualities among the boys, it engenders loyalty and patriotism and truthfulness and independence. We do not believe that any other system can so well create these faculties among boys.[84]

Sir Richard Jebb, speaking at the dedication of Charterhouse School's memorial transept, was equally keen to extol the formative qualities of a public school education. The public schoolboy was, he asserted, equipped to assume a leading role in the pressing task of national defence for 'at school he will have learned, not by mechanical and rigid routine but in a large and liberal sense, the two supreme functions of a soldier – to obey and command'.[85]

The true champion of this line of reasoning was Lord Roberts. Having been a long-term advocate of compulsory military service, Roberts seized on the concerns over national efficiency which the army's performance in South Africa had prompted to promote the National Service League's campaign for the introduction of conscription. A key battleground in this campaign was the public schools, the products of which would be expected to command Britain's new mass army. Roberts's address to the boys of Glenalmond School, at the dedication of their memorial library in 1906, typified his approach:

I look to you public school boys to set an example. Let it be your ambition to render yourself capable of becoming leaders of those others who have not had your advantages, should you ever be called upon to fight for your country ... Public school training inculcates just those qualities which are required in leaders of men: self-reliance, determination, and a certain amount of give and take, exacting obedience to authority more by an appeal to honour and sound common sense than by severity, and by a happy mixture of prudence and audacity.[86]

Although conscription was his ultimate goal, there were also some short-term practical reforms which Roberts was keen to have implemented by the public schools. Volunteer corps had been established at a number of schools in the last decades of the nineteenth century but, with a few notable exceptions, these had not flourished in the years before the South African War. However, with their fortunes revived by the surge of patriotism which had gripped the

---

[84] HSA, *Harrovian*, Vol. XIV, No. 8 (16 November 1901), p. 98.
[85] CSA, 83/3/2, Sir Richard Jebb's unveiling address, 4 July 1903.
[86] Quoted in Simon and Bradley (eds), *The Victorian Public School*, p. 137.

country in the first few months of the fighting against the Boers, the corps became an obvious platform for the militarisation of the public school system in the immediate aftermath of the conflict.[87] At the laying of the foundation stone for the college's memorial gate in 1902, Roberts urged the authorities at Winchester to furnish the pupils with ample opportunity to replicate the feats of the 308 Old Wykehamists they were honouring 'by letting the boys have time for practising at rifle shooting and learning gymnastics and physical exercises'.[88] But it was not just the practical aspects of curriculum time that were of concern to Roberts but rather the status of such activities. They must not, he insisted, be restricted only to 'boys who show a taste for military pursuits' but extended to encompass 'even those boys who aspire to be Lord Chancellors or Archbishops'.[89]

The war as a clarion call for the reawakening of the nation's military spirit was also the theme of the Marquess of Camden's address to the boys of Tonbridge School at the unveiling of the memorial window in the school chapel in August 1905. The lessons of the war should, he felt, not only have had the practical effect of encouraging army reform by 'awakening a serious desire to fill up that which is lacking in our military organisation', but should also have served to provoke in the public school community some serious soul-searching:

> The public schoolboy, we are afraid, is by nature rather narrow, and we cannot help being glad that something has happened to rouse him from the selfish and isolated pursuits of his own amusements. This memorial might serve to raise him for a moment above his own narrow circle of thought; it will be an incentive to his public sympathies.[90]

Self-abnegation similarly served as the central message of Lieutenant-General Robert Baden-Powell's speech at the laying of the foundation stone of the memorial cloisters at his alma mater, Charterhouse, in September 1901. He told the current crop of Carthusians that the war should have taught them, 'not to try to shove yourself forward, but help your neighbours and try to play the game, and play it right through as you play football or any other game. Right through for your side and not for yourself'.[91]

---

[87] Geoffrey Best notes that Eton College had a flourishing volunteer corps throughout the 1880s and 1890s. This was largely due to the influence of the headmaster, Edmond Warre, who was a staunch supporter of compulsory military training for all school pupils. Best, 'Militarism and the Victorian Public School', pp. 133–134. See also B. Porter, *The Absent-Minded Imperialists: Empire, Society and Culture in Britain* (Oxford: Oxford University Press, 2004), pp. 48–57.

[88] WinCA, *Wykehamist*, No. 396 (October 1902), p. 448.

[89] WinCA, *Wykehamist*, No. 396 (October 1902), p. 448.

[90] Tonbridge School Archives, *Tonbridgian*, August 1905, p. 129.

[91] CSA, *Carthusian*, Vol. VIII, No. 263 (November 1901), p. 140.

Indeed, messages about duty and service were staples of dedication addresses at schools. The didactic nature of memorialisation rituals made them particularly suited to a young audience and it was especially common for pupils to be urged to emulate those being commemorated. The mayor of Canterbury was insistent that the pupils of Simon Langton Boys' School should be 'proud of those boys who served in time of need' and should regard the names listed on the commemorative tablet as 'an incentive ... to do likewise when the occasion presented itself'.[92] In a sermon delivered after the unveiling of the memorial window in Tonbridge School chapel, the Bishop of Kensington, an Old Tonbridgian, reminded the pupils present that the reason why the fallen had sacrificed their lives 'was written on their graves; it was for King and Country'.[93] He then proceeded to outline and exemplify for his young audience, in a rhetorical flourish redolent with the images of Newbolt's *Vitai Lampada*, the conduct and qualities expected of the products of the Edwardian public school system:

> The young officer who died with the colours for his shroud which he tried to save, the man in the bridge of the warship who refused to leave the vessel, and went down, saluting as he went, and the boy who forfeited popularity because the sense of duty was rooted in his soul; were these things hard? Or did it tell them of the most pathetic feature, of the magic power, the influence and the strength of character which duty produced?[94]

Equally conformist messages underscored the dedication speeches at the unveiling of memorials at Merchant Taylors' School, Eton, Harrow and Charterhouse.[95]

If such calls to patriotic service were to have the desired effect on young audiences, then it was vital that both the cause and manner in which the sacrifices had been made should be seen as pure. The contentious nature of the memory of the South African War, both in terms of motivation and conduct, encouraged some officiating dignitaries to revisit old debates. Lord Harris, who as honorary colonel of the Royal East Kent Mounted Rifles had successfully encouraged eleven of his men to volunteer for active service as early as November 1899, was determined that any lingering doubts over the justness of Britain's involvement in the recent conflict should not be allowed to cloud the minds of the pupils of Simon Langton Boys' School. He informed his young audience at

92 *Kentish Gazette and Canterbury Press*, 28 November 1903.
93 Tonbridge School Archives, *Tonbridgian*, August 1905, p. 129.
94 Tonbridge School Archives, *Tonbridgian*, August 1905, p. 130.
95 *City Press*, 14 October 1903; ECA, *Eton College Chronicle*, No. 1251 (26 November 1908), p. 383; HSA, *Harrovian*, Vol. XVI, No. 8 (November 1903), p. 104; CSA, *Carthusian*, Vol. VIII, No. 279 (August 1903), p. 370.

the unveiling of the memorial tablet in honour of the Old Langtonians who had served in the war that:

> Just as the Boers have been held up as great patriots and as gallant defenders of their land, so it was perfectly legitimate for them, who were doing honour to those, many of whom were volunteers, to remember that the service they gave was just as much in defence of their country as the service given by the Boers in defence of the Transvaal. Because for a long time the action was fought, not on Transvaal territory, not on the Orange River, but on British territory. In fact, it was to force back that invasion that many of those men volunteered.[96]

Lord Selborne, who was to be appointed High Commissioner to South Africa in 1905, was prepared to accept that government policy towards the Boer Republics during the war might justifiably have its critics but drew the line at any denigration of British military conduct. Insistent that all should take pride in the 'glorious crown of sacrifice' shown by Wykehamists who had served and fallen, he concluded the final committee meeting before the dedication of the college's memorial gate with an attack on those who took their criticism too far:

> While each one of us can understand an honest conviction that the war could have been avoided, it is almost incomprehensible why such a large proportion of those who hold that opinion should seem to be drawn by some irresistible influence into revelling in every vile aspersion that was cast upon their fellow countrymen who had fought in the war and laid down their lives.[97]

Bishop J. Taylor Smith, the chaplain-general to the forces, was also keen to defend the professionalism and integrity of the British soldier. At the unveiling of the commemorative reredos in Cheltenham College chapel, in April 1904, he regaled his young audience with a stirring tale of self-sacrifice and heroism:

> Two days ago I was told of a Medical Officer who was shot through the side, and laid down, but who called to a corporal and said: 'Take the bandage and wave it.' The corporal held up the white triangular bandage and waved it and immediately a shot pierced his hand. The brave fellow took the bandage into the other hand and held it up and waved it again, to have the left hand riddled with shot as he fell back, both hands gone. After a time the Boers came. And the doctor said: 'Attend to the corporal first, and take this case and give him a dose of morphine, for he is suffering terrible pain.' The doctor

---

[96] Simon Langton Boys' School Archives, *Langtonian*, Vol. II (December 1903), p. 245. It should be noted that it was not just Harris's service record but also his business interests, he was chairman of the Rhodes Consolidated Goldfields and the South African Gold Trust, that help to provide a rationale for the views presented to the boys of Simon Langton Boys' School.
[97] WinCA, *Wykehamist*, No. 396 (October 1902), p. 247.

then fell over dead, but the corporal lives today and he is now in London, and tells the story of that noble and unselfish act of kindness.

Yet, anxious not to undermine the reintegration of the defeated Boer Republics into the imperial family, Taylor Smith ended his tale on a note of reconciliation by maintaining that, 'our enemies are not to be blamed because anything was sufficient to try them at a time like that'.[98]

Peter Parker has noted that South African War 'memorials [in public schools] testified to the chivalric nature of death upon the battlefield'.[99] That this was so owes much to the controlling influence of old boys in the memorialisation process. Educated at a time when the idealisation of the Middle Ages was at its height and in institutions where the importance of the historic community was stressed, the alumni of Britain's public schools took great pride in the perceived bonds of tradition that underpinned the values of their alma maters.[100] It is hardly surprising, therefore, that frequently these men, as they were to do again in the aftermath of the Great War, drew on an understanding of a 'remote yet meaningful past' to encode with a sense of coherence and purpose the deaths of former pupils in the war in South Africa.[101] Lines of continuity were drawn with the recent as well as mythic past to tie the conflict with the Boers into an unbroken heroic narrative. The fallen of 1899–1902 were viewed and remembered as the most recent incarnation of a long line of warrior-patriots, the purpose of whom was, in J. A. Mangan's words, 'noble and sacrificial – to fight and die for England's greatness'.[102] At the heart of this narrative of remembrance were the personal attributes that the fallen were deemed to embody: service, duty, self-abnegation. Dedication ceremonies were used to restate these shared beliefs and values for the benefit of the school community and to extol institutional pride and worth to a wider audience.

Memorials built in communities of the young did, therefore, present schoolchildren with highly controlled representations of the past where the didactic function of the memorialisation process took precedence over any sense of loss or consolation. The service of old boys, and the sacrifice of those who had given their lives, was used to validate institutional traditions and endorse the wider public school ethos of duty, manliness and honour. Although acknowledged, the feelings of the bereaved were not allowed to detract from the overriding sense of collective pride. When the Bishop of London addressed a congregation of boys and parents at the consecration of Harrow's memorial transepts he ensured that the presence of grieving relatives was not allowed to

---

[98]   Cheltenham College Archive, *Cheltonian*, April 1904, p. 21.
[99]   Parker, *The Old Lie*, p. 105.
[100] Sanderson, *Education and Economic Decline*, pp. 39–41.
[101] Goebel, *The Great War and Medieval Memory*, p. 286.
[102] Mangan, 'Images of Empire', p. 32.

distort his inspirational message: 'And it is a great day and a good day for a Harrow boy when, with his company of 10 or 12 men, he holds a post for England against the enemy, and it is a good day – yes, I say it, knowing the sorrowing hearts, some of whom are in this Chapel, – it is a good day even when he falls, and lays down his life for his School and his Country'.[103] Although grief may, at least in part, have been assuaged by such uplifting messages, the public school war memorial in honour of the old boys who served and died in South Africa was, in essence, a definition of values and ethos. It was a monument to those principles that a school community held sacred. As such it lay closer to George Mosse's 'site of mobilisation' than it did to Jay Winter's 'site of mourning'.[104]

---

[103] HSA, *Harrovian*, Vol. XVI, No. 8 (November 1903), p. 105.
[104] Mosse, *Fallen Soldiers*; Winter, *Sites of Memory*.

Chapter 4

Alternative Affiliations: Remembering the War in Families, Workplaces and Places of Worship

LTHOUGH the nineteenth century was a period of change in memorialisation practice with a move towards the democratisation of the process occurring, the celebration of the individual remained at the heart of commemorative activity throughout this period. Yet, with the volunteer movement of 1899–1902 playing such a prominent role in the public imagery of the army, the South African War was, undoubtedly, a crucial stimulus for civilian organisations to celebrate the contributions of their members to the collective war effort. Thus, at every level of society where people shared a common identity or could perceive a unifying bond, communities were eager to raise monuments to their war dead and to honour those who served.

i Memorials to Individuals

The bonds of kinship were, and are, for most people the ties that most firmly connect them to others and, therefore, it should come as no surprise that memorials in honour of individuals were by far the most common commemorative sites constructed during and in the immediate aftermath of the South African War.[1] Where raised by members of the fallen's immediate family, these sites were relatively straightforward both in terms of design and purpose. Typical was the memorial window in St Oswald's Church, Malpas, in honour of Lieutenant George Lockhart of the Shropshire Company Imperial Yeomanry. Commissioned by his parents and siblings and designed by the renowned stained glass artist, Charles Eamer Kempe, the figurative representations of Bravery, Duty, Love and Faith in the lower lights of the window presented a comforting message of martial prowess underscored by Christian

---

[1]   Jones, 'A Survey of Memorials to the Second Anglo-Boer War'.

8 Bertie Moeller memorial, St Peter's Church, Belsize Park.

virtues.[2] Memorial tablets or panels were also considered particularly apt for the commemoration of individuals. An especially fine memorial plaque was the centre-piece of the Bertie Moeller memorial at his parish church of St Peter, Belsize Park, London. Moeller, an Honourable Artillery Company man, was commemorated by his father who commissioned the tablet as part of an impressive improvement scheme to the church which included a chancel screen and steps in marble and that most Victorian of funerary materials, alabaster. That these types of memorials were largely the preserve of the affluent is shown by the Lockharts's ability to secure the services of such a highly fashionable and exclusive artist as Kempe and by Moeller's address in a well-to-do London suburb and his membership of the socially elite Honourable Artillery Company.[3] Indeed, Moeller's status was reinforced still further by his father's decision to have his South African diaries, *Two Years at the Front with the Mounted Infantry*,

---

2   Gildea, *For Remembrance*, p. 22.

3   Such commemorative sites were not, however, exclusively the preserve of the rich. A grant of £100 for the erection of a memorial plaque was provided to the next of kin of each of the seventy-two men from the City of London Imperial Volunteers who had died in the war. Designed by Frederick Wheeler, the bronze plaques were framed with the coat of arms of the City of London and engraved with the name of the deceased, the unit from which he had volunteered and the date and full circumstances of his death. Jones, 'A Survey of Memorials to the Second Anglo-Boer War'.

posthumously published and the willingness of the Bishop of Kensington to unveil the memorial.[4]

Occasionally whole communities looked to preserve the memory of individual members. The officers and men of the 1st battalion, the Royal Sussex Regiment, chose to commemorate the death of Lieutenant-Colonel Louis Eugene du Moulin, who was killed leading a charge against Boer positions at Abraham's Kraal on 28 January 1902, by completing and publishing his unfinished regimental history of the war under the title, *Two Years on Trek: Being Some Account of the Royal Sussex Regiment in South Africa*.[5] The residents of the small West Yorkshire community of Elland, led by the chairman of the parish council, Lewis Mackrell, raised sufficient money to pay for not only a memorial tablet but also a drinking fountain in the public baths in honour of Sergeant Joshua Hemingway, who had been the first person from the village to volunteer for active service and who had died at Kimberley in February 1901. The unveiling ceremony, in June 1902, combined tributes to Hemingway's personal qualities with messages of comfort for grieving friends and relatives. Mackrell was anxious to stress the community's high regard for the deceased by underlining the purity of emotion that had seen the memorialisation project through to fruition. The fact, he told the assembled crowd, that 'the work had not been carried through by any club or organisation, and no subscription list had been published and canvassing had been debarred', should be seen as proof that the 'motivation for the memorial was entirely one of sympathy and love'.[6] For Major Edwards, the recently retired commanding officer of Elland's volunteers, the manner of Hemingway's death meant that sorrow could be mitigated by pride: 'This was no wasted life; he gave it to his country – he lived a good man; he died a hero. What more can be wished for?'[7]

Unsurprisingly, these twin themes of love and condolence underscored the vast majority of commemorative schemes at this highly charged individual level. The intimacy of the connections between deceased and mourners ensured that the needs of grieving family members played a much more prominent part in proceedings than they did at collective tributes to regimental or civic fallen. At the unveiling of the memorial to Bertie Moeller, the Bishop of Kensington

---

[4]   For the Moeller memorials' history see HACA Court Minutes, 20 January, 17 February, 1 December 1902; HACA, Moeller Papers; British Library Grant Richards Archive, Moeller correspondence, which shows the increasingly tense relations between Moeller's father and the Grant Richards company; L. R. C. Boyle, *Two Years at the Front with the Mounted Infantry. Being the Diary of Lieutenant B. Moeller. With a Memoir by Lieutenant-Colonel L. R. C. Boyle, HAC* (London: Grant Richards, 1903); *Hampstead and Highgate Express*, 20, 27 December 1902; *Hampstead Advertiser*, 18, 23 December 1902.

[5]   Lieutenant-Colonel Louis Eugene du Moulin, *Two Years on Trek: Being Some Account of the Royal Sussex Regiment in South Africa* (London: Murray and Co., 1907).

[6]   *Halifax Courier*, 21 June 1902.

[7]   *Halifax Courier*, 21 June 1902.

sought, first and foremost, to comfort the congregation of friends and relatives gathered in St Peter's Church:

> In this case Lieutenant Moeller had not died in vain. His country's greatness was being built-up by the death of her sons, and the shutting of the doors of their young lives meant probably the swinging back of the door of South Africa for fuller civilisation and Christianity. By his death, too, Lieutenant Moeller had shown the beauty of self-sacrifice; the reality of life to come was forced upon one by it, and had established a stronger and more tender bond of brotherhood, and had sealed and cemented regimental cords of sympathy. The memorial did not tell of what was premature and untimely, but that in the greatest tragedies of life God did see one thing over and against another.[8]

Lieutenant-Colonel L. R. C. Boyle reinforced the bishop's theme by reassuring the bereaved that: 'Lieutenant Moeller was a dutiful, affectionate son, a kind brother, and a warm-hearted and true comrade. Well might his family and his country be proud of such a son!'[9] A similar line was adopted at the dedication of the stained glass window in St Peter's Church, Bennington, to the memory of Second Lieutenant George Mills of the Sherwood Foresters. Having first had the full details of the deceased's eighteen months' service in South Africa outlined by Lieutenant-Colonel Viscount Cranbourne, who unveiled the window, the address by Dr John Cox Edghill, a former chaplain-general, 'dwelt upon the good soldiery qualities exhibited by Lieutenant Mills, his courage and well deserved popularity'.[10]

Messages of consolation were frequently buttressed by memorial symbolism. The assertion by the vicar of St Mary's Church, Wootton, that Lieutenant Charles Henry Dillon had died 'a true soldier's death, a hero's death' found visual realisation in the commemorative stained glass window erected in Dillon's honour.[11] Based on Sir Noel Paton's painting, *Mors Janua Vitae*, the window's twin lights depict 'an angel showing the uses of life to a young knight'.[12] An equally comforting motif was adopted by the family of Lieutenant Francis Sowerby, of the Durham Light Infantry, for the memorial window in St Peter's Church, Luton. Designed by the well-known stained glass firm of Heaton, Butler and Bayne, the window portrays an elaborate scene of the Ascension bearing the inscription, 'Suffer hardship with me as a good soldier of Christ'.[13] Such chivalric tropes in commemorative art served to remove the fallen from the harsh realities of life and death on the veldt and re-site them in a mythical

---

8   *Hampstead Advertiser*, 23 December 1902.
9   *Hampstead Advertiser*, 23 December 1902.
10   *The Times*, 27 January 1902.
11   Wootton parish magazine, July 1901.
12   Gildea, *For Remembrance*, p. 2; Wootton parish magazine, July 1901.
13   Gildea, *For Remembrance*, p. 83.

age when warfare adhered to a more gentlemanly and noble code of behaviour. Implicit in this depiction of the fallen as Christian warriors was not only a certainty about the righteousness of Britain's cause in South Africa but also an unshakeable faith in the promise of resurrection. The popularity of the Christian soldier-hero in familial memorial imagery in this period not only reflected a heartfelt desire by the bereaved to receive some form of mitigation from their grief but also mirrored a growing acceptance of, and admiration for, the army by civil society.[14] As Stefan Goebel, in his study of medievalism in the remembrance rituals of the interwar years, has shown, commemorative imagery of this type was to become one of the dominant themes in the memorialisation of the Great War.[15]

It was not only, however, the self-sacrifice of men that was remembered. The war was also an important chapter in the development of British nursing, with over 1,800 nurses serving in civilian and military hospitals in South Africa and twenty-nine dying as a result of disease.[16] For many, such an egregious manifestation of loyalty to the imperial cause merited some public recognition. Authorities in Leeds, Rochdale, St Helens and Yorkshire decided to include the names of nurses who had contributed to the war effort on the civic rolls of honour.[17] There was also a memorial tablet in honour of the fallen of the Army Nursing Service and Army Nursing Reserve erected in St George's Church, Aldershot.[18] For the editor of the *St Helens Advertiser* there was little to differentiate the service of the combatant and non-combatant. Choosing to announce the death of local army nursing sister Clara Evans, who had died from enteric while working in a hospital in Bloemfontein, alongside the news that three of the town's volunteers had been injured in action, he made explicit the connection between the two events:

> We couple the lady's name with the names of the Yeomanry because it cannot
> be doubted that, in going to South Africa as she did, Miss Evans was doing
> just as much to advance her country's cause as were the men who shouldered

---

[14]   Spiers, *The Late Victorian Army*, pp. 187–192; Olive Anderson, 'The Growth of Christian Militarism in Mid-Victorian Britain', *English Historical Review*, 86 (1971), pp. 46–72.

[15]   Goebel, *The Great War and Medieval Memory*; see particularly chapter 4.

[16]   S. Marks, 'Imperial Nursing and the South African War', in Cuthbertson, Grundlingh and Suttie (eds), *Writing a Wider War*; Jones, 'A Survey of Memorials to the Second Anglo-Boer War'.

[17]   Indeed, not only were the names of two nurses inscribed on the bronze plates at the foot of the Yorkshire County Memorial but one of the eight niches on the upper portion of the Edwardian Cross set aside for the figures of service personnel was occupied by the statue of a nurse. Although it should, perhaps, be pointed out that it was one of the last figures to attract a financial backer and was not ready in time for the memorial's unveiling. *Yorkshire Evening Post*, 3 October 1905.

[18]   Gildea, *For Remembrance*, p. 71.

the rifle in the field. Her conduct is equally worthy of the highest admiration and respect: and this the townspeople will, I am sure, readily accord.[19]

This latter assumption proved correct. At a meeting of the borough council the following week it was unanimously agreed that an earlier resolution to have the names of all local volunteers inscribed on a commemorative tablet should be amended so that, 'the word "men" might also include women'.[20]

Equality of sacrifice was also the leitmotif of the dedication service for a memorial window in Clara Evans's honour at St John's Church, Ravenhead in December 1901, although this time, unsurprisingly, it was service to Christ not Empire that was the focus. Taking as the text for his address 'devotion to duty', the vicar of St John's, the Reverend J. S. Bolton, reminded the congregation how, in the final reckoning, their lives would be judged:

> The speeches of orators, the exploits of warriors, the works of poets or painters shall not be mentioned on that day, but the least work that the weakest Christian woman has done for Christ or his remembrance shall be found written in the book of everlasting remembrance. Not a single word or deed, not a cup of cold water, not the binding up of a wound, or a box of ointment, will be omitted from the record. Of silver and Gold [Clara Evans] may have had but little; of rank, power, and influence she may not have possessed much, but if she has loved Christ and confessed Christ, and worked for Christ, her memorial shall be found on high and she shall be commended before assembled worlds.[21]

The memorial, designed by the well-known London-based firm, Whitefriars Glass, further reinforced this message. Paid for by her sisters and consisting of three lights, the window depicted Evans in nursing uniform flanked on the left by fighting at Bloemfontein and on the right by the tending of the sick in hospital.[22]

Occasionally, friends and families opted to remember their fallen by constructing utilitarian memorials. However, where this course of action was followed it was still considered important that a memory site's function should be associated with a noble or worthy purpose. Thus, Lieutenant F. G. Tait, twice Scottish amateur golfing champion, who was killed in action at Koodoosberg on 7 February 1900, had a wing of St Andrew's Memorial Hospital named in his honour following the raising of subscriptions by friends

19 *St Helens Advertiser*, 8 June 1900.
20 *Nursing Record and Hospital World*, 16 June 1900, p. 478. The fact that Evans was the sister-in-law of the mayor of St Helens, Alderman Joseph Massey, may have also had some part to play in the decision of the council to include her name on the role of honour.
21 *Prescot Reporter*, 7 January 1902.
22 *Nursing Record and Hospital World*, 22 February 1902.

and fellow players.[23] The wealthy financier and chairman of the South West Africa Company, George Cawston, endowed his home village of Cawston with a memorial institute in memory of his son, Cecil, a lieutenant in the 18th Hussars.[24] To safeguard the institute's function as a place for the wholesome recreation of the villagers, Cawston established a board of trustees whose task was 'to ensure that the provision of the Trust shall be fulfilled, in that the entire Premises and Recreation Grounds shall be retained for all time … for the purpose of recreation in strict accordance with the spirit and letter of the rules and regulations originally laid down'.[25] Equally keen to preserve the purity of his memorial gift to Middlesbrough town council was the steel magnate, Arthur Dorman. To commemorate his son, Lieutenant Charles Lockwood Dorman, who had died of enteric at Kroonstad military hospital on 30 March 1901, Dorman had provided the £15,000 required to finance the council's plans to construct a natural history museum.[26] To ensure that the monumental function that underpinned such largesse should not be lost as a result of the local government's involvement in the project, it was stipulated in the agreement transferring responsibility for upkeep to the Corporation that the building would 'be called the Dorman Memorial Museum and an inscribed marble tablet affixed to the wall thereof setting forth the commemorative purpose of the Institution shall for ever hereafter be preserved and kept up, and the purpose expressed by the inscription thereon observed'.[27] To safeguard further the sanctity of the site, Dorman was appointed 'Life Protector' with the power of veto over any move to amend the museum's founding charter.[28]

More senior officers were frequently commemorated beyond the bounds of the immediate family through the opening of subscription lists to a wider public. In such cases memorials served a more complex function than simply providing solace for the bereaved. The unveiling, at Windsor Castle on 6 November 1903, of Goscombe John's bronze statue of Prince Christian Victor

---

[23]   McFarland, 'Commemoration of the South African War in Scotland', p. 202; the sixteenth hole of the Jubilee Course at St Andrew's was also renamed in honour of Tait.

[24]   The fact that George Cawston and the village where he lived had identical names is no more than coincidence.

[25]   Cawston Historical Society, www.cawstonparish.info (accessed 7 March 2011); Lieutenant Cecil Cawston is also commemorated with a more traditional memorial in Norwich Cathedral. A stained glass widow, designed by Harold East and paid for by Cawston's family, depicts three figures representing Devotion, Faith and Courage. *Norwich Mercury*, 19 November 1904.

[26]   Dorman Memorial Museum Archive (DMMA), Proceedings of Middlesbrough Town Council, minutes, 3 May 1901, p. 513; *Dorman Memorial Museum: History and Guide* (Middlesbrough: County Borough of Middlesbrough, 1959), pp. 2–3.

[27]   DMMA, Proceedings of Middlesbrough Town Council 1903–1904, minutes, 28 June 1904, p. 809.

[28]   DMMA, Proceedings of Middlesbrough Town Council 1903–1904, minutes, 28 June 1904, p. 808.

of Schleswig-Holstein, who had died of enteric in a military hospital in Natal on 29 October 1900, was used to disseminate wider messages about duty and patriotic self-sacrifice. Although the subscriptions had been raised by 'the school fellows, college friends, comrades-in-arms and admirers of the late Prince', the dedication addresses focused on didactic lessons rather than personal reminiscences.[29] For the Dean of Windsor, the statue 'would be a perpetual stimulus to others to follow the Prince's good example', while Lord Roberts, seizing on the chance to advance, albeit obliquely, the cause of national service, insisted that the Prince's death 'was another instance of the readiness of all the King's subjects to lay down their lives in the defence of their country'.[30]

The commemoration of Colonel Lord Airlie, a major landholder in Perthshire who died while leading the 12th Lancers at Diamond Hill in June 1900, was similarly suffused with the high rhetoric of personal honour and national glory. At the laying of the memorial stone on Tulloch Hill, Cortachy, on 31 August 1901, the Reverend Mr Paisley expressed the hope that Airlie's death may be 'the means of stirring the hearts of young and old with more fervent loyalty, and devoted patriotism, with a growing and strengthening sense of duty'.[31] An acrostic, composed especially for the occasion by D. D. Beaton, the Provincial Grand Bard of Forfarshire, elevated Airlie into the pantheon of Scottish national heroes:

> **A**ngus worthy sons and daughters sadly mourns to-day
> **I**n deep and loving sympathy with those dear hearts,
> **R**eaved of their best beloved, so deeply, keenly pierced!
> **L**ong may dear Scotia raise such worthy gallant sons!
> **I**ncitingly this pile on Tulloch Hill proclaims
> **'E**xcelsior! Ye Angus youths, Excelsior!'[32]

Beaton's sentiment was reinforced by the monumental iconography. In Scotch Baronial style, the memorial took the form of a traditional Border beacon complete with signal platform which was to be lit 'on occasions of national or estate rejoicings'.[33]

To ensure that the lessons to be drawn from the loss of such a privileged elite resonated as deeply as possible, it was not uncommon for great emphasis to be placed on the strength of the bonds that existed between the deceased and those over whom they held sway. At the initial public meeting in Kirriemuir

---

[29] *The Times*, 7 November 1903.
[30] *The Times*, 7 November 1903.
[31] Forfar Local History Library, 25:B/OGI, 'Inscription on the Airlie Monument, Tulloch Hill, Cortachy', n.d.
[32] Forfar Local History Library, 25:B/OGI, 'Inscription on the Airlie Monument, Tulloch Hill, Cortachy', n.d.
[33] *Forfar Herald*, 6 September 1903.

to discuss the proposed Airlie memorial, the chairman, John Ogilvy, made a point of noting that the impetus for the project had come from the tenantry of the Airlie estates. Ogilvy proceeded to underline further the Earl's credentials as a man of the people, by informing those gathered that:

> it was one of the noblest features of Lord Airlie's character that he was ever ready to do all in his power for those in less favourable circumstances than himself. There were none who loved him more than the rank and file of the army, and had he been spared he would doubtless, in a more exalted sphere in the army, have done all he could in the reorganisation which would likely take place for the benefit of the British soldier.[34]

An equally philanthropic claim underpinned a public appeal for subscriptions in the memory of Prince Christian Victor. Announcing, through the letters' columns of the national press, the launch of the Prince Christian Cottage Homes for Disabled Soldiers and Sailors Fund, Sir Redvers Buller and Field Marshal Lord Roberts sought to recommend the utilitarian nature of the scheme by observing that it was 'in harmony with the spirit and aims of the young Prince, who always had the interests of soldiers at heart'.[35] It was not just in the rhetoric of remembrance that such professions of cross-class empathy were made. The inscriptions on the memorials to both the Marquis of Winchester and Lionel Fortescue, the third son of the Earl of Fortescue, laid great stress on the fact that tributes had come from across the social spectrum. The plaque at the base of the Octagon Cross in Filleigh Church in honour of Fortescue noted that the monument had been 'erected by his friends and neighbours of all conditions in the county of Devon', while the inscription beneath Winchester's memorial tablet in Amport parish church informed the viewer that funds had been contributed by 'Coldstreamers of all Ranks, by whom he was universally beloved'.[36] Such claims not only spoke highly of the deceased's personal qualities but also went some way towards legitimising aristocratic authority in an increasingly meritocratic world.

Occasionally, parochial pride could be stirred by a perceived slight to the reputation of a local commander. Major-General Andrew Wauchope was the subject of veiled criticism in the despatches of Lord Methuen, and subsequently the national press, following his death at the head of the Highland Brigade during its ill-fated assault on Boer positions at Magersfontein on 11 December 1899.[37] Communities associated with Wauchope, already a Scottish national

[34] *Forfar Herald*, 29 June 1900.
[35] *Star*, 2 May 1901.
[36] Gildea, *For Remembrance*, pp. 43, 77.
[37] TNA, WO132/14, Lord Methuen's Despatches, 4 January 1900; *London Gazette*, 16 March 1900; *The Times*, 17 March 1900; *Daily Mail*, 17 March 1900. In fact Methuen edited out some of the more explicit criticism of Wauchope in his final despatch but

hero for his role in the reconquest of the Sudan in 1898, quickly sprang to his defence with a flurry of commemorative activity. Stained glass windows in his honour were placed in St Giles's Cathedral, Edinburgh, the Presbyterian Church, York, Liberton Kirk, Niddrie and Newcraighall parish church as well as monuments at Perth, Yetholm and on the village green at Niddrie. The dominant leitmotif in all these memorials was Wauchope as the archetypal hero-warrior meeting a glorious battlefield death and as such, as Elaine McFarland has noted, 'represented a defiant endorsement of his military reputation'.[38]

Regional pride in a tarnished local hero was also on show at the unveiling of the equestrian statue in honour of Sir Redvers Buller in Exeter on 6 September 1905, although the memorial's gestation had proved to be considerably more contentious than the harmony of the occasion suggested. Buller had commanded the British forces in South Africa during the disastrous early stages of the war before being superseded by Lord Roberts's arrival as commander-in-chief in January 1900. Although Buller retained responsibility for the defence of Natal, eventually relieving the beleaguered garrison town of Ladysmith on 28 February 1900, doubts continued to be aired about his professional competence and, on his return to England in November 1900, he faced a concerted press campaign against his reappointment as general officer commanding at Aldershot. The matter came to a head during a luncheon thrown in Buller's honour by the Queen's Westminster Volunteers on 10 October 1900. Still smarting from a particularly vitriolic attack by Leo Amery which had appeared in *The Times* a few days earlier, Buller used the platform of his after-dinner speech to defend his record in the Ladysmith campaign by quoting confidential military telegrams. This minor, but nonetheless public, breach of military discipline provided his critics at the War Office with the excuse they had been looking for and on 21 October it was announced that he had been relieved of his command.[39]

---

by then the damage had been done. See Stephen Miller, *Lord Methuen and the British Army: Failure and Redemption in South Africa* (Abingdon: Frank Cass, 1999), p. 141, 156. Even those who sought to defend Wauchope's reputation by insisting that Methuen had brushed off Wauchope's misgivings about the Highland Brigade's deployment on the eve of Magersfontein found they merely added fuel to the flames of the scandal by raising the suspicion of disloyalty. Indeed, so persistent were the rumours that Wauchope had publicly criticised Methuen than Lady Wauchope felt obliged to issue a denial through the letters' pages of the *Standard*. *Standard*, 23 January 1900.

38   McFarland, 'Commemoration of the South African War in Scotland', p. 202.
39   Leo Amery, *My Political Life, Volume One: England before the Storm, 1896–1914* (London: Hutchinson, 1953), pp. 152–157; Ian Beckett, 'Buller, Sir Redvers Henry (1839–1908)', *Oxford Dictionary of National Biography* (Oxford: Oxford University Press, 2004), online edition, January. 2008: www.oxforddnb.com/view/article/32165 (accessed 24 March 2011).

Buller's cause was immediately taken up in the letters' column of his local paper, the *Devon and Exeter Gazette*.[40] Citing the example of an earlier West Country hero who had suffered unjust treatment at the hands of the established powers, a 'Colonial Colonel' demanded some explanation for such shoddy treatment of a faithful public servant:

---

[40] Sympathy for Buller as the forgotten hero of the war had already been expressed in the pages of the *Devon and Exeter Gazette* in June 1900 in the aftermath of Roberts's victorious entry into the Transvaal capital, Pretoria. In a parody of Kipling's *The Absent-Minded Beggar*, the paper published the following poem in which Buller's role in the British forces' changing fortunes was made abundantly clear.

> When you shout at news of victory,
> And you hip hurray for 'Bobs',
> When next you feel you're 'cheerily' disposed
> Don't forget the man who chose himself
> The hardest of the jobs,
> And 'fought it to a finish' with 'mouth closed'.
>
> He's a grim and silent soldier,
> And his luck was awful bad,
> But he never 'squealed'
> Or blamed 'the other man',
> He shouldered blame and carping,
> And drove 'the critics' mad,
> 'Cause he looked as though he didn't care a d__n.
>
> When 'some one's blunder' at Colenso lost his guns,
> Recovery meant fame – their loss disgrace
> Did he hesitate? Oh No! He said the lives
> Of Britain's sons
> Were worth more than fame – the guns he could replace.
>
> Then that cool and sturdy leader
> 'Hammered at it' till he won,
> He never grumbled, or 'despatches altered',
> But took his 'medicine' silently,
> And when the work was done,
> Said 'twas due to men whose trust
> Had never faltered
>
> Rough job, tough job,
> 'Nough to daunt anyone,
> He didn't send somebody else to tackle it,
> When defeat looked near,
> 'Twas 'Buller the Bulldog' who 'hung right on',
> And now that the job's near done,
> Remember his silence, work and pluck –
> So cheer, cheer, cheer!

In the case of 'Trelawney' it was 20,000 Cornishmen would 'know the reason why' and now it will be something like 100,000 or more Devon men will know why Buller has gone, and would like to kick 'Reformer' of the 'Times' and a few other 'tinkling cymbals' to call them nothing worse.[41]

Further backing for Buller came from the mayor of Exeter, Mr A. E. Dunn, who announced that a public meeting would be held in the Guildhall the following day 'to express unabated confidence in General Buller, and to consider what steps shall be taken to give effect to this feeling'.[42] Yet local support was by no means universal. William Ball, the mayor of Torquay, Lord Morley, the chairman of Devon County Council and John Kennaway, Conservative MP for Honiton, all used the pages of the *Devon and Exeter Gazette* to express their misgivings about Dunn's scheme and to make known that they would not be attending the Guildhall meeting. Ball and Morley were adamant that any public discussion of what they considered to be a matter of internal army discipline would be *ultra vires*, while Kennaway insisted that, 'in this great crisis in our history, we should do nothing to weaken Lord Roberts's hands and to endanger the prestige – I had almost said existence – of the British Army'. The editor of the *Devon and Exeter Gazette*, a staunch supporter of Buller, was equally unsure that Dunn's scheme had been fully thought through. The likelihood was, he argued in the paper's editorial, that the movement 'will be utilised in Radical circles for the purposes of making party capital'.[43] Such a concern was evidently shared by the *Pall Mall Gazette*, although it fell short of explicitly articulating it. Having roundly condemned Dunn's proposal, the paper alerted its readers to the possibility of political undercurrents by concluding somewhat disingenuously that 'A. E. Dunn happens to be a Radical and unsuccessful Parliamentary candidate, but we will not lay any stress upon his political past'.[44]

In his opening remarks to those assembled at the Guildhall on 26 October, Dunn attempted to deflect this criticism by insisting that the meeting was 'devoid of political significance' and had been called 'in no antagonistic spirit, nor for the purposes of condemning or criticising the actions of His Majesty's Ministers or the commander-in-chief of His Majesty's forces, but simply to show their high appreciation of the services rendered to the commonwealth by Sir Redvers Buller'.[45] To further underscore the prevailing mood of civic

---

[41] *Devon and Exeter Gazette*, 25 October 1901.
[42] *Devon and Exeter Gazette*, 25 October 1901.
[43] *Devon and Exeter Gazette*, 25 October 1901.
[44] *Pall Mall Gazette*, 25 October 1901. Dunn had unsuccessfully contested Exeter for the Liberal Party at the 1892 general election. He was eventually elected as MP for Camborne in the Liberal landslide of 1906. F. Craig, *British Parliamentary Election Results, 1885–1918* (Chichester: Parliamentary Research Services, 1989), pp. 109, 239.
[45] DRO, 2065Madd28/Z9, *Official Souvenir of the Unveiling of the Buller Memorial*, 6 September 1905.

harmony, the meeting appointed, in absentia, a representative committee of county notables to oversee the commemorative work. Yet, if Dunn thought this move towards inclusion would silence his adversaries he was quickly disabused of such a notion. Lord Clinton, the Lord Lieutenant of Devon, immediately informed him that he could 'take no part whatever in proceedings which appear to question a decision of the War Department in a matter connected with military discipline', while the mayors of Plymouth, Devonport and Barnstable all chose to make their disapproval clear by simply not acknowledging their nomination to the memorial committee.[46] With, as the editor of the *Devon and Exeter Gazette* noted, support for the scheme only coming from 'those who share the political views of the mayor', the project appeared to have become fatally tainted by Dunn's Liberal sympathies. In the opinion of the *Gazette*, the whole matter had become so 'party and one-sided in character' that it would be better if responsibility for completion was deferred to Buller's immediate neighbours in Crediton as they were 'more intimate and, therefore, less controversial'.[47]

Despite this unpropitious beginning, a reconfigured committee of political allies from the Liberal controlled Exeter council, under the chairmanship of Dunn, persevered with the task of raising funds for the memorial. In an attempt to capitalise on Buller's reputation as the soldier's general, and to promote the memorial as a thanks-offering from all citizens not just the privileged elite, a ceiling was imposed on subscriptions with the launching of a shilling fund in November 1901.[48] Although a large number of the regional and national papers, including the *Devon and Exeter Gazette*, refused to run the committee's call for donations, the response was, nonetheless, enthusiastic.[49] Over £2,000 was raised from 50,000 subscribers.[50]

By the time of the statue's unveiling in September 1905, the elapse of time had allowed passions to cool. Even the editor of the *Devon and Exeter Gazette* was prepared to admit that the paper's earlier opposition to the scheme might have been over hasty: 'We have to stand away from the mountain to see its size. Genius and work are often more highly valued when looked at through the vista of long years, and when the din of controversy, which attends the life and acts of most great men, has died away'.[51] The *Sunday Times* was equally sure that the dedication of the monument in Exeter should be taken as the

[46] *Devon and Exeter Gazette*, 27 October 1901.
[47] *Devon and Exeter Gazette*, 31 October 1901.
[48] *Devon and Exeter Gazette*, 7 September 1905; *Observer*, 10 September 1905.
[49] The *Official Souvenir* programme suggests that many papers were reluctant to open up their columns to the appeal for funds 'through fear that the scheme would be a failure'. Although this may well have been the case, the contentious nature of the project must also have had a large part to play in the lukewarm response of the press. DRO, 2065Madd28/Z9, *Official Souvenir*.
[50] *Devon and Exeter Gazette*, 7 September 1901.
[51] *Devon and Exeter Gazette*, 7 September 1905.

signal for a reassessment of Buller's role in South Africa. In an article entitled 'Devonia's Tribute to Her Soldier Son', the paper argued for the rehabilitation of Buller's reputation:

> We are forcibly reminded of the hard measures meted out at times to our generals by the tribute just paid to Sir Redvers Buller at Exeter, in the unveiling of an equestrian statue raised in his honour. The events, some untoward, some notably the reverse, in which he was the central figure are even now too near for decisive comment, but it is perfectly clear from the following he has in this country that a large section of the public is satisfied that he was hardly used. Fifty thousand subscribers have testified to this by a memorial that proves their appreciation of a man who always, to use his own words, 'did his level best'. It is not easy, indeed, to understand the acrimony with which he has been attacked ever since those dark days when he stood as the chief scapegoat to bear the sins of an effete Government and an enraged people clamouring for a victim to suffer for their own sins. Let it be granted that in the earlier phases of the Colenso campaign the failure was lamentable in at least two instances, but Buller subsequently vindicated his generalship, and his advance through the Eastern Transvaal, and the successful action at Machadodorp was distinctly creditable. There was nothing really to justify the virulence with which Buller was subsequently assailed.[52]

The traditional heroic motif of the completed memorial provided visible proof of such sentiments. Designed by Captain Adrian Jones, the twelve feet high statue of a mounted Buller, resplendent in general's uniform complete with Victoria Cross, exuded power and authority.[53] Engraved on the granite pedestal was the unambiguous inscription, 'He Saved Natal'.

The unveiling of Jones's equestrian statue further confirmed Buller's reintegration into the Pantheon of British war heroes. In stark contrast to the divisions and acrimony that had punctuated the early stages of the scheme, the dedication service on 6 September 1905 was suffused by a harmony borne of local pride and solidarity. With the list of those invited to attend serving as a roll-call for Devon's political and social elite, the late replacement as officiating dignitary of a flu-stricken Sir Garnet Wolseley with Lord Ebrington, the Lord Lieutenant of the Country, was viewed as something of a blessing in disguise. Not only, according to the *Devon and Exeter Gazette*, was Ebrington's appointment more in keeping with the regional nature of the occasion but it had the additional advantage of averting any threat of discord. Reminding his readers that the 'existence of rings' within the army had resulted in 'a tendency to pit one distinguished soldier against another and to indulge in contrasts

---

[52] *The Sunday Times*, 10 October 1905.

[53] For more on the heroic imagery of the equestrian figure see Borg, *War Memorials*, pp. 37–39.

and comparison', the *Gazette*'s editor was insistent that any disappointment at Wolseley's absence was more than compensated for by the fact that his indisposition had 'relieved us from the risk of disharmony'.[54] With unanimity of purpose assured, the way was clear for the focus of the day to fall firmly on Devonian glory. Speech after speech extolled the virtues of Buller and, by extension, the region. Typical was the address by the mayor of Exeter who, having taken custody of the memorial on behalf of the municipal council, made clear for a receptive audience the site's significance as a symbol of local pride:

> There is no part of His Majesty's dominions where greater love and admiration is shown for Sir Redvers Buller than in the city of Exeter. He is a very near neighbour of ours and is a very large landowner in our midst. He is, and his ancestors before him have been, upon our roll of freemen for many years. Devonshire has produced many great men who, in all the various walks of life and in all climes, have contributed materially to our beloved Sovereign. (Applause.) It is peculiarly fitting that in this old city, which has played so very important a part in the history of the country, and within and without whose walls so many valiant deeds have been done on behalf of the country, that you should have unveiled this statue and asked the city to accept it.[55]

Indeed, so universal were such sentiments, and so dramatic had been the transformation in the attitude of the local elite over the course of the memorial's gestation, that the committee felt able to conclude the souvenir programme on the following self-congratulatory note: 'So after a long and stern fight against prejudice and hostility, the Buller Memorial Committee have brought their labours to a successful issue, and by their labour of love have earned the thanks and gratitude of all who appreciate the paying of "Honour to whom Honour is due."'[56]

ii Memorials in Places of Work and Worship

Although the family played a defining role in much of the commemoration of the South African War, the ties of kinship were by no means the only bonds of belonging that connected the fallen to their pre-war civilian identities. Beyond the obvious attachments to locality, be they civic or county, we have already

---

[54] *Devon and Exeter Gazette*, 25 August 1905. In this period, the army high command appeared divided into two opposing cliques. On one side was a group of officers who had built their careers campaigning under Garnet Wolseley in Africa, the 'African Ring', and, on the other, a group whose service had primarily been on the Indian sub-continent with Frederick Roberts, the 'Indian Ring'. See Miller, *Lord Methuen and the British Army*, pp. 18–19.

[55] *The Sunday Times*, 10 September 1905.

[56] DRO, 2065Madd28/Z9, *Official Souvenir*.

seen how schools and colleges looked to claim the dead as unique products of institutional tradition and ethos. Equally important in this layering of memory was the commemorative activity in sites of worship and employment. For the vast majority of the population, religion and work were central in defining identity and belonging. Although churchgoing had been declining since the mid-nineteenth century, attendance by the turn of the twentieth century remained relatively buoyant amounting to between a quarter and a third of the population.[57] Yet, the reach of the church and religion went beyond the purely spiritual. Despite the dramatic changes in urban topography brought about by the rapid industrial growth of the preceding half century, residential solidarities for much of Edwardian Britain were still based on parish boundaries. Evidence for this can be found in the unlikely field of association football and the proliferation of amateur and semi-professional teams in the last quarter of the nineteenth century. As Richard Holt, in his excellent survey of sport in Britain, has noted the vast majority of these new teams, most of which were based in the new urban centres, were either directly organised by or had strong affiliations to local churches.[58] In a rapidly changing urban landscape, parish churches and religious institutions provided threads of continuity to the more tightly defined communities of a pre-industrial age; they served as symbols of community, as sites to which a sense of belonging and identity could be attached. In much the same way work and the workplace were vital components in tying the individual into the collective. Fellow workers functioned as an alternative family based on the shared experience of employment. The role of the workplace as a communal focal point has been noted by the sociologists Willmott and Young in their study of attitudes to work in London:

> Whether or not labour is, in Marx's terms, a 'commodity', it is a link with the collective life. Work also creates a time-ordering of the sort that is necessary not only to social structure. Routines in the way people organise their lives are indispensable to almost everyone.[59]

Although the influence and importance of both workplaces and sites of worship in local communities went well beyond their formally prescribed functions, the decision to construct a memorial was invariably left to a few leading individuals. Unsurprisingly, at parish level, it was more often than not the local vicar who took the lead. In Tonbridge in Kent, Cuckfield in Sussex and the Nottingham suburb of Lenton, sole responsibility for initiating the

---

[57]   Robin Gill, *The Myth of the Empty Church* (London: SPCK Publishing, 1993), chapters 6 and 7.

[58]   Richard Holt, *Sport and the British: A Modern History* (Broadbridge: Clarendon Press, 1990), pp. 150–151.

[59]   M. Young and P. Willmott, *The Symmetrical Family: A Study of Work and Leisure in the London Region* (London: Routledge and Kegan Paul, 1973), p. 151.

memorialisation schemes lay with the local vicars.[60] Indeed in Lenton, the local vicar, the Reverend Alan Watts, not only first raised the idea of constructing a memorial but even presented the parish council with a fully worked and costed proposal which it unanimously accepted.[61] Elsewhere, collaboration between a few influential parishioners and the vicar was the order of the day. The memorial committee for Holy Trinity, Barkingside, a village on the edge of Ilford Urban District, was chaired by the vicar and included a local JP and councillors.[62] In the parish of St Jude, Kensington, the presence of a number of affluent parishioners and vestry members must have played an important part in memorial activity, particularly as the membership contained a major, two colonels, a major-general and General Lord Chelmsford.[63] A small group of influential British Jews also controlled the scheme to erect a London memorial to mark the sacrifices of British Jewry. Chaired by Isidore Spielmann of the Jewish Historical Society of England, the committee also included many of the scions of Anglo-Jewry: J. Waley Cohen, Cecil Sebag-Montefiore, S. J. Solomon and Colonel A. E. Goldsmid, founder of the Jewish Lads' Brigade in 1895.[64]

Similar structures can be found in works' communities. The memorial proposed by the London and North Western Railway (LNWR) for its Euston station main terminus was instigated by the chairman of the company, Lord Stalbridge, and organised by his fellow directors.[65] The same held true for the leatherworks firm Turney Brothers, where the managing director, Sir John Turney, chaired a committee of senior executives to oversee the erection of a commemorative plaque at its Trent Bridge factory.[66] Frederick Taylor, the senior physician at Guy's Hospital, co-ordinated the task of his institution's memorial committee; while a special sub-committee of the Institute of Journalists was established to oversee its plans to commemorate the war correspondents lost in South Africa.[67]

An exception to this top-down model appears to have occurred at the London and North Western Railway's Crewe works. In a special edition to celebrate the unveiling of the memorial in 1903, the *Crewe Chronicle* charted the gestation of the scheme, pinpointing its genesis in the unrestrained rejoicing that greeted

[60]   *Tonbridge Free Press*, 15 April 1904; West Sussex Records Office, Par301/4/31, Holy Trinity Cuckfield parish magazine, July 1903; *Lenton Times: The Magazine of the Lenton Local History Society*, No. 18 (May 2002), p. 3.
[61]   *Lenton Times*, No. 18 (May 2002), p. 3.
[62]   *Ilford Recorder*, 26 December 1902.
[63]   London Metropolitan Archives, P84/JUD/58 Vestry Minutes Book, St Jude, Kensington, 1901; *Kensington News*, 27 June 1902.
[64]   *Jewish Chronicle*, 24 March 1905.
[65]   *The Times*, 24 April 1903.
[66]   Denise Amos, 'The Boer War', www.nottsheritagegateway.org.uk/events/boerwar/boerwarstructural.htm (accessed 19 October 2011).
[67]   *The Times*, 5 November 1902; 16 January 1905.

the news of the relief of Mafeking in May 1900. It was, the paper noted, this manifestation of unbridled patriotic fervour that encouraged representatives of the various workshops to explore ways in which the 'artisans' enthusiasm' might be brought under some sort of control and turned into a proper and at the same time popular channel. A subsequent meeting of works' foremen agreed to arrange 'a series of processions' at which collections would be made 'with the object of founding some memorial to commemorate in a permanent way the services which Crewe railwaymen had rendered the Empire'.[68] It should, however, be noted that, notwithstanding the scheme's apparently spontaneous grass-roots origins, formal control was quickly passed on to a self-appointed committee presided over by the president of the works, James Atkinson.

One of the first tasks of these largely self-appointed committees was the establishment of the boundaries of the community. This was a two-fold process which involved determining who was eligible for inclusion on the memorial and who had the right to contribute to the various schemes. Establishing eligibility for inclusion was a potentially challenging task as it touched upon issues of membership and also forced committees to consider whether the memorial was solely for the dead or for all who had served. At the parish level decisions had to be made whether to include all residents or only the active parishioners. The latter course was adopted at the parish churches in Tonbridge and Cuckfield while at St Jude's, Kensington, Lenton parish church and Holy Trinity, Barkingside, the decision was taken to embrace the wider community.[69] In the case of Barkingside, contributions were sought from across the parish, but it is highly likely that the majority of the money was raised by active parishioners given that the scheme originated with members of the church. Similarly, in Lenton, although two house-to-house canvasses were organised, a significant percentage of the funds appears to have come from a few well-to-do stalwarts of the congregation.[70] For the British Jewish community, the clear definition of belonging complicated the issue of contribution. Having agreed that a central Jewish war memorial should be erected in the Central Synagogue, Upper Regent Street, the problem lay in making the memorial seem relevant to those outside the immediate congregation. A major form of assistance came from the support given by the Jewish charitable organisation, the Maccabean Society, which largely circumvented this potential problem.[71]

Disputes occasionally broke out over inclusion and contributions. The writer, Hammond Hall, was annoyed by a misunderstanding concerning the War

68   *Crewe Chronicle*, 15 August 1903.
69   *Tonbridge Free Press*, 15 April 1904; Cuckfield parish magazine, July 1903; *Ilford Recorder*, 26 December 1902; *Lenton Times*, No. 18 (May 2002), p. 3; Gildea, *For Remembrance*, p. 146.
70   *Lenton Times*, No. 18 (May 2002), p. 3.
71   *Jewish Chronicle*, 29 January 1904.

Correspondents' memorial. He wrote to *The Times* stating that initially he was informed that the memorial was to be erected by the Institute of Journalists, to which he did not belong, and so was ineligible to contribute. However, having been assured that that was not the case, he made his donation, but now believed the tablet would include the words, 'Erected by the Institute of Journalists'. Pointing out the fact that a good many of the contributors on the subscriptions list were not members of the institute, he was upset by the implication that the memorial was its work alone and he hoped 'that before Lord Roberts unveils the memorial the misleading line will have been erased'.[72] The offending line was not on the unveiled memorial, although it is uncertain whether this was because the allegation was incorrect, or whether it was indeed erased.

For the London and North Western Railway memorial in Crewe a blurring of the boundaries between work and civic communities saw the scope of the memorialisation scheme extend beyond the margins established by those eligible to subscribe. Although, as we have already seen, the funds for the project were raised at a series of works' festival days, it was unanimously agreed by the memorial committee that the site should be dedicated to not just those veterans of the war who were employees of the railway company but to all the men of Crewe who had served. Such a move was, in many ways, simply a reflection of the LNWR's dominance of the town's civic culture. The company's decision to relocate its engineering works from Liverpool to Crewe in 1843, and the inevitable demographic transformation this had had on the locality, had encouraged the LNWR's board of directors to assume responsibility for a range of civic amenities from the provision of fresh water and medical services to the upkeep of the public baths and the construction of Christ Church parish church.[73] Yet, this extension of the remembered community to encompass citizens as well as employees was not allowed to detract from the scheme's origins in the workplace. The memorial's location in Queen's Park, land gifted to the town by the LNWR in 1889, the choice of Lord Stalbridge, the company's chairman, to undertake the unveiling and the timing of the ceremony, on the works' annual festival, all served to underline with whom ownership resided.[74]

The definition of community in workplace and religious schemes may not always have been precisely identified, but the intimacy of the ties that bound fellow workers or co-religionists together nonetheless ensured that, in sharp

---

[72] *The Times*, 11 January 1905.

[73] 'Crewe History', *Crewe Chronicle*, 29 July 2008. An indication of just how central the railway was to Crewe can be gleaned from the towns' demographics. In the sixty years following the relocation of the engineering works, the population grew from 498 in 1841 to 42,000 by 1901. Allan Redfern, 'Crewe: Leisure in a Railway Town', in John K. Walton and James Walvin (eds), *Leisure in Britain, 1780–1939* (Manchester: Manchester University Press, 1983), p. 118.

[74] *Crewe Chronicle*, 15 August 1903; Crewe Local Studies Centre, CP/Crew/O Crewe Memorial Unveiling Programme, no date.

contrast to civic commemoration, concentration on grief and mourning were much more pronounced. At parish level, Christian messages of self-sacrifice and ever-lasting life provided some measure of comfort and catharsis for the bereaved. Typical was the Reverend W. S. Lach-Szyrma's address at the unveiling of the memorial plaque in Holy Trinity Church, Barkingside, in which he referred to the dead as Christian martyrs and implied their joyful resurrection.[75] Frequently, this language of consolation and hope was reinforced by the iconographic symbolism of the memorials. The central Christian symbol, the cross, perfectly served this purpose but was, surprisingly, a relatively rare choice.[76] Financial expediency may, at least in part, account for this; the construction of a cross involved considerably greater outlay than a simple plaque or tablet. However, the relative rarity with which the cross was used as a symbol compared with the Great War may also reflect the generally lower emotional temperature experienced during the South African War, aside from a few major outbursts such as Mafeking night. Unlike the Great War, the South African War did not lend itself to the idea that the whole of the civilised world was in danger. The thundering sermons of Bishop A. F. Winnington-Ingram and the widespread use of apocalyptic imagery during the Great War made the cross, as the symbol of Christian redemption, much more applicable and ubiquitous.[77]

The provision of comfort and solace through commemorative iconography was still evident in other forms of memorial, however. The bronze mural tablet in Tonbridge parish church to the thirteen local men who fell in the war was an artful admixture of sorrow and pride. The central frieze depicting a recumbent soldier holding the palm branch of victory was flanked on either side by reliefs of two angels, 'the figure on the left in the attitude of prayer and grief, symbolical of a nation sorrowing over her soldiers that are no more; while that on the right may be described as representing the nation showing her pride in the victories of her armies and her gratitude to those who died for their country'.[78] William Goscombe John's War Correspondents' memorial plaque in St Paul's Cathedral addressed the same themes. The bronze panel encased in marble featured a figure of Victory holding a laurel wreath, but hooded in mourning, set against the South African landscape.

Although sorrow and mourning were significant features of commemorative practice for these tight-knit communities, pride remained the key leitmotif, in particular institutional pride. The London and North Western Railway, the Institute of Journalists and Guy's Hospital all laid claim to corporate

[75] *Ilford Recorder*, 26 December 1902.
[76] Meurig Jones has estimated that just 4.2 per cent of memorials took the form of a cross. Jones, 'A Survey of Memorials to the Second Anglo-Boer War'.
[77] For a general discussion of Christian symbolism and war memorials during the Great War see Moriarty, 'Christian Iconography and First World War Memorials', pp. 63–76.
[78] *Tonbridge Free Press*, 15 April 1904.

9 War Correspondents' memorial, St Paul's Cathedral.

ownership by recalling the fallen as employees rather than combatants. Thus, on the memorial plaque at the LNWR's Euston terminus the fallen were listed along with their grades and the stations at which they served; the Institute of Journalists chose to include the names of the companies for whom the thirteen correspondents who had lost their lives in the conflict had worked; on the Guy's Hospital memorial the names of the dead were arranged by order of the dates they had commenced their student internships. Ownership could be further reinforced by the choice of monumental form. The decision of the Guy's Hospital memorial committee to opt for Frederick Wheeler's classically designed drinking fountain was particularly apt as it played on firmly embedded notions about civic obligation. Not only were water fountains extremely common forms of Victorian street ornamentation but the provision of fresh, clean drinking water was regarded as a great public service to the health of the nation which would cause the drinker to reflect on the qualities of those who provided it.[79] John Whitehead's standard bronze figure of a khaki-clad trooper for the LNWR's Crewe works' memorial was firmly located within the confines of the company by the inclusion of a model of the latest locomotive. For their memorial in the Central Synagogue in London, the British Jewish community signalled institutional ownership by opting for a variant on the highly traditional Victorian funereal form of a commemorative plaque. Much advice was taken on the design of the memorial including comments from the Jewish artist, Solomon J. Solomon, and Sir Purdon Clarke of the Victoria and Albert Museum. The result was a diptych of bronze plaques in an elaborate

[79] See Lynda Nead, *Victorian Babylon: People, Streets and Images in Nineteenth-century London* (New Haven and London: Yale University Press, 2000), pp. 9, 23.

frame which deliberately recalled the Mediterranean roots of Judaism as its decoration drew on Moorish and Byzantine forms.[80]

Yet, for the Jewish war memorial committee, it was not just the form that warranted attention, but the precise location was of extreme importance and provoked much discussion. Highly sensitive to any accusation of unpatriotic or alien sympathies, the leaders of the Anglo-Jewish community were very keen to promote the Jewish role in the war. During the course of the conflict there had been anti-Semitic sentiments expressed by those who believed that the British were fighting to secure the mining rights of Jewish-owned companies.[81] The war's end had seen a continued debate about the role of Jews in British society and culminated in the Aliens Act of 1905, which was aimed mainly at curbing Jewish emigration from Eastern Europe.[82] It was against this backdrop that the Jewish war memorial was debated and formed. At the initial meeting to discuss the memorial it was noted that some had 'said that the Jewish community did not do enough in the way of sending men to the South African campaign and it was right that some record should be kept of those who went to the front'.[83] One participant then suggested that the memorial should be placed in a Jewish cemetery, but others demurred believing it would lack visibility to the wider world. Yet another took exception to the idea of the memorial being public, explaining that Jews had played a proud role in the war and there was no need to advertise it so overtly. The interior of the Central Synagogue, he went on to advocate, was a perfectly good place where a memorial could be inspected by anyone interested in Jewish affairs. Isidore Spielmann, the chair of the committee, took the opposite position. For him, an exterior site clearly proclaiming the Jewish contribution was vital, for the memorial would commemorate men who 'had not only fallen as Jews, but as English Jews, and, therefore, the exterior of the building did not seem improper'.[84] As a warning he added that if it was not erected at the Central Synagogue, then it might well end up being placed in an East London synagogue. Spielmann's remarks reveal a pronounced concern about the nature of the Jewish community. The East End was home to a significant number of poor, unassimilated Eastern European Jews and formed the main target of anti-Semitic comment in Britain. He was therefore highly sensitive to the idea that the memorial might be located in the 'wrong' sort of synagogue. For Spielmann, it was important that assimilated, affluent, respectable, anglicised Jewry make the public statement. British Jews

---

[80] *Jewish Chronicle*, 24 March 1905.
[81] See Bernard Porter, 'The Pro-Boers in Britain', in Warwick (ed.), *The South African War*, pp. 239–258.
[82] See David Feldman, *Englishmen and Jews: Social Relations and Political Culture, 1840–1914* (New Haven and London: Yale University Press, 1994), pp. 261–311.
[83] *Jewish Chronicle*, 15 July 1904.
[84] *Jewish Chronicle*, 15 July 1904.

10 Jewish memorial, Central Synagogue, Great Portland Street, London.

were to be caught in precisely the same bind after the Great War when the same arguments were rehearsed in an almost identical fashion.[85]

Having secured the Central Synagogue as the site for the memorial, the leading representatives of Britain's Jewish community then seized on the unveiling ceremony as a crucial opportunity to promote an image of loyalty and conformity. In the course of his dedication address, Isidore Spielmann informed the congregation of the memorial's meaning: 'This memorial stands here in eloquent testimony to the fact that British Jews are inspired by a love of King and Country no less enthusiastic and no less devoted than that which animates their fellow-subjects'. Following on, the Chief Rabbi stated that 'surely

---

[85] See Mark Connelly, *The Great War: Memory and Ritual: Commemoration in the City and East London, 1916–1939* (Woodbridge: Boydell and Brewer, 2002), pp. 212–229.

England deserves that we, her Jewish children, should gladly live and die for her ... since here, as in no other empire in the whole world, there breathes a passionate love for freedom'.[86]

The organisers of workplace memorials were equally keen to use unveiling ceremonies to disseminate messages about corporate values and institutional worth. The presiding dignitaries at the dedication services for the Guy's Hospital, the War Correspondents' and the LNWR's Euston station memorials were all quick to emphasise that the war service given by their fallen was no less valuable and heroic than that offered by combatants. General Sir Richard Harrison, a governor of Guy's Hospital, having noted that with a 10 per cent attrition rate a high proportion of Guy's men had lost their lives, stressed the impact medical volunteers had had on army practice: 'members of the profession who went out to the war from the hospitals had let light into Army methods, and those whose names were inscribed on Guy's and other memorials had not shed their blood in vain'.[87]

The twin themes of honour and courage also underpinned the president of the Institute of Journalists' address at St Paul's. War correspondents had, he insisted, 'all done their duty to their newspapers, to their country and to their Sovereign. They took their lives in their hands almost to an equal extent as did the officers and the rank and file of the Army, and if they died they laid down their lives in a noble cause'.[88] This sentiment was then endorsed by Field Marshal Lord Roberts. Something of an exception in the ranks of the high command for his cordial relations with journalists during the conflict in South Africa, Roberts seized the moment to eulogise on the press corps' contribution to the war effort. Insisting that the invitation to unveil the commemorative plaque was a particularly pleasing one because it 'gave him the opportunity of showing his appreciation of the work done for their country by [the fallen]', he continued with a tribute to the work of the newspaper industry as a whole:

> The men we are commemorating today died, as so many of their brethren had died before them, in the loyal performance of arduous duties, and they proved themselves worthy of belonging to a high and honourable profession, the members of which, in all quarters of the globe, had rendered valuable service, not only to the journals which they represented, but also to the public at large.[89]

---

[86]   *Jewish Chronicle*, 24 March 1905.

[87]   *The Times*, 4 July 1903.

[88]   *The Times*, 16 January 1905.

[89]   *The Times*, 16 January 1905. For more on the role of the media in the war, and on Roberts's relationship with the press, see Stephen Badsey, 'The Boer War as a Media War', in Peter Dennis and Jeffrey Grey (eds), *The Boer War: Army, Nation and Empire* (Canberra: Army History Unit, 2000).

A similar scene was played out at Euston station for the unveiling of the LNWR's memorial to the ninety-nine railway volunteers who had died in the war. Adamant that, despite dying of disease, the men 'had looked on death as their comrades in arms', Lord Stalbridge, in his unveiling address, drew a parallel between the honourable self-sacrifice of the fallen and the selfless duty performed by the company in 'maintaining, while the men were at the front, those who were near and dear to them'. His concluding hope that, as presiding dignitary, Lord Roberts would underline these points for the assembled crowd was, unsurprisingly, fully realised. Evidently carefully briefed, the Field Marshal's address was a paean to the company's largesse and patriotic spirit. The military authorities, he was happy to confirm, were not only fully aware of the generous arrangements made to support the volunteers' families while they were at the front, but also conscious that, on their return, they had, 'with few exceptions, all been reinstated in the service of the company, and some of them in higher and better paid positions than they had occupied before they went out'.[90] That the occasion was a corporate celebration rather than a rite of remembrance was further evidenced by the absence of the bereaved. Uninvited due to lack of space, the immediate families of the fallen were each sent a framed photograph of the memorial plaque so that, in the words of the company's deputy manager, Frank Rees, 'they might have something by them to show what had been done in memory of their relatives'.[91]

Four months later, on 8 August 1903, the company's benevolence was once again celebrated, this time for the benefit of the vast crowds gathered to witness the unveiling of the Crewe Reservists' and Volunteers' Memorial in Queen's Park. Scheduled to coincide with the town's annual patriotic carnival, the day attracted between forty and fifty thousand people, with special trains being laid on from Liverpool and Manchester.[92] The day began with a grand procession consisting of 104 displays led by the Crewe Carriage Works, while a series of sporting, musical and theatrical entertainments were staged to keep the visitors amused throughout the afternoon and early evening.[93] In such a festive atmosphere, it is hardly surprising that the unveiling and dedication of the memorial, sandwiched as it was between a 'Bell and Balloon Contest' in the morning and 'a programme of dance music by the silver band' in the late afternoon, had little to do with formal mourning. The tone for the occasion was set by Lord Stalbridge. Striking the same chord as he had at Euston in April, he attributed the high recruitment level in Crewe to the 'public spiritedness

[90] *The Times*, 24 April 1903.
[91] *Crewe Chronicle*, 15 August 1903.
[92] *Crewe Chronicle*, 15 August 1903.
[93] Crewe Local Studies Centre, C/Crew/C *Programme for the Crewe Patriotic Carnival and Demonstration to celebrate the Unveiling of the Crewe (South Africa) Volunteers' and Reservists' Memorial,* no date.

of the [LNWR] Board' which had kept the men's 'places open for them'. Indeed, for Stalbridge, the lesson of the war was to be found in the actions of the survivors not the fallen. The high proportion of LNWR veterans who had resumed their former employment showed, he argued, 'that their hearts were with the company'. Ringing endorsements of the workers' loyalty and the Board's governance followed on from the company's general manager, Lieutenant-Colonel Sir F. Harrison, and his deputy, Frank Rees. The only discordant note was sounded by the town's Liberal mayor, Mr H. Taylor. The only officiating dignitary with no formal connection with the LNWR, Taylor had taken a consistently anti-war line throughout the conflict and was not now prepared to let sleeping dogs lie. In reply to Stalbridge, he accepted that all were in agreement that 'the men of Crewe did their duty nobly', but was less certain that unanimity existed 'as to the policy which culminated in the war; or as to the conduct of the war itself'.[94]

As might be expected, commemoration at the familial, parish and work level was a much more intimate affair than it was in the grander schemes of civic communities and military organisations. It was in the tight-knit social structures of family, work and religious grouping that individuals were most sorely missed and grief and solace were most in evidence. Yet pride, be it regional or institutional, was never far away. Those being commemorated frequently served as representatives of their parent communities. As such, the qualities and characteristics which they were deemed to have embodied were used as proof of collective rather than personal worth.

---

[94]   *Crewe Chronicle*, 15 August 1903.

Chapter 5

Writing the Anglo-Boer War: Leo Amery, Frederick Maurice and the History of the South African War

*I*N the introduction to his magisterial 1979 overview of the Boer War, Thomas Pakenham noted that the history of the conflict for the past seventy years had been dominated by two contemporary works ; *The Times History of the War in South Africa*, edited by Leo Amery, and Sir Frederick Maurice's (official) *History of the War in South Africa*.[1] Indeed, until Pakenham's study, little serious research into the conflict had been undertaken. Although there had been brief revivals of interest in the 1930s, with Ian Hamilton's *Anti-Commando* and J. F. C. Fuller's *The Last of the Gentlemen's Wars*, and in the late 1950s, with such populist works as Edgar Holt's *The Boer War* and Rayne Kruger's *Goodbye Dolly Gray: The Story of the Boer War*, these books had deviated little from the line established by Amery and Maurice.[2] Pakenham was not alone in dismissing the glut of war-related memoirs and histories released in the first decade of the twentieth century as a 'barrage' from which the 'Long Toms' of Amery and Maurice stood apart.[3] An anonymous 'British Officer', commissioned to survey 'The Literature of the South African War' for the *American Historical Review* in 1907, was equally contemptuous of 'popular books, which profess to lay before their readers history, red-hot from its making like a baker's rolls'. 'These works', he argued:

---

[1]   Pakenham, *The Boer War*, p. xv.
[2]   Ian Hamilton and Victor Sampson, *Anti-Commando* (London: Faber & Faber, 1931); J. F. C. Fuller, *The Last of the Gentlemen's Wars: A Subaltern's Journal of the War in South Africa, 1899–1902* (London: Faber & Faber, 1937); Edgar Holt, *The Boer War* (London: Putnam, 1958); Rayne Kruger, *Goodbye Dolly Gray: The Story of the Boer War* (London: Cassell, 1959).
[3]   Pakenham, *The Boer War*, p. xv.

no doubt answer their publishers' purpose. They have a considerable although purely ephemeral sale, and in the case of a national struggle fan a healthy spirit of patriotism. But it must be confessed that they have no pretension to be included in the historian's library. Their text is for the most part compiled by the scissors and paste process from the columns of newspapers. Their illustrations are strangely dissimilar to the realities of modern war, and are often palpably the work of artists who have never been under fire, and whose acquaintance with battlefields is limited to a study of Napoleonic pictures and of melodrama as presented by the suburban stage. It is unnecessary therefore to trouble the readers of this review by enumerating works of this class given birth to by the South African War. Their brief day has passed and, save to satisfy curiosity, it would be [a] waste of time to dip into their pages.[4]

By contrast, both *The Times History* and the official history were immediately recognised as works of lasting significance. First off the presses was *The Times History of the War in South Africa*, published in seven volumes between 1900 and 1909. For the reviewer in the *Observer*, the publication of the final two volumes represented the 'completion of a great historical work of permanent national importance' that would 'always remain the standard history of the war'. The *Globe* was equally fulsome in its praise, asserting that, 'From its first inception *The Times History of the War in South Africa* has been a national undertaking, and it fills a place in our literature from which no rival can dislodge it', while the *Daily Mail* viewed the seven volumes as 'a national work of the first importance'.[5] Such acclaim was by no means exceptional and was a reflection of not only the quality of the work but also *The Times'* position as a national institution. Although increased competition had resulted in circulation figures dropping from a peak of approximately 65,000 in the 1870s to an average of 35,000 by the end of the nineteenth century, the paper still retained a disproportionate influence in British political and cultural life. Leading politicians used its letters columns to debate key policy issues while its rivals, although often critical, invariably took their lead from the paper's editorials.[6] Using Stephen Koss's criteria that the stature of a journal should be measured by 'the gratitude it received from those whom it praised, the resentment it incurred from those whom it censured, and, above all, ... by the number of lesser journals that duplicated it contents', then *The Times* was still Britain's pre-eminent newspaper.[7]

---

[4]   A British Officer, 'The Literature of the South African War, 1899–1902', *American Historical Review*, 12 (1907), pp. 313.

[5]   Churchill College Archives (ChCA), Leopold Amery papers, AMEL 1/1/9, Reviews – *The Times History of the War*.

[6]   Jacqueline Beaumont, '*The Times* at War, 1899–1902', in Donal Lowry (ed.), *The South African War Reappraised* (Manchester: Manchester University Press, 2000), pp. 67–68.

[7]   Stephen Koss, *The Rise and Fall of the Political Press in Britain* (London: Hamish Hamilton, 1984), p. 9.

Indeed, the extent of *The Times*' power was fully recognised by Sir Frederick Maurice. Embroiled in a long-running dispute over pay and conditions with the Treasury in 1903, he set out, in a memorandum to the War Office, what the consequences would be of denying him the staffing and funding enjoyed by Amery. Without adequate resources, he warned, *The Times History* would become 'the one authoritative History in England' with the result that, 'its influence upon the electorate and both indirectly through them and directly by itself on the House of Commons will make it very hard not to adopt a view of the short service system and of other matters involved in the proposals embodied in the plan of army reform set forth by that newspaper'.[8]

Just as eagerly anticipated by both the general public and the country's political leaders was the official history of the war, published in four volumes between 1906 and 1910. The scope and, consequently, the appeal of official histories had widened considerably in the half-century since the Crimean War. Originally restricted to little more than the compilation of artillery and engineering records, the remit of the official historian had been extended in 1873, when the newly formed Intelligence Branch had assumed responsibility for the histories' production, to include a broad overview of the various small wars in which Britain was engaged.[9] By 1901, the public's fascination with the war in South Africa was such that there was 'a clamour from publishers' to secure the rights over the official history, with the eventual winners, Hurst and Blackett, predicting sales in excess of 10,000.[10] Interest was no less keen at Westminster and Pall Mall. In a letter to Leopold Amery, Lieutenant-Colonel Charles à Court, the British military attaché at Brussels and The Hague, hinted at the excitement that publication of the official history was expected to arouse within the political and military elite when, only half-jokingly, he suggested that the recently appointed official historian, Colonel G. F. R. Henderson, would 'have to go about armed to the teeth for the rest of his days'.[11]

In an addendum to his survey of South African war literature, the anonymous British officer referred to in the opening paragraph of this chapter had a chance to assess the importance of the recently released first volume of the official history. It would, he felt, in combination with *The Times History*, dominate the record of the war. While Amery's vision of the war would 'live for many generations … amongst amateurs', professional readers would, he was certain,

[8]   TNA, WO32/4756 Memorandum from Sir Frederick Maurice to the War Office, 24 April 1903.
[9]   Jay Luvaas, *The Education of an Army: British Military Thought, 1815–1940* (London: Cassell, 1965), pp. 184–185.
[10]   TNA, WO32/4755, Memorandum from Major G. L. Gretton to the Sir E. W. D. Ward, 21 March 1903.
[11]   ChCA, Leopold Amery papers, AMEL 1/1/11, Colonel Charles à Court to Amery, 7 October 1900.

turn to Maurice for an 'accurate and final record of that campaign'.[12] In holding sway over the written memory of the conflict, *The Times History* and the official history played vital roles in the construction of a publicly accepted version of the past. To uncover just how this collective narrative developed, it is important to examine the production processes of these two histories. In the same way that the apparently consensual vision of the past enshrined in war memorials was cast during the memorialisation process, so the works of Amery and Maurice were shaped by the external pressures of finance and political intrigue. Indeed, for one reviewer in the *Standard* the parallel is particularly apt, for Amery's volumes were, he insisted, more than a mere history of the war, they were and would remain 'a lasting monument'.[13] This chapter will, therefore, investigate the evolution and impact of these two key written memory sites, exploring both their preparation and reception.

Recalling his work during the South African War as a *Times*' correspondent, Leopold Amery claimed that the idea for a history sprang from a throwaway line in a letter he sent from Cape Town in December 1900 to the paper's manager, Moberly Bell. Replying to a 'pitiful wail' from Bell about excessive journalistic expenditure, Amery suggested, 'as a pure jest', a 'history of the South African War in sixty volumes'. It was, he continued, 'to his complete surprise' that the proposal was taken seriously.[14] Although Amery's diary suggests he pressed the matter with rather more urgency, it was undoubtedly the case that serendipity played a part in committing him to a task which was, in his own estimation, to occupy five of the next nine years of his life.[15] Having spent a year as a history fellow at All Souls, Oxford, Amery joined *The Times* in early 1899 as an assistant to Sir Valentine Chirol, the paper's foreign editor. On 26 August he was despatched to Cape Town to cover what was expected to be a peaceful settlement to the growing diplomatic crisis and, as tensions increased, travelled to Pretoria to report on the Boer view of negotiations. Expelled from the Transvaal on the outbreak of hostilities, he found himself in the right place at the right time and was directed by Bell to assemble a team of correspondents to cover hostilities.[16]

The war caught *The Times* at a critical point in its evolution. Still regarded by the British public as the most authoritative broadsheet, its precarious financial position made it increasingly difficult to live up to this mantle. With an operating profit for newspaper sales in 1896 of £29,955 transformed into a loss of £18,498 by 1900, and with the need to maintain an expensive network

12   A British Officer, 'The Literature of the South African War', p. 320.
13   ChCA, Leopold Amery papers, AMEL 1/1/9, Reviews – *The Times History of the War*.
14   Amery, *Political Life*, p. 133.
15   John Barnes and David Nicholson (eds), *The Leo Amery Diaries, Volume 1: 1896–1929* (London: Hutchinson, 1980), pp. 31–33; Amery, *Political Life*, p. 158.
16   Beaumont, '*The Times* at War', pp. 67–70; Amery, *Political Life*, pp. 55–90.

of correspondents in South Africa adding to the financial strain, Bell turned towards the one buoyant branch of the business, the book publishing section, for salvation. Both *The Times Atlas* and *The Times* edition of the *Encyclopaedia Britannica* had brought in substantial profits in the two years before the war in South Africa.[17] Thus, Amery's proposal, facetious or otherwise, for a serialised history was enthusiastically adopted by Bell who, within the space of three months, had acquired a publisher, Sampson Low, and fleshed out details on price, format, number of volumes and publication dates.[18] All these negotiations taking place, of course, while the war was still in its early stages.

For Amery and Bell then the initial impetus for the production of *The Times History* was profit. To maximise potential earnings, both recognised it was vital to seize the moment and publish 'while public interest was at its height'.[19] Both were also acutely aware that they did not have the field to themselves. In January 1900, Amery, using Valentine Chirol as an intermediary, urged Bell to commit to publishing a history 'soon to prevent all the correspondents writing huge books of their own', while the following month the roles were reversed with Bell imploring Amery 'to get on with it as soon as possible as I hear Winston Churchill and others are going to bring [a history] out in parts'.[20] The need to rush into print before the market became saturated or interest waned shaped the format that the enterprise was to take. The prelude to hostilities, which it was assumed would take up much of the first volume, was to be little more than a rehash of the hugely successful pamphlet on Great Britain and the Boer Republics by Flora Shaw, the paper's colonial editor, while the military operations were to be covered by simply editing the reports from the paper's war correspondents to form a coherent narrative.[21] Indeed, the populist nature of the publication that Bell envisaged can be discerned by his rejection of Samson Low's choice for editor of Sir Herbert Maxwell, whose biography of Wellington, Bell claimed, was 'a cure for insomnia', and by his, albeit flippant, suggestion that they might go in for alliterative chapter titles along the lines of: 'Buller's Blunders, Gatacre's Gaffes, Methuen's Madness, White's Wobblings, Rhodes' Roars, Kruger's Krimes [sic]'.[22] A subsequent proposal that the history 'should

---

[17]   *The History of* The Times: *The Twentieth Century Test, 1884–1912* (London: *The Times*, 1947), pp. 433–457.

[18]   ChCA, Leopold Amery papers, AMEL 1/1/6, Bell to Amery 12 January 1900; 19 January 1900; 1 February 1900; 9 February 1900; 16 February 1900; 26 February 1900; 15 March 1900; 20 March 1900; 23 March 1900.

[19]   Amery, *Political Life*, p. 151.

[20]   Amery to Chirol, 23 January 1900 quoted in Barnes and Nicholson, *Diaries*, p. 33; ChCA, Leopold Amery papers, AMEL 1/1/6, Bell to Amery, 26 February 1900.

[21]   ChCA, Leopold Amery papers, AMEL 1/1/6, Bell to Amery, 19 January 1900; 16 February 1900; 7 March 1900; Amery, *Political Life*, p. 151.

[22]   ChCA, Leopold Amery papers, AMEL 1/1/6, Bell to Amery, 12 January 1900; 19 January 1900.

mention as many officers as possible especially when they are killed', was, Bell freely admitted, made from a purely 'mercenary motive'.[23]

As work progressed, however, Amery's attitude to the enterprise radically shifted. Swamped by official despatches and operational reports from serving officers, he became increasingly convinced that if the history was to alert the public to the deficiencies in the army's performance that the early months of the war had brought into high relief it would need to be both comprehensive and meticulously accurate. As he explained to General Sir George White, when asking him to review an early draft of Volume II, he 'was very anxious indeed to make *The Times History* a really accurate and impartial work, and nothing could distress me more than if through imperfect information I allowed a garbled version of events or an unfair criticism to be incorporated in it'.[24] Bell was having a similar though by no means so profound change of heart. In a letter to Amery in the spring of 1900 he reluctantly accepted that, as 'histories of the war now abound', they should 'try to make ours <u>The</u> [sic] History of the War'.[25] However, he had far from given up hope of turning a handsome profit. Although still adamant, in a letter sent to Amery in the summer of 1900, that he did 'not want to sacrifice the worth of the book to undue haste', he nonetheless could not restrain himself from adding the caveat that an early publication was still vital if public interest was to be caught before events in South Africa became overshadowed by the deepening crisis in China.[26]

With Volume I completed in draft form by May 1900 and published by December, Bell became increasingly anxious that subsequent volumes, dealing with the military events, should follow in swift succession. No doubt adding to his impatience was Sampson Low's rash pledge in their advertising circular for Volume I that future volumes would be issued at an interval of six weeks with the set complete by May 1901. Even Bell recognised that it would be impossible to keep to this schedule, but with no sign of Volume II by the beginning of 1901, and with some subscribers to the whole set now demanding their money back, mounting frustration drove him to inform Amery that he was 'inclined to cut my losses'. At issue was Amery's decision to abandon a populist approach. In Bell's view, in attempting to produce the definitive account of the conflict, Amery was 'trying to write a history in 1901 which can never be written until 1911'.[27] Although Bell's trust in the project was briefly rekindled, in May 1902, by the positive critical reception for Volume II, the correspondence between Bell and Amery charts an increasingly fractious relationship as continuing delays

[23]   ChCA, Leopold Amery papers, AMEL 1/1/6, Bell to Amery, 27 March 1900.
[24]   Amery, *Political Life*, pp. 151–152; British Library, Field Marshal Sir George White paper,s Mss Eur F108/66, Amery to White, 22 February 1901.
[25]   ChCA, Leopold Amery papers, AMEL 1/1/6, Bell to Amery, 26 April 1900.
[26]   ChCA, Leopold Amery papers, AMEL 1/1/6, Bell to Amery, 7 June 1900.
[27]   ChCA, Leopold Amery papers, AMEL 1/16, Bell to Amery, 20 January 1901.

saw any chance of profit disappear completely.[28] In February 1909, with the concluding volume yet to be published, Bell finally ran out of patience. Insisting that 'the matter had become a public disgrace', Bell concluded a stinging letter to Amery with a heartfelt personal rebuke; 'Because I have hitherto tried to treat the matter jocularly you have chosen to treat all our representations with contempt and absolutely to neglect fulfilling an engagement for which you have been very liberally paid'.[29]

The root cause of what, in Bell's view, was an unnecessarily extended production period was Amery's switch from a populist to a self-confessed propagandist approach and his concomitant belief that if the project was to have any impact then it would have to be scrupulously accurate.[30] To achieve the required veracity the manuscript went through an elaborate process of drafting, reviewing and editing. The scope of the task was such that a number of the *Times*' war correspondents were charged with preparing draft chapters. Thus, the early operations in Natal were covered by Lionel James, Lord Methuen's advance on Kimberley by Perceval Landon, Stormberg by Major A. W. A. Pollock and Colenso by Bron Herbert.[31] By far the most useful of the former *Times*' correspondents was Lionel James. A professionally trained journalist, not only did he contribute much of the final copy on the siege of Ladysmith and Roberts's subsequent advance on Pretoria but he also acted as assistant editor on the first three volumes of the history. Outside experts were also invited to contribute, although the results were occasionally disappointing. A chapter on the British army at the outbreak of hostilities by the future Secretary of State for War, Hugh Arnold-Foster, was dismissed as consisting of 'mainly figures and statistics', while Unionist MP J. Parker Smith's submission was deemed 'too verbose'.[32] Spenser Wilkinson, lead writer on the *Morning Post* and soon to be elected as the first Chichele Professor of Military History at Oxford, and Major-General Robert Baden-Powell, the hero of Mafeking, were both rejected as potential contributors. Wilkinson, whom Bell had suggested might cover 'the patriotic government in England', on the grounds that he was liable to 'gush' and Baden-Powell because they 'would be running the risk of a chapter that would be undiluted Baden-Powell'.[33]

Amery, nonetheless, retained tight editorial control. He cross-checked all work with a mass of official and unofficial material before having it sent out

---

[28] ChCA, Leopold Amery papers, AMEL 1/1/6, Bell to Amery, 28 August 1902; 17 April 1903.

[29] Bell to Amery, 13 February 1909, quoted in Barnes and Nicholson, *Diaries*, p. 63.

[30] Amery, *Political Life*, p. 192.

[31] Amery, *Political Life*, p. 157.

[32] ChCA, Leopold Amery papers, AMEL1/1/6, Bell to Amery, 11 May 1900; 22 June 1900.

[33] ChCA, Leopold Amery papers, AMEL 1/1/6, Bell to Amery, 22 June 1900; 20 June 1900.

to a variety of experts and protagonists for comment; 'in some cases to over one hundred correspondents'. Suggestions for revisions were then collated with Amery assuming sole responsibility for the production of the final manuscript.[34] Not only was this a lengthy process but it was also one which, inevitably, led to professional tension. Perceval Landon, who had served as a war correspondent for *The Times* between September 1899 and April 1900, found the experience of working for Amery 'a difficult and unpleasant one'. Piqued to find that his account of the battle of Magersfontein had been substantially reworked, he complained, in a letter to Amery in February 1901, that he 'had not expected such a complete "Ameryisation" of the words and phrases used by me'.[35] Although much more latitude was given to Basil Williams, Erskine Childers and Ian MacAlistir who were, respectively, appointed to act as editors on the final three volumes dealing with Roberts's operations after the fall of Bloemfontein, the guerrilla war under Kitchener and various technical aspects of the war, conflict could still arise.[36] Largely in agreement in their reading of military operations during the conflict's long drawn-out endgame, Amery and Childers clashed violently over their interpretation of the post-war reconstruction programme under Lord Milner, the High Commissioner for Southern Africa and first governor of the Transvaal and Orange River Colony. Amery, who held 'a great personal affection as well as admiration' for Milner, having nearly joined his staff in the summer of 1901, was appalled by what he felt was an overly critical final chapter from Childers on British policy following the Peace of Vereeniging.[37] His decision to rewrite the piece from scratch resulted in a breakdown in relations between the two, with Childers insisting that he should be allowed to use the preface to the volume to disassociate himself completely from the views expressed.[38]

In his autobiography Amery explained why he had attached so much weight to Childers's final chapter. It was in this political epilogue, he argued, that 'the key to the whole work' lay, for the war in South Africa was more than just a 'military story', it was 'a great historical and political event and a turning-point in the history of the Commonwealth'.[39] During the war, Amery had been one of only a few British correspondents who had had any sympathy for the

---

[34] Amery, *Political Life*, p. 158.

[35] ChCA, Leopold Amery papers, AMEL 1/1/11, Landon to Amery, 15 February 1901.

[36] In fact ill-health forced MacAlistir to resign as editor leaving the volume to be completed by Amery, Lionel James and Charles à Court. ChCA, Leopold Amery papers, AMEL 2/5/6, MacAlistir to Bell, 22 June 1907; Amery, *Political Life*, p. 334.

[37] ChCA, Leopold Amery papers, AMEL 1/1/11, Childers to Amery, 19 June 1905; Amery, *Political Life*, pp. 150–151.

[38] *Times History of the War*, Vol. V, pp. xii–xiii; Andrew Boyle, *The Riddle of Erskine Childers* (London: Hutchinson, 1977), pp. 127–133.

[39] Amery, *Political Life*, p. 334.

Boers, admiring what he called their 'force and passion'.[40] However, this regard had remained firmly constrained by his conservative political outlook and, throughout the crisis in South Africa, he had maintained that the only way 'to break the power of Krugerism' was through recourse to arms.[41] It was almost inevitable, therefore, that *The Times History* would reflect Amery's imperialistic certainty. The reviewer in the *Manchester Courier* regarded the complete work as 'a great lesson in imperialism, its ideals and its duties, which should appeal most strongly to all political thinkers'.[42] Although, unsurprisingly, taking issue with Amery's 'general outlook', the eminent historian and Liberal politician, H. A. L. Fisher, writing in *The Times Literary Supplement*, was equally certain that this was 'history with a mission'. 'Its aim', Fisher asserted, was 'to defend Imperialism in the past, to make Imperialists in the present, and by displaying not only the virtues but also the faults of British organisation to strengthen the Empire against the perils of the future'.[43]

The propagation of Britain's imperial mission may have provided the overarching rationale for *The Times History*, but it was the means by which this was to be achieved that most excited Amery. It was, he claimed in later life, the innumerable eye-witness accounts he received in preparation for the writing of Volumes II and III that not only reinforced his belief in the inadequacy of Britain's military preparedness but also convinced him that 'the story of the war could be made the best instrument for preaching Army Reform'.[44] Certainly no attempt was made to mask the unashamedly propagandist nature of the history. The preface to Volume II, which covered the first three months of hostilities up to Buller's defeat at Colenso, made explicit the underlying moral that readers should draw from this dark period in British military history:

> The description [of British and Boer military systems] may, I hope, help the reader … to see underlying the story the real and deeper causes of success and failure, to trace the influence of national characteristics and national organisation for war in the seemingly fortuitous sequence of events, and in the often almost incomprehensible actions of generals and politicians. It is in the realisation of those more deeply rooted causes of our past failures, quite as much as in the indiscriminate adoption of methods found useful in the South African veld, that lie the best hopes of the reforms required to insure the safety and the full development of the British Empire.[45]

[40] Amery, *Political Life*, p. 114.
[41] Amery, *Political Life*, p. 114; Beaumont, 'The Times at War', p. 81.
[42] *Manchester Courier*, 7 July 1909.
[43] *The Times Literary Supplement*, 1 July 1909.
[44] Amery, *Political Life*, p. 152.
[45] *Times History of the War*, Vol. II, pp. v–vi.

It would certainly appear that the 'unflinching frankness' of *The Times History*'s criticism had the desired effect on Field Marshal Lord Roberts, the commander-in-chief of the forces.[46] Amery recalled how Roberts, having read the account of the battle of Colenso in the concluding chapter of Volume II, felt compelled to write to Ian Hamilton to tell him that, 'It is enough to make a dead man turn in his grave, and the worst of it is that every word of it is true'.[47] Increasingly convinced that national service was the only solution to the nation's military deficiencies, Roberts subsequently provided substantial assistance with the preparation of Volume III of the history, which advanced the narrative up to the fall of Bloemfontein, offering unfettered access to his war diaries, returning detailed commentaries on draft chapters and inviting both Amery and Lionel James to Englemere, his palatial house in Virginia Water, to use his papers.[48] Lord Kitchener, Roberts's successor as chief of staff in South Africa, was equally approving of Amery's approach and objectives. Before leaving South Africa in June 1902, he informed Amery that the Colenso chapter was not at all 'too severe and that it is necessary to speak out if you wish to reform the army'.[49]

Roberts and Kitchener were by no means the only ones to voice approval of the reformist agenda that underpinned Volumes II and III of the history. Published in 1902 and 1905 respectively, the two volumes were accorded, for the most part, a favourable critical reception. Review after review pointed to the works as object lessons in past military failings and blueprints for future army reform. Writing for *The Times Literary Supplement*, Sir George Goldie, fresh from service on the Esher Commission, was adamant that Volume III raised 'matters of vital importance to our continued existence as an Imperial or even independent people'. Contending that the opening chapters examining the effects of Black Week were of such consequence that they warranted a separate review, he concluded by suggesting that Amery's closing words 'should be posted on every church and chapel door throughout the country: "National military training is the bed-rock on which alone we can hope to carry through the great struggles which the future may have in store for us."'[50] Herbert Maxwell, in the *Bookman*, was equally sure that 'the chief lesson' of Volume III, the 'necessity for the youth of the nation being trained to arms', was 'vital to the security and endurance of the Empire'.[51] The reviewer in the *Graphic* was insistent that the 'wholesome and disagreeable truths' which the volume contained would leave

[46]   Amery, *Political Life*, p. 152.
[47]   News International Archive, Moberly Bell papers, Bell Letter Book 23, Amery to Bell, 19 June 1902.
[48]   ChCA, Leopold Amery papers, AMEL 1/1/11, Roberts to Amery, 1 January 1903; 29 November 1903.
[49]   News International Archive, Moberly Bell papers, Bell Letter Book 23, Amery to Bell, 19 June 1902.
[50]   *The Times Literary Supplement*, 2 June 1905.
[51]   ChCA, Leopold Amery papers, AMEL 5/4, Reviews, *Bookman*, July 1905.

no one in 'any doubt as to whether the British Army is what it ought to be', while the *Spectator*, in a belated review of Volume II, worried that:

> unless the bulk of the population realise to the full the true import of this writing on the wall – that, as the late Colonel Henderson put it, 'adequate military knowledge should be part of the intellectual equipment of every educated man,' and, above all, that our Army and our Army system are what the nation choose to make them – nothing can save us from irretrievable disaster and ruin.[52]

Indeed, for the *Spectator*, the only glimmer of hope lay in the growing public acceptance of Amery's position. It was both 'significant' and 'hopeful', posited the paper's reviewer, that the 'sternly uncompromising criticisms and ruthless dissection of facts and motives, which ten years ago would probably have resulted in sending its authors to Coventry, should have been received by military and non-military reviewers alike with an almost unanimous chorus of agreement and approval'.[53]

There were, however, dissenting voices. Amery received a number of complaints from senior army officers who felt that their treatment in the pages of the history had been unduly harsh. Most notable of these was Sir Redvers Buller who, battling to save an already tarnished military reputation, was particularly aggrieved by Amery's damning indictment of his command during the opening stages of the war.[54] At the root of Buller's complaint was his belief that *The Times History*'s interpretation of his abortive campaign to relieve Ladysmith was based on a garbled version of official telegrams which a banning order from the War Office, put in place at the time of his dismissal from the Aldershot command in October 1901, prohibited him from effectively challenging.[55] In an effort to set the record straight, he campaigned both publicly, through the press, and privately, through a protracted correspondence with the War Office, for the full publication of the relevant despatches.[56] Concerned that Buller intended to pursue the matter through the courts, the War Office decided, in June 1902, to place all the contested material in the hands of Parliament and

---

[52] *Graphic*, 24 June 1905; *Spectator*, 24 June 1905.

[53] *Spectator*, 24 June 1905. Amery was of the same opinion. He felt that critics of *The Times History* had been much less vocal since the publication of the findings of the Esher and Norfolk Commissions, which had made public many of the shortcomings of the army's performance in South Africa. Amery, *Political Life*, p. 219.

[54] Ian Beckett views Amery's trenchant condemnation of Buller as a particular flaw of *The Times History*. See Ian F. W. Beckett, 'The Historiography of Small Wars: Early Historians and the South African War', *Small Wars and Insurgencies*, 2: 2 (1991), p. 287.

[55] Amery had, in fact, been at the forefront of the campaign to have Buller removed. See Amery, *Political Life*, pp. 152–157.

[56] *The Times*, 28 May 1902; TNA, CAB 37/61, papers on alleged libel on Sir Redvers Buller in *The Times History*.

the dispute fizzled out the following month when the full text of the telegrams was published in *The Times*.[57] Indeed, that the whole issue was never considered a threat to the historical integrity of *The Times History*, or for that matter to its financial viability, can be discerned from the publisher's 'jubilant' assertion, on being informed that Buller might sue for libel, that a court case would 'be a splendid advertisement'.[58]

Criticism, although largely overshadowed by acclaim, also surfaced in press reviews. Unsurprisingly, the influential Liberal paper, the *Westminster Gazette*, was unimpressed by the opening volume of *The Times History*, seeing in it no more than 'a restatement of the causes of the war and of events which led up to it from the point of view which *The Times* has adopted during the last five years'.[59] Undoubtedly more aggravating for Amery than such political sniping was the allegation in one popular daily that his criticisms of the army's performance in South Africa were unpatriotic. Under the banner headline, 'Unwarrantable!', the *Daily Mirror* expressed outrage at what it perceived to be an 'amazing attack', in Volume III, on the 'physical and moral endurance' of British soldiers at Spion Kop. It was, fulminated the paper's reviewer, not only an opinion which would 'arouse universal indignation' but also a clear sign of the declining standards of *The Times* generally.[60] This was followed up three days later by an angry letter to the *Mirror*'s editor from a retired major-general, who, insisting that 'the British soldier cannot be excelled by those of any nation', dismissed Amery's views as 'perfect nonsense and not worth contradicting'.[61]

However, such outright condemnation was rare. More often than not, when critics found fault, it was with Amery's analysis of specific technical aspects of military operations rather than his broader conclusions. Typical was the verdict of the distinguished American naval theoretician, Captain T. Mahan, in *The Times Literary Supplement*. Although taking issue with the claim in Volume II that the war had 'finally established the unqualified supremacy of firearms over any form of the more primitive weapons', he nonetheless concluded on a note of harmony, agreeing that, in highlighting Britain's military and political unpreparedness for war, 'Mr. Amery correctly sees the leading lesson of these hostilities'.[62] In a similar vein, the reservations that both *The Regiment* and the *Army and Navy Gazette* had about the third volume's critical assessment

---

[57] *The Times*, 8 July 1902.
[58] ChCA, Leopold Amery papers, AMEL 1/1/6, Bell to Amery, 5 May 1902.
[59] *Westminster Gazette*, 12 December 1900.
[60] *Daily Mirror*, 27 May 1905.
[61] *Daily Mirror*, 30 May 1905.
[62] *The Times Literary Supplement*, 23 May 1902.

of the role of volunteers were all but lost in what were otherwise wholehearted endorsements of the *History*'s standpoint.[63]

Debates over the finer points of operational tactics may have animated Mahan and other military specialists but they were of only marginal significance for the general public and popular press. Reviewers for the new mass circulation papers, with little time or space for detailed critiques, seized on the controversial tone of *The Times History* as a means of engaging the interest of their readers. Typical were the *Evening News* and the *Daily Mail*, two of the country's best-selling dailies. Aware of a good story when they saw one, both papers employed eye-catching headlines to bolster their reviews of Volume III; the *Evening News* opting for, 'The Army and the Nation: Sensational Indictment' while the *Daily Mail* settled on the not dissimilar, 'Sensational Indictment of Army Methods'.[64] Volume II, as Amery was to concede in the first instalment of his autobiography, *My Political Life*, had been subjected to equally superficial treatment at the hands of the mass dailies. 'Reviewers were', he noted, 'laudatory, but very few of them showed any real appreciation of the extent of the new light thrown on the actual operations as a whole. Most of them, indeed, were more concerned with such high lights [sic] as my criticism of Buller's conduct at Colenso'.[65] This process of critical distillation, a process that monumental narratives such as *The Times History* are inevitably subjected to, may have disappointed Amery but it undoubtedly played an important part in shaping the public memory of the war in South Africa in the years following the conflict. As our anonymous 'British Officer' disapprovingly observed in the *American Historical Review*, the British public, who 'revel in … pungency', were bound to be attracted by 'the sting and virulence of its irresponsible criticism'.[66]

The officially produced *History of the War in South Africa*, by contrast, contained little that was designed to enflame public passions. However, this is not to say that its genesis was any less protracted or its impact on the public's vision of the war any less important. The decision to produce an official account of the conflict was taken in the autumn of 1900 when Colonel G. F. R. Henderson, Roberts's former director of intelligence in South Africa, was appointed to the task. Having already established a first-class reputation as a military writer, Henderson was anxious that the project's appeal should not be restricted to the narrow confines of the military and governmental cognoscenti. His suggestion that a more populist approach could result in a not insubstantial financial return for the government persuaded the Secretary of State for War, St John Brodrick, to waive the War Office's right to arrange publication and in

---

[63] *The Regiment: An Illustrated Military Journal for Everybody*, No. 488 (May 1905), p. 34; *Army and Navy Gazette: Journal of the Militia and Volunteer Forces*, 27 May 1905, p. 411.
[64] *Evening News*, 31 May 1905; *Daily Mail*, 31 May 1905.
[65] Amery, *Political Life*, p. 160.
[66] A British Soldier, 'Literature of the South African War', p. 321.

June 1901 a contract for a seven volume history was signed between Henderson and the commercial publishers, Hurst and Blackett.[67] The terms of the contract stipulated that the work would not only contain 'commentaries on the strategy, tactics and organisation' of the army but that, by ensuring the 'political history' of the conflict was fully treated, 'every effort [would] be made to make it picturesque and popular'.[68]

On Henderson's death in March 1903, Major-General Sir John Frederick Maurice, the author of the official history of the 1882 Egyptian campaign, was brought out of retirement to assume responsibility for the project. Although ready to concede that Henderson's work, which dealt with the political backdrop to the war, was 'certainly not in the ordinary form of official history', Maurice was nonetheless keen that the scheme should not revert to the more traditional 'blue book' approach.[69] 'A dry statistical record of the war will no doubt be useful for future reference', he informed Field Marshal Lord Roberts shortly after his appointment, 'but it will be read by hardly anyone, and is certainly not the form of history which the public everywhere has been led to expect and for which those who had relations engaged in the war have been looking'.[70] Trained from an early age for an academic career, Maurice eschewed some of the more 'partisan expressions' of Henderson, arguing instead that the task of the historian was 'solely to get at the facts ... and to allow inferences to be drawn from the success or failure that attended the action taken'.[71] Yet, his insistence that it was not the official historian's 'business to pronounce private opinions' was not meant to challenge the terms of the original contract with Hurst and Blackett that the work should appeal to the general public and should include a full examination of the preparations for, and political context of, the war.[72]

Throughout Henderson's time overseeing the official history, the government had little interest in the project beyond a mild concern that the work should be completed in good time and on budget. Initially, the only change that Maurice's appointment brought about was to exacerbate this concern. Arguing that at the current rate of progress the history would take a further twenty-eight years to

---

[67]   TNA, WO32/4759, Note from Major G. L. Gretton to Sir Edward Ward, Permanent Under-Secretary of State for War, 21 March 1903.

[68]   TNA, WO32/4759, Memorandum on 'Proposed Official History of the South African War in 1901', 2 January 1903. Indeed, just how popular Hurst and Blackett anticipated the history would be can be seen in the remarkably generous contract they drew up with Henderson. Terms of a £300 advance on each volume and 30 per cent royalties were, noted Henderson's aide, Major G. L. Greton, 'almost unprecedented'. TNA, WO32/4759, Gretton to Ward, 21 March 1903.

[69]   TNA, WO32/4758, Maurice to Roberts, 20 October 1903.

[70]   TNA, WO32/4758, Maurice to Roberts, 20 October 1903.

[71]   Luvaas, *Education of an Army*, pp. 174–176; TNA, WO32/4758, Maurice to Sir Edward Ward, 28 September 1903.

[72]   TNA, WO32/4758, Maurice to Ward, 28 September 1903.

write and stretch to fourteen volumes, Maurice insisted, in a memorandum sent to the War Office a month after his appointment, that he would require a staff of twenty-one officers at a cost of £10,000 per annum, plus his own salary of £800 per annum, if the work was to be completed within the three year period to which Henderson had originally agreed.[73] Anxious to see 'the volumes brought out as rapidly as they could be before interest has gone back', St John Brodrick attempted unsuccessfully to persuade a reluctant Treasury to accede to Maurice's requests.[74] After protracted negotiations the best Brodrick could procure was a staffing budget of £6,000 per annum for three years in addition to Maurice's salary of £800 per annum.[75] Although the Treasury's insistence on savings is hardly surprising at a time of army spending cuts, the decision to restrict the official history's funding was not simply a financial one. Both the Treasury and Brodrick were uncertain that any study of the conflict in South Africa warranted such an extravagant deployment of resources as those demanded by Maurice. The Treasury initially suggested that if it was impossible to complete the history on the original budget granted to Henderson then the best solution would be simply 'to omit the less important details', while Brodrick intimated to Maurice that he was unlikely to receive the support he wanted 'because, though a great war for us, it is hardly a Franco-Prussian war in its lessons – especially after the first twelve months'.[76]

The death of Henderson and subsequent dispute over Maurice's terms and conditions of employment had the effect of galvanising Brodrick's interest in the project and towards the end of September 1903 he ordered a detailed review of the completed chapters to be undertaken. The results did not make happy reading. The anonymous War Office reader was not only doubtful about the literary merits of Henderson's work but also its suitability as a government publication. Noting that the third chapter covering the diplomacy in the immediate lead up to the war 'bristles with controversial matter', he concluded by suggesting that it would be more fitting if an official history were to 'begin with the declaration of war and end with the declaration of peace'.[77] This was a view that was shared at the highest levels of government. Alerted to the controversial nature of Henderson's work by the Secretary of State for

[73] TNA, WO32/4756, Memorandum from Maurice to the War Office, 24 April 1903.
[74] King's College, LHCMA, Maurice Mss, 2/3/79, St John Brodrick to Maurice, 8 May 1903.
[75] TNA, WO32/4761, Financial Secretary to the Treasury to War Office, 23 July 1903.
[76] TNA, WO32/4757, Memorandum from the Treasury to the War Office, 8 July 1903; King's College, LHCMA, Maurice Mss, 2/3/79, Brodrick to Maurice, 8 May 1903. In a later memorandum, Brodrick identified the aspects of the war that he felt deserved 'special treatment'. These were: '1) The Natal Campaign, October 1899 to February 1900; 2) Stormberg; 3) Lord Methuen's battles; 4) Kimberley; 5) March on Bloemfontein'. TNA, WO32/4757, Memorandum, Brodrick to Treasury, 13 July 1903.
[77] TNA, WO32/4758, Memorandum, unsigned to Brodrick, 7 October 1903.

Foreign Affairs, Lord Lansdowne, the cabinet informed the War Office that 'a dry narrative of the actual events of the war would be preferable to a political history'.[78] Unsurprisingly, Hugh Arnold-Foster, who by this time had succeeded Brodrick as Secretary of State for War, acceded to the cabinet's recommendation and instructed Maurice to start work afresh, producing 'strictly an official account of the war,' written as nearly as circumstances will allow upon the lines of the German Official History of the War of 1870'.[79]

Although Maurice agreed to tone down 'all expressions of party proclivities' and to reduce the political context to a bare minimum, his revised manuscript proved to be no more acceptable to the authorities than Henderson's original.[80] Of particular concern, as exemplified by the following extract from the new introduction which Maurice submitted for review in October 1904, were passages which passed judgement on the former Boer leadership:

> The war, which these volumes record, was in nothing more remarkable than in this, that it was a contest most unwillingly waged by a great peace-loving empire against small states which, at the time when the war began, had come under the dominion of an autocracy based on an oligarchy. For many years the one purpose of the autocrat and his agents had been to organise the whole people for war. That preparation had only one object, the expulsion of British authority and the substitution for it of the autocracy as supreme throughout South Africa.[81]

For General Sir Neville Lyttleton, the newly appointed Chief of the Imperial General Staff, such views had no place in an official publication. Having read the proofs of the re-worked first three chapters, he informed Maurice that by stating 'officially to the Boers that they fought and died not for their Republic but for the personal autocracy of Mr Kruger', he was highly likely 'to give offence to our new fellow subjects in South Africa'. Lyttleton concluded by insisting that political expediency had to take priority over literary merit:

---

[78] TNA, WO32/4758, Brodrick to Sir Edward Ward, 25 September 1903.
[79] TNA, WO32/4758, Memorandum, Arnold-Foster to Maurice, 17 November 1903. Indeed, the strength of the War Office's objections to Henderson's work can be gauged by the lengths they went to in order to have publication suppressed. Maurice, Henderson's executors and his typist were all contacted to ensure that they did not possess copies of the manuscript and legal advice taken to confirm that anyone pirating the work could be prosecuted. Furthermore, a request by the publishers, Hurst and Blackett, to produce an edition of the first three chapters with all reference to the official history removed was denied. TNA, WO32/4758, War Office memorandum, 4 March 1904. Despite these precautions, some copies of the original manuscript did survive and Henderson's chapter on the state of the British army in 1899 appeared in a posthumous collection of his essays, *The Science War*. See Beckett, 'The Historiography of Small Wars', pp. 289–290.
[80] TNA, WO32/4758, Maurice to Sir Edward Ward, 28 September 1903.
[81] Quoted in Beckett, 'The Historiography of Small Wars', p. 290.

The political history contained in the official history of the war should be made as concise as possible and should be limited to a colourless narrative of events and conditions and that all expressions that might be regarded as of His Majesty's Government on controversial points should be omitted. He is particularly moved to make this suggestion by his desire that nothing, which can be avoided, should be done to impede the reconciliation of races in South Africa.[82]

Hugh Arnold-Foster and Lord Lansdowne were equally perturbed by Maurice's efforts. While Arnold-Foster dismissed the work as little more than a 'political romance', Lord Lansdowne was concerned that the multiplicity of 'irrelevant' passages would be 'taken hold of', particularly if the book comes out under the auspices of a government department'.[83] Despite support from a characteristically bullish Joseph Chamberlain, the former Secretary of State for the Colonies, for whom the authorities were 'so fearful of offending our enemies that they are unable to defend ourselves', Maurice was left with no option but to remove all the offending sections and restrict himself solely to an examination of the military operations.[84] His only consolation was the inclusion of a partial disclaimer in the preface to Volume I in which he explained that the absence of any political commentary was the result of the government's belief that it would be 'undesirable to discuss here any question that had been at issue between them and the rulers of the two republics, or any points that had been in dispute at home, and to confine this history to the military context'.[85]

When Volume I was eventually published in June 1906 the press reception was, according to Andrew Green in his study of the official history of the Great War, favourable but not enthusiastic.[86] Certainly, the anonymous British officer, surveying the literature of the South African war for the *American Historical Review*, although impressed by Maurice's industry was, nonetheless, doubtful that the work would be a commercial success. Arguing that Maurice's 'impartial narrative' was worthy but lacking in popular appeal, he reasoned that the British public, overcome by an apathetic cynicism towards all military questions, was:

unlikely ... to study a book like the official *History* which fails to afford the attraction of the impalement of unsuccessful generals. By the soldier, however, who desires to master his profession, the official *History of the War in South Africa* will be found a mine in which true ore can be dug. To the

[82]   TNA, WO32/4760, General Sir Neville Lyttleton to Maurice, 16 January 1905.
[83]   TNA, WO32/4760, Arnold-Foster to Lansdowne, 23 December 1904; Lansdowne to Arnold-Foster, 22 December 1904.
[84]   King's College, LHCMA, Maurice Mss, 2/3/97, Chamberlain to Maurice, 6 February 1905.
[85]   Maurice, *History of the War in South Africa*, Vol. I, Preface and p. 1.
[86]   Andrew Green, *Writing the Great War: Sir James Edmonds and the Official Histories, 1915–1916* (London: Frank Cass, 2003), p. 7.

impartial historical student it presents evidence which may be accepted as above suspicion.[87]

The sales figures would appear to support this verdict. Only 4,500 sets of the history were sold with the project as a whole making a loss of over £30,000.[88]

For many reviewers, of much greater interest than the actual content of the official history was its controversial genesis. Indeed, press interest in the chequered beginnings of the history pre-dated the publication of the first volume. In March 1906, the *Spectator* concluded its review of *The Official Account of the South African War* by the Historical Section of the German General Staff, by noting that, 'It has been rumoured that the preliminary chapters of [the official history], as prepared by Colonel Henderson, showed the ungarbled truth to be so unpalatable that the late government absolutely forbade their publication and went so far as to have the entire manuscript burned'.[89] Despite a letter of correction, carefully concocted by the War Office in collaboration with the editor of the *Spectator*, Lytton Strachey, appearing three months later, speculation about government interference continued to dominate the press coverage.[90] Typical was the notice which appeared in *The Times Literary Supplement* in July 1906. The opening paragraph indicated that the history had failed to live up to expectations, observing that it was originally:

> to have been a work conceived in the great style, one which was not only to illustrate the great principles of the art of war by the example of our failures and successes against the Boers, but also to bring out the place of that campaign in the history of the political development of the British Empire, and the national, as well as purely military, lessons which that campaign could furnish to statesmen as well as citizens.[91]

The remainder of the piece then moved on to a detailed examination of the obstacles that had prevented such lofty ambitions being fulfilled. Chief among these, so the reviewer argued, was 'the action of the War Office authorities'.[92] Indeed, criticism of this nature gained such currency that Maurice felt obliged to open Volume II with a rebuttal. A 'Note to the Reader', dismissing the 'fiction that has gone abroad that the official history has been much "sub-edited" in the interest of Departments concerned', insisted that 'the only subject on which

---

[87]   A British Officer, 'Literature of the South African War', p. 321.
[88]   Beckett, 'Historiography of Small Wars', p. 293; *The Times*, 6 April 1911.
[89]   *Spectator*, 24 March 1906, p. 461.
[90]   TNA, WO32/4762, Strachey to Sir Edward Ward, 31 March 1906; Ward to Strachey, 4 April 1906; *Spectator*, 7 June 1906, p. 535.
[91]   *The Times Literary Supplement*, 13 July 1906, p. 246.
[92]   *The Times Literary Supplement*, 13 July 1906, p. 246.

any officer asked for change [was to] any phrase that might affect our relations with our Boer fellow subjects'.[93]

Although Maurice persevered with the task of producing an account of the war as comprehensive and objective as the constraints of his War Office remit would allow, the pressure of work, exacerbated by on-going disputes with the Treasury over spiralling costs, undermined his health and he was compelled to retire in 1908. The project was eventually put under the direction of the newly established Historical Section of the Committee of Imperial Defence and the fourth and concluding volume was finally published in 1910.[94] The finished history had, then, clearly failed to live up to Maurice's original aspirations. By omitting any reference to the political context of the conflict it had fallen short of educating the general public in the complexities of modern warfare and, notwithstanding the disclaimer in the second volume, it had never been able to shrug off the widely held belief that it had been tainted by the dead hand of official censorship. The sense of an opportunity missed was perhaps best given in Maurice's obituary which appeared in *The Times* on 13 January 1912:

> If he had been given a free hand, then these volumes [of the *History of the War in South Africa*] would, without the smallest doubt, have been among some of the most interesting ever written, but the actions of the authorities did not do much to lighten the historian's task. It was decided that it was undesirable to discuss any questions that had been at issue between ourselves and the Boer Republics or any points that had been in dispute at home, while the earlier period was only to be mentioned so far as it concerned the necessary modifications in the plan of campaign, which were influenced by the unwillingness of Her Majesty's Government to believe in the necessity of war. It was, perhaps, in all circumstances inevitable that Sir Frederick should have decided not to discuss controversial military questions, but the result of the decision was equally inevitably to make the official history a colourless statement of facts rather than one which might guide and form the opinions of soldiers.[95]

In Volume II of *The Times History*, Amery opened the account of military operations in South Africa with a sweeping indictment of the British army. As an institution, he argued, it flattered to deceive: 'The numbers on its roll were large, the uniforms of the members through all the ranks of the military hierarchy most distinctive, their traditional ceremonies, known as parades, inspections, guards, elaborate and pleasing to the eye, the regulations to which

---

[93]   Maurice, *History of the War in South Africa*, Vol. II, 'Note to the Reader'.
[94]   Volume III was published in 1908 with no author being credited; Volume IV appeared two years later with Captain Grant of the newly established Committee of Imperial Defence's Historical Section as the acknowledged author.
[95]   *The Times*, 13 January 1912.

they submitted, infinitely complex. As a fighting machine it was largely a sham'.[96] Although Maurice disagreed fundamentally with this viewpoint, he was realistic enough to recognise that his scrupulously detailed and objective exploration of the problems facing the British army in South Africa would do little to mitigate the criticism. 'It was', he resignedly admitted in Volume II of the official history, 'much more popular to ignore all this and throw the whole blame on our "ignorant generals" and our "stupid soldiers"'.[97] In this, Maurice was undoubtedly correct. Not only did Amery's stirring narrative trump the 'colourless statement of facts' contained in the official history, but, by reopening contentious debates, *The Times History*'s polemics pandered to the public's appetite for scandal. In turn, the protracted and problematic genesis of the official history raised rumours about a War Office cover-up which served to reinforce Amery's critical interpretation of the conflict. It is this version of the war, of a poorly prepared and ill-led army outwitted by a resourceful enemy, which set the tone for subsequent histories and, as we will see in the next chapter, continued to colour the popular memory of the war for the rest of the century.[98]

---

[96] *The Times History*, Vol. II, p. 40.
[97] Maurice, *History of the War in South Africa*, Vol. II, p. 206.
[98] See Howard Bailes, 'Technology and Imperialism: A Case Study of the Victorian Army in Africa', *Victorian Studies*, 24: 1 (Autumn 1980), pp. 84–85.

Chapter 6

Filming the War:
Television, Kenneth Griffith
and the Boer War

*I*N her study of the presentation of the Great War in television documentaries, Emma Hanna notes that such histories serve much the same purpose as war memorials. Both, she argues, are carefully constructed representations of the past, artfully composed so that the story they portray 'will be accepted in the moment of their creation and by the society for whom they are created'.[1] But here Hanna is ploughing a lone furrow. Invariably, the small screen, as distinct from cinema, is ignored by cultural historians, dismissed as nothing more than mere entertainment. Yet, the past enshrined in historical documentaries has an immediacy, power and influence that no single monument or, for that matter, written history, could ever attain. Indeed, so all pervasive is television that many academic historians fear that it undermines the public's ability to appreciate the complexity of historical events by propagating inaccuracies and myths, an 'agreed' version of the past. Simon Schama has neatly summarised such academic navel-gazing as:

> the usual moan of the Common Room and the opinion columns that 'serious television' is a 'contradiction in terms'; that the subtlety of history is too elusive, too fine and slippery to be caught in television's big hammy fist; that try as it might, television can't help but simplify the complications; personalise the abstract; sentimentalise the ideological and just forget about the deep structure – all of which are assumed to be at the heart of what my colleagues (on that side of the fence) like to call real history.[2]

---

[1] Emma Hanna, *The Great War on the Small Screen: Representing the First World War in Contemporary Britain* (Edinburgh: Edinburgh University Press, 2009), p. 163.
[2] Simon Schama, 'Television and the Trouble with History', in David Cannadine (ed.), *History and the Media* (London: Palgrave Macmillan, 2004), p. 20.

In articulating these fears, academics are not only tacitly admitting to the power of television but also acknowledging the influence that the medium has in shaping public memory. Such power has, unsurprisingly, long been appreciated by those within the television industry. Producers and directors have consistently maintained that the medium is particularly suited to the broadcasting of history, as its strengths lie in 'telling stories and anecdotes, creating atmosphere and mood, giving diffuse impressions'.[3]

This chapter will focus on the work of Kenneth Griffith. Obsessed with Britain's imperial past in general and the conflict in South Africa in particular, Griffith wrote and presented three seminal works for television between 1967 and 1999 that not only reacquainted the viewing public with the events of 1899 to 1902 but also tackled head on the orthodoxy of an honourable war. Although, as we have seen in the previous chapter, Leo Amery, in *The Times History of the War*, had raised concerns about the army's management and leadership in South Africa, this criticism had fallen well short of questioning the conflict's moral justification. For Amery, the war had been a necessary step in the nation's imperial mission. Such certainty mirrored the filmic version of the war presented in a series of short 'entertainments' to the avid cinema-going public of late Victorian and early Edwardian Britain.[4] The forty-four 'entertainment' films of the Boer War that were exhibited in Britain between November 1899 and December 1912 resolutely portrayed the fighting as part of a grand heroic narrative, a natural extension of the patriotic colonial campaigning of the late nineteenth century.[5] With the killing grounds of France and Flanders quickly supplanting the kopjes and veldt of South Africa in the public consciousness, the Boer War largely escaped the revisionism and debunking of the First World War and continued to be portrayed as the last good war.[6] Indeed, for some, the mechanised slaughter of total war served only to reinforce the myth of the noble Boer and chivalrous Tommy. The journalist, E. W. Smith, who covered the siege of Ladysmith for the *Morning Leader*, noted that the Boer War lacked the sustained horror of the Western Front, while J. F. C. Fuller, the military historian and theorist who served in both wars, insisted in his 1937 memoir, *The Last of the Gentlemen's Wars*, that 'by fighting in a sporting way we endowed the

---

[3]   Jerry Kuehl, 'History on the Public Screen', in Paul Smith (ed.), *The Historian and Film* (Cambridge: Cambridge University Press, 1976), pp. 178–179.

[4]   For a definition of 'entertainments' see Denis Gifford, *The British Film Catalogue 1895–1970: A Guide to Entertainment Films* (Newton Abbot: David & Charles, 1973).

[5]   Richard Schellhammer, 'How the Boer War Saved the Movies: The Depiction of the Boer War in Early British Cinema', http://westalabama.academia.edu/RichardSchellhammer/Papers (accessed 22 June 2010).

[6]   For more on the changing representations of the Great War, see Brian Bond, *The Unquiet Western Front: Britain's Role in Literature and History* (Cambridge: Cambridge University Press, 2007) and Todman, *The Great War*.

[Boer] war with a chivalrous atmosphere'.[7] Even Kitchener's bloody endgame of sweeping the veldt was sanitised in Winston Churchill's interwar autobiography as a time when 'humanity and civilization were never wholly banished, and both sides preserved amid frightful reciprocal injuries some mutual respect'.[8] This romanticised version of the fighting in South Africa, as Kenneth O. Morgan has noted, remained firmly entrenched in the public memory of the war for much of the twentieth century.[9] It was only with Kenneth Griffith's one-off documentary about the siege of Ladysmith, *Soldiers of the Widow* (BBC2, 1967), that the first serious challenge to the orthodoxy was mounted. This was followed up five years later by the four-part series *Sons of the Blood: The Great Boer War 1899–1902* (BBC 2, 1972) and, for the conflict's centenary, a two-part documentary, *Against the Empire: The Boer War* (BBC 2, 1999). To explore just how these three works raised new questions about the war and tested public perceptions, it will be necessary to look beyond the programmes' content and instead examine the process of selection and the editorial decisions that shaped Griffith's presentation.

Born in Tenby, Pembrokeshire, Kenneth Griffith was raised in a strictly Nonconformist household by his paternal grandparents. Later in life he would attribute his obsession for challenging the establishment line to the influence the dissenting tradition of Wesleyan Methodism had during his formative years.[10] Although he first came to national prominence as an actor, appearing in a number of British cinematic hits in the late 1950s and early 1960s, it was in what was effectively a second career as a documentary-maker that he was able to indulge fully his passion for questioning authority.[11] Described by the *Independent* as 'one of the most distinguished trouble-makers of his time', Griffith was drawn towards subjects that were calculated to antagonise opinion-makers on both the Right and the Left.[12] Thus, he supported Sinn Fein in *Hang Out your Brightest Colours: The Life and Death of Michael Collins* (ATV, 1972) and defended Afrikaners in *Zola Budd: The Girl Who Didn't Run* (BBC2, 1989). To Griffith, there was no contradiction in such eclecticism. In a nod towards the Nonconformity of his childhood, he described television as

[7] E. W Smith, quoted in Kenneth O. Morgan, 'The Boer War and the Media (1899–1902)', *Twentieth Century British History*, 13: 1 (2002), pp. 1–16; J. F. C. Fuller, *The Last of the Gentlemen's Wars*, p. xxv.

[8] Winston S. Churchill, *My Early Life: A Roving Commission* (London: Odhams Press Ltd, 1930), p. 351.

[9] Morgan, 'The Boer War and the Media', pp. 14–16.

[10] Dennis Baker, 'Griffith, Kenneth Reginald (1921–2006)', *Oxford Dictionary of National Biography* (Oxford: Oxford University Press, 2004); Kenneth Griffith, *The Fool's Pardon: The Autobiography of Kenneth Griffith* (London: Little Brown and Co., 1994), pp. 1–31.

[11] Among the more notable of Griffith's acting credits were roles in such films as *Lucky Jim* (1957), *I'm All Right Jack* (1959) and *Only Two Can Play* (1962).

[12] *Independent*, 26 June 2006.

'the biggest pulpit ever devised' where it would be possible to challenge the complacency of the nation's leaders and the viewing public by 'speaking up for those who were often ignored or suppressed'.[13] To this end, he told the controller of BBC2 in 1972, he felt compelled to address Britain's imperial past and what he saw as 'the terrible unconfessed questions hanging over it'. It was, he insisted, 'only by answering a few of these painful questions truthfully that the country would gain greater dignity in the eyes of the miserable world'.[14] The South African War was to be the battleground where Griffith would confront the British public with these uncomfortable truths.

Soldiers of the Widow (BBC2, 1967)

Kenneth Griffith was first and foremost an actor. In 1937, at the age of sixteen, he joined the Cambridge Festival Theatre as a bit player and was to continue appearing on stage, television and cinema screens until shortly before his death in 2004. Indeed, it was his renown as an actor, and his ability to hold an audience, that provided him with his first break as a documentary film-maker in 1965. On the back of a successful interview on BBC2's *Tonight* programme, in which he had talked at length about his fascination for the South African War, he was approached by the then controller of the channel, David Attenborough, to produce and present a film on the subject. Understandably apprehensive about his lack of professional experience, Griffith was, nevertheless, confident that 'new ground could be broken in the style of television communication'.[15] The 'pulpit' of the television documentary was, he later argued, the perfect platform for his particular skills set. By fusing the hobbyist's infectious enthusiasm with the actor's rhetorical flair he would, he claimed, be able to move on from the anodyne objectivity of the historian and tell 'his personal deeply felt truth'.[16]

Griffith chose the siege of Ladysmith as the focus for the documentary. He had first visited the town fifteen years earlier when on tour with the Old Vic and although he states in his autobiography that at the time he knew little about the South African War, the battlefield is, nonetheless, infused with a brooding prescience:

> The dead soldiers and the awful suffering they had endured were about to look at me and wink and smile and perhaps even hope that I would speak for them. The poor innocent British 'Tommies' and the shaggy strange ghosts of Dutch and Huguenot farmers: the Boers. Perhaps all of them hoped that

[13]   Griffith, *Fool's Pardon*, p. 184.
[14]   BBC Written Archives Centre (hereafter BBCWAC), T41/535/1, Kenneth Griffith to Robin Scott, 11 September 1972, p. 5.
[15]   Griffith, *Fool's Pardon*, p. 173.
[16]   Griffith, *Fool's Pardon*, pp. 178–179.

I would be interested enough in their old strivings and sufferings to listen carefully and perhaps even say something about it.[17]

Even allowing for the wisdom of hindsight, the passage provides an interesting insight into Griffith's approach to film-making. Fiercely passionate about the South African War, with a deeply held sense of right and wrong, he saw it as his duty to uncover the injustices of Britain's imperial past and to 'reveal the truths which even our political leaders ... preferred not to know'.[18] Central to this crusade were the ordinary soldiers, Boer and British. Committed to providing a voice for the 'exploited against the exploiters', Griffith felt a deep empathy for, and responsibility to, the rank and file troops of both sides.[19] He was, he argued, 'commissioned to be their advocate'.[20]

Unsurprisingly, perhaps, this highly personalised approach to documentary-making resulted in Griffith clashing with his BBC appointed director, Lawrence Gordon Clark. Given the responsibility for turning Griffith's somewhat rambling research notes into a coherent narrative, Clark produced, by Griffith's own admission, 'a typical, well-written, objective BBC television documentary script'.[21] However, to Griffith, Clark's work lacked passion. Not only, therefore, did he insist on rewriting the entire script but he also demanded that the completed film be re-edited to emphasise the 'dramatic continuity and tension' of the story.[22] For Griffith it was essential that he had personal control over all aspects of production if he was to fulfil his responsibilities as presenter and 'speak for those old soldiers, both Boers and Britons'.[23]

Aired on BBC2 on Saturday 27 May 1967 *Soldiers of the Widow* certainly bore the stamp of Griffith's passions and prejudices. The opening sequence sets the tone. Griffith, standing on top of Spion Kop by the graves of three soldiers from the Lancashire Fusiliers, stares sternly into the camera and asks accusingly, 'Why were these men executed and who executed them?'[24] A brief summary of the negotiations between Chamberlain, Milner and Kruger over the rights of the Uitlanders, the disenfranchised immigrants who flocked to Johannesburg to work in the goldmines, soon provides the answer: 'These Lancashire men were executed ... because of British greed for someone else's gold'.[25] The narrative swiftly moves on to the repeated attempts by the British under Sir Redvers Buller to relieve Sir George White's beleaguered garrison in Ladysmith. Charting the

---

17   Griffith, *Fool's Pardon*, p. 126.
18   Griffith, *Fool's Pardon*, p. 172.
19   BBCWAC, T41/535/1,Griffith to Scott, 11 September 1972, p. 6.
20   Griffith, *Fool's Pardon*, p. 176.
21   Griffith, *Fool's Pardon*, p. 175.
22   Griffith, *Fool's Pardon*, p. 182.
23   Griffith, *Fool's Pardon*, p. 175.
24   BBCWAC, T5426/2031, Post Production Script, dated 18 March 1967, p. 1.
25   BBCWAC, T5426/2031, Post Production Script, dated 18 March 1967, p. 2.

halting progress of the British army, from the first ill-fated engagement with the Boers at Colenso on 15 December 1899 to Ladysmith's eventual relief on 28 February 1900, Griffith directs his anger towards the senior commanders. Buller, in particular, is roundly condemned. Depicted as dithering and defeatist, the tragic consequences of his decision to ignore the advice of his subordinates and order a frontal assault of Boer positions at Colenso are brought home graphically. Accompanied by a soundtrack of martial music and rifle fire, Griffith intones that, 'not one man crossed the Tugela and lived – at this point the river was 10' deep'.[26] The programme then lingers on Buller's moral collapse in the aftermath of this debacle. As if inviting the viewer to explore the defeated general's inner demons, the camera zooms in for an intense close-up of Buller's face while the script goes through the details of his pessimistic heliograph exchange with White, in which it was suggested that the garrison should look to negotiate the best terms they could with the Boers.

Although the greatest censure is undoubtedly reserved for Buller, other commanders do not get off scot-free. Colonel Long's incompetence in allowing his artillery to be fatally exposed at Colenso is used to reinforce the impression that the army was officered by a corps of bungling reactionaries. Similarly, Brigadier-General Neville Lyttleton is held up by Griffith as a typical example of inept British leadership, but this time through indifference rather than incompetence:

> A Boer commandant named Pretorius addressed General Lyttleton on the battlefield [during a truce on 25 February 1900]: 'You British have had a rough time'. 'A rough time', replied Lyttleton, 'I suppose so, but we are all well paid for it'. 'Great God', said the Boer. Of course, Lyttleton was not telling the whole truth – many of the soldiers were not used to it – and most of them were appallingly paid – 1/– per day before deductions for doing the dying. The General must have temporarily forgotten his men.[27]

The programme concludes with a visual reminder that the relief was a British victory but one gained at too high a cost. With 'Land of Hope and Glory' playing in the background, a picture of Queen Victoria being greeted by rejoicing crowds in London soon fades into a final scene showing Griffith silhouetted against the sunset walking past the graves of Spion Kop.[28]

In its pre-screening advertising, the BBC was at pains to promote the documentary's subjective nature. Listed in the *Radio Times* as 'a personal view of the siege of Ladysmith', this signal about the programme's partisan approach was buttressed by an accompanying human interest piece which stressed that Griffith's enthusiasm for the subject and empathy for the British soldier had

---

[26]   BBCWAC, T5426/2031, Post Production Script, dated 18 March 1967, p. 5.
[27]   BBCWAC, T5426/2031, Post Production Script, dated 18 March 1967, p. 12.
[28]   BBCWAC, T5426/2031, Post Production Script, dated 18 March 1967, p. 14.

resulted in a 'very personal narrative'.[29] Although only achieving moderately low viewing figures, just 3.7 per cent of the viewing public, *Soldiers of the Widow* was, nonetheless, received relatively positively.[30] In part, this favourable response seems to have been directly due to, rather than in spite of, Griffith's lack of objectivity. The BBC's audience research department found that viewers were 'particularly impressed by the narrator's sincerity, his knowledge of and dedication to his subject', with one of the survey panel noting that, 'the programme served as an excellent, involved guide to the horror. In general, one would not want a professional actor as such a guide, but Mr Griffith was superb; so clearly a keen student of this period'.[31]

There were some dissenting voices. One viewer informed the BBC that, 'The biased commentary almost ruined the programme for me. I became more and more irritated and less and less interested'.[32] This was an opinion that was shared by the *Daily Telegraph*'s veteran TV critic Marsland Gander. Arguing that Griffith was 'too obviously pro-Boer and unnecessarily sarcastic and unsympathetic towards the British cause', Gander dismissed the programme as nothing more than 'anti-British propaganda'.[33] Yet, in the paper's letters column the following week, Griffith received support from an unlikely quarter. Adam Burnett, secretary of the Royal Overseas League, insisted that the 'programme was not "anti-British" but simply anti certain British attitudes at the time of the Relief of Ladysmith'. 'Mr Griffith was', Burnett continued, 'clearly full of sympathy for the ordinary soldier. His scorn was reserved for the folly of their leaders and for the wrong-headedness of the then Government. Such an attitude is surely no more "anti-British" than that of those who opposed Government action at the time of Suez'.[34] For Burnett, then, there was little to distinguish the militaristic adventuring of 1956 from that of 1899–1902; both smacked equally of imperial hubris.

Writing in the *Guardian*, Stanley Reynolds drew a parallel with an even more recent conflict. *Soldiers of the Widow* was, he claimed, 'more than a mere kick up the Empire's backside. No one could have watched it without thinking of Vietnam and the poor hillbillies, Negroes, and high school drop-outs who are fighting the war for the Rotarians'.[35] Reynolds agreed with Marsland Gander that the documentary was propaganda: 'but propaganda for the humanity of the common man, in this case, the Liverpool, Manchester and Dublin private

---

29   *Radio Times*, 25 May 1967, p. 4
30   BBCWAC, TFVR/67/346, BBC Audience Research Barometer of Viewing, 27 May 1967. By way of comparison programmes aired at the same time on BBC1 and ITV received audience shares of 9.8 per cent and 18.6 per cent respectively.
31   BBCWAC, TFVR/67/346, Audience Research Report, 28 June 1967.
32   BBCWAC, TFVR/67/346, Audience Research Report, 28 June 1967.
33   *Daily Telegraph*, 29 May 1967.
34   *Daily Telegraph*, 9 June 1967.
35   *Guardian*, 29 May 1967.

soldiers who fought in the Boer War'.[36] As such, he argued, Griffith's piece acted as a corrective to the 'stone statues, bronze plaques and civilised placenames' that celebrated the makers of the war.[37]

The comparisons drawn by Burnett and Reynolds to Suez and Vietnam serve as a useful reminder that television programmes do not appear in a vacuum. *Soldiers of the Widow* was broadcast in the wake of a number of books, plays and documentaries produced to coincide with the 50th anniversary of the outbreak of the First World War, the most notable of which was the BBC's twenty-six-part series *The Great War*. These commemorative productions buttressed the popular image of war as a futile waste in which a bungling officer class needlessly sacrificed the lives of the nation's youth.[38] Griffith's script captured perfectly this public mood. The BBC audience research report noted that although Griffith made 'no attempt to hide his dislike, anger and despair at the incompetence of British commanders ... viewers usually saw no reason to quarrel with him'.[39]

Indeed, in many ways, the South African War, more than the Great War, was better suited to Griffith's stated intention of 'evoking the horrors of war'.[40] With fewer surviving veterans and lacking the emotional intensity borne of the enormous losses of 1914–1918, the conflict against the Boers presented a televisual blank canvass upon which viewers' perceptions and attitudes could be shaped. Even those who had some knowledge of the period seemed prepared to accept Griffith's take on events. 'Please may we have more of these post mortems of British and foreign episodes of folly?' asked one respondent to the BBC's audience research poll: 'It's a good thing to see the story slightly slanted in favour of the Boers – after school history books'.[41]

Sons of the Blood: The Great Boer War 1899–1902 (BBC2, 1972)

In 1967, the *Guardian*'s television critic, Stanley Reynolds, had concluded his glowing review of *Soldiers of the Widow* on a note of concern. Certain that Griffith's foray into television history could have been nothing other than 'a cul-de-sac', he had voiced the fear that the actor would 'now retreat into his own profession leaving the television field to the mundane and merely professional makers of documentaries'.[42] In fact, Reynolds could not have been more wrong.

---

[36]   *Guardian*, 29 May 1967.
[37]   *Guardian*, 29 May 1967.
[38]   A. Danchev, 'Bunking and Debunking: The Controversies of the 1960s', in Brian Bond (ed.), *The First World War and British Military History* (Oxford: Oxford University Press, 1991), pp. 263–288. See also Mark Connelly, 'The Great War, Part 13: The Devil Is Coming', *Historical Journal of Film, Radio and Television*, 22: 1 (2002), pp. 21–28.
[39]   BBCWAC, TFVR/67/346, Audience Research Report, 28 June 1967.
[40]   *The Sunday Times*, 21 May 1967.
[41]   BBCWAC, TFVR/67/346, Audience Research Report, 28 June 1967.
[42]   *Guardian*, 29 May 1967.

Indeed, in his autobiography, Griffith cited the *Guardian*'s review as the critical factor in his decision to alter his career trajectory. It was, he recalled, only after reading Reynolds's lavish praise that he realised he was 'on the edge of terminating my life as an actor'.[43] Although the transformation was not quite as abrupt as this, as any filmography will reveal, it was nevertheless the case that Griffith did, from the beginning of the 1970s onwards, devote more and more of his time and energy to documentary-making. After writing and presenting a critical study of the life of Cecil Rhodes for the BBC in 1971, he returned the following year to the South African War for what was to be his most ambitious project, a four-part series charting the course of the conflict in its entirety.[44]

The gestation of *Sons of the Blood* was protracted and troubled. Disappointed by the BBC's failure to commission any more work on the back of the critical success of *Soldiers of the Widow*, Griffith looked elsewhere for support, eventually acquiring funding from an independent production company owned by the actor Patrick McGoohan. Although committed to an ambitious project charting the rise and fall of the British Empire, he chose to return to his first love, the war in South Africa, and began the process of recording interviews with veterans from both sides of the fighting. In late 1969, with fourteen hours of film from twenty-four veterans taped, Gordon Watkins, the chief assistant for programme development at the BBC, was approached about the possibility of turning the interviews into a four-part series covering all aspects of the conflict. However, lengthy negotiations over the financial terms of the contract meant that it was not until over a year later that a deal was finally secured.[45]

The difficulties did not end there. A greater stumbling block to the eventual realisation of the project lay with Griffith himself and, in particular, with his passionate commitment to the series and his absolute devotion to the old men he had interviewed. In a memorandum entitled 'How I would like to use the veterans' material and why', he made abundantly clear for Chris Brasher, the head of general features at the BBC, just how significant he considered the work to be:

> Personally, I cannot escape the importance of this material. It is now irreplaceable. I think it is the most important opportunity of my life. I managed, by the skin of my teeth, to get the story of our empire inscribed on film by the men who did the killing. And whatever we may think of that empire today, the truth is that our house is built on the rubble of it and the world is still rocking from the effects of it. I find it surprising that so few people – even in Britain – seem aware of this fact. We British are responsible for monumental crimes and often major moral contributions which are still

---

[43] Griffith, *Fool's Pardon*, p. 184.
[44] *A Touch of Churchill, a Touch of Hitler: The Life of Cecil Rhodes* (BBC, 1971).
[45] Griffith, *Fools Pardon*, pp. 201–205; BBCWAC, T41/535/1, Gordon Watkins to Chris Brasher, 28 January 1971.

bristling dangerously all around our globe … and few have begun to even swallow our significance, leave alone digest it. And the awful lessons to be learnt for today and tomorrow!

If the above is true, I believe that our only hope of even hearing that extraordinary heart really beat is by listening very carefully to these old warriors. We must give them a *full* hearing for so many reasons.[46]

Such fervour presented the BBC with a dilemma. Gordon Watkins, aware that the success of the enterprise depended on Griffith's 'enthusiasm, both in his to camera pieces and linking passages within the interviews', was anxious that the veterans should not be upstaged.[47] It was they, he insisted, 'who, without doubt, must be the stars of the films'.[48] The BBC thus insisted on tight editing, ensuring that the unmediated, in televisual terms at least, testimony of the veterans made up a large proportion of the on-screen time. Although Griffith was adamant that his narration was needed to turn 'the raw interviews … into a coherent story' and this would require each programme to be a minimum of fifty minutes long, the BBC remained unmoved and eventually four thirty-minute episodes were aired in August 1972.[49]

The series adopted a conventional chronological approach to the conflict. Yet, as one might expect given Griffith's guiding hand, this was no traditional account of imperial adventuring. A clear indication of the tenor of the programme can be found in Griffith's original pitch to Christopher Brasher. Having first been informed that the narrative would need to be divided into four parts, Brasher was provided with an unashamedly partisan breakdown of each episode:

First: Attitudes of Britain on the eve of war – in 1899. And the attitudes of a nation of farmers – the Boers – as they faced the onslaught of the British Empire.

Second: The great battles where passionate, puritan farmers fought the regiments of Waterloo and Sebastopol. And how the British lion was smitten from one end of southern Africa to the other.

Third: The heroic resistance. We burnt their homes and put their women and children into concentration camps, refugee camps or Burgher camps – call them what you will – where nearly 30,000 died from 'enteric fever' etc. The

[46] BBCWAC, T41/535/1, memorandum, 'How I would like to use the veterans' material and why', Kenneth Griffith to Chris Brasher, undated (emphasis in original).

[47] BBCWAC, T41/535/1, memorandum, Gordon Watkins to Chris Brasher, 8 December 1970.

[48] BBCWAC, T41/535/1, memorandum, Gordon Watkins to Chris Brasher, 8 December 1970.

[49] BBCWAC, T41/535/1, Griffith to Scott, 11 September 1972, p. 11

Boers finally came to terms – riding in from the high-veldt in their rags having previously smashed their Mausers. With justifiable pride they are called by white South Africans: The Bitter-Enders.

And *Fourth*: The Peace. The world that was forever changed. The responsibility. Who was to blame for the enormous crime? One charitable old Boer 'outstryder' answers the question: 'God; He should never have allowed it to happen'. I would have preferred the opportunity to have kicked Jo Chamberlain, Milner and Rhodes up the arse.[50]

For the viewer, the tone for the whole series was set in the opening sequence. The camera lingers on a few frail old men in uniform before panning away to watch Colonel Lang, the president of the South African War Veterans' Association, read out a brief communiqué from the Queen's Treasurer, Sir Charles Tryon, acknowledging the Association's disbandment as a result of 'old age and physical infirmities'. The scene then cuts to an indignant Griffith who, quivering with righteous fury, tells the viewer: 'I understand Tryon is the assistant to Sir Michael Adeane, secretary to Her Majesty the Queen. And his miserable reply from Buckingham Palace, I presume, is the very last royal response to the warriors of the Empire, upon which the sun never set'.[51] The following episodes continue to grind out a message of stoic and courageous Tommies being betrayed by uncaring and incompetent superiors. The needless suffering of the troops as a result of inept British leadership is brought home graphically. Thus episode two, *You Can't Miss a Man at 800 Yards …!*, focuses on the senior command's failure to adapt to Boer tactics at the battles of Modder River and Spion Kop. As the programme synopsis in the *Radio Times* made clear, the real heroes of the fighting were the rank and filers of both sides: 'But, as their memories of these tragic months reveal, the ordinary soldiers, Boer and British, retained their humanity – and their sense of humour'.[52]

Unsurprisingly, as had been the case with *Soldiers of the Widow*, the BBC was anxious that the series should be differentiated from its usual run of historical documentaries. The billing in the *Radio Times* gave prominence to the fact that the series was a personal interpretation of events and this point was reinforced by an interview with Griffith in the 12–18 August edition of the magazine, in which he decried the BBC's avowed impartiality. 'I've always been fascinated by militant objectivity', he confided to the interviewer, 'though it's not a failing of mine. I hope I never sink so low as to be objective about anything myself. I

[50]   BBCWAC, T41/535/1, memorandum, 'How I would like to use the veterans' material and why', Kenneth Griffith to Chris Brasher, undated. *Outstryder* is the Afrikaans word for a veteran of the South African War from the Boer side.
[51]   Griffith, *Fool's Pardon*, pp. 204–205.
[52]   *Radio Times*, 5–11 August 1972, p. 37.

do wish the BBC would stick its neck out a bit more'.[53] Yet, the Corporation was also keen to establish Griffith's credentials as an expert. A promotional piece for the documentary, which again appeared in the *Radio Times*, featured his extensive collection of South African War memorabilia.[54] *Sons of the Blood* may just be one man's view of the conflict, BBC viewers were being told, but it was nonetheless, a fully informed one.

Despite this attempt at reassurance, the partisan nature of Griffith's script did receive criticism. A number of viewers were angered by what they felt was the programme's anti-Empire bias. 'I am getting rather sick of all this British breast-beating' was how one respondent to the BBC's audience research survey put it.[55] Another viewer, W. G. Webber of Bristol, was equally concerned that it seemed to be 'fashionable nowadays to mock at the Empire and everything associated with it', and called on Griffith to 'study an impartial history of the time so he would see that all the faults do not lie with us'. Interestingly, Webber went on to support his argument by raising the issue of unprovoked Boer aggression through the invasion of Natal and the Cape Colony, a justification for British action that had featured in many of the dedication addresses at the unveiling of war memorials in the immediate aftermath of the fighting.[56]

Within the ranks of the BBC there was similar unease that the programme had strayed too far into polemic. Reviewing episode three, which had dealt with the guerrilla stage of the war, the Controller of Programme Schedules questioned whether what had been aired should have been labelled a documentary. Likening Griffith 'to a psychopath splitting spleen [sic] all over the screen', he said he 'would have preferred [the series] to have been presented as one disturbed man's view of the Boer War'.[57] Robin Scott, the Controller of BBC2, although more restrained in his language, was equally uncertain that the right note had been struck. 'I felt', he told Griffith in a letter nominally thanking him for his efforts, 'on some occasions more than others, that you could have allowed the facts and the reminiscences to speak for themselves without drawing personal conclusions or philosophising on the rights and wrongs of the whole episode in our history'.[58] Even Huw Wheldon, the BBC's managing director and a long-time champion of Griffith, was forced to admit to some reservations: 'I have always liked [Griffith] enormously and have always admired him as a narrator.

53 *Radio Times*, 12–18 August 1972, p. 5.
54 *Radio Times*, 29 July–4 August 1972, pp. 6–7.
55 BBCWAC, TFVR/72/462, Audience Research Report, 8 September 1972.
56 *Radio Times*, 9–15 September 1972, p. 64.
57 BBCWAC, T41/535/1, Television Weekly Programme Review, 23 August 1972.
58 BBCWAC, T41/535/1, Robin Scott to Kenneth Griffith, 1 September 1972.

What I distrust is his moralising. I do not feel that he is in a position to lay down precepts on moral philosophy with any authority'.[59]

Griffith, as one would expect, refuted outright such accusations. Having been asked to act as 'link-man', he told Scott in reply to his criticism, he was obligated to present the truth as he saw it. 'Since it was me in vision', he argued, 'I was there for what I stand for'.[60] This line of reasoning received support in the television reviews of the *Daily Telegraph* and *The Times*. For both papers, the success of *Sons of the Blood* lay not in its merits as academic history but rather in the drawing power of Griffith's passion and prejudice. The *Telegraph* attributed the fascination of the series to Griffith's 'obvious love-hate attitude to the Imperial past',[61] while Barry Norman of *The Times* positively revelled in the brazen partiality of the whole exercise. 'Whether it stands up as history or not I am unable to say', he told the paper's readers after the first episode, 'having no qualifications as an historian; but the man is quite magnificently and enjoyably biased'.[62]

Although Griffith's narration undoubtedly divided critical opinion, where there does seem to have been unanimity is in the positive response to the eye-witness testimony. Gordon Watkins, who as co-producer on the BBC's 1964 Great War documentary had worked closely with a number of war veterans, felt that the key to the success of *Sons of the Blood* lay in the interviews with the twenty-four old men who had served in the Boer and British ranks during the conflict.[63] Certainly all the evidence, from viewers as well as professional critics, would appear to support this contention.[64] In part, this popular acclaim can be attributed to the general upsurge in interest in this period for the stories and experiences of the ordinary man, for the history of everyday life. This was especially true for military history. The BBC's seminal 1964 documentary, *The Great War*, had established in the viewing public's mind the eyewitness account as an indispensable feature of television history.[65] The audience research report, commissioned by the BBC after the first episode of *Sons of the Blood* had been broadcast, confirmed this fact. The authors noted that there was general agreement within the viewing panel that the veterans' interviews had been

[59] BBCWAC, T41/535/1, Huw Wheldon to Head of Programme Purchasing, 30 January 1973; Griffith, *Fool's Pardon*, pp. 184–189.
[60] BBCWAC, T41/535/1, Griffith to Scott, 11 September 1972, p. 11.
[61] *Daily Telegraph*, 4 August 1972.
[62] *The Times*, 4 August 1972
[63] BBCWAC, T41/535/1, Television Weekly Programme Review, 23 August 1972.
[64] BBCWAC, TFVR/72/462, Audience Research Report, 8 September 1972; *Daily Telegraph*, 4 August 1972; *The Times*, 4 August 1972; *Sun*, 4 August 1972; *Radio Times*, 9–15 September 1972, p. 64.
[65] Hanna, *The Great War*, pp. 70–72.

central to the programme's success, 'because history is about people, and these were real people with something to say'.[66]

Yet, not only were viewers understandably captivated by seeing men in their nineties and above vividly recalling an event that two world wars had appeared to consign to a remote past, but they were also inclined to accept what was being said as the truth. Samuel Hynes, in his study of soldiers' frontline experience in the twentieth century, has observed that it is the memories of veterans that give war a human dimension that the objectivity of the professional historian or documentary-maker is unable to capture. 'If we would understand', he has argued, 'what war is like, and how it feels, we must turn away from history and its numbers, and seek the reality in the personal testimonies of the men who were there'.[67] Certainly the audience research report for *Sons of Blood* would appear to support Hynes's line of argument. By adding 'the substance of first-hand experience to Kenneth Griffith's narrative', it pointed out, 'the viewers' esteem for the informative qualities of the programme had been upheld'.[68] Indeed, the final paragraph of the report indicated that, for the majority of viewers, this 'esteem' extended beyond the recollections of the old men: 65 per cent of the viewing panel thought that Griffith's linking commentary helped to make the story clear and 68 per cent felt that his personality and opinions were given the right degree of prominence.[69] The report's authors attributed this high satisfaction rating to the nexus between Kenneth Griffith and the veterans. It was, they concluded, the obvious affection of the interviewer for his interviewees that added credibility to an otherwise contentious script.

In many ways, then, *Sons of the Blood* built on the questions raised in *Soldiers of the Widow*. Extensive use of veterans' testimony buttressed Griffith's anti-imperial slant. Although his insistence that 'because these old men were *there* they are too old to shovel any cant', falls foul of what Stéphane Audoin-Rouzeau and Annette Becker have called the 'tyranny of witness' – the assumption that only those who have experienced war have 'the moral, generational and historical right to discuss it' – it was, nonetheless, an assertion that seems to have resonated with large sections of the programme's audience.[70] Of the vast correspondence that the BBC received about the series, only one letter in every twenty-five took issue with Griffith's 'disapproval of Empire'.[71] For

---

[66]   BBCWAC, TFVR/72/462, Audience Research Report, 8 September 1972.
[67]   Samuel Hynes, *The Soldiers' Tale: Bearing Witness to Modern War* (London: Pimlico, 1997), pp. xii–xiii.
[68]   BBCWAC, TFVR/72/462, Audience Research Report, 8 September 1972.
[69]   BBCWAC, TFVR/72/462, Audience Research Report, 8 September 1972.
[70]   BBCWAC, T41/535/1,Griffith to Scott, 8 August 1971 (emphasis in the original); Stéphane Audoin-Rouzeau and Annette Becker, *1914–1918: Understanding the Great War* (London: Profile, 2000), pp. 37–39.
[71]   *Sun*, 17 August 1972.

the majority, the general feeling was that the programme had provided a 'new slant on events that were now old history'.[72] As one viewer told the *Radio Times*:

> [Griffith's] evocative and compassionate television … and his keen dramatic irony renders both the moment and the sweep of history extraordinarily vivid, and his piercing irony, biting down to the bedrock of character and the profound ambivalences of historical movements, is always at the service of a scepticism as compassionate as it is ruthless.[73]

For the centenary of the outbreak of the South African War, Griffith was to employ the piercing irony of his dramatic talents to their fullest extent as he undertook to produce for the BBC one final television history of the conflict.

Against the Empire: The Boer War (BBC2, 1999)

To mark the centenary anniversary of the South African War, Griffith was commissioned by the BBC to write and present a two-part documentary on the conflict. Although well into his late seventies, he approached the project with characteristic vigour. Interweaving interview clips culled from the *Sons of the Blood* archive with dramatic reconstructions of events in which the presenter impersonated key personalities (including, bizarrely, Emily Hobhouse), the programme saw Griffith at his impassioned best.

Once again, at the heart of his interpretation of the war was a desire to present the human cost of the conflict as the outcome of rapacious Randlords, duplicitous politicians and inept army commanders. A constant thread throughout the documentary was the causal significance of the newly discovered mineral wealth of the Transvaal and Orange Free State. Having outlined at length, in the first episode, the economic imperatives that he felt underpinned British diplomacy in the lead up to hostilities, Griffith ensured that his audience was not allowed to lose sight of such materialistic motives once the fighting started. A breathless account of the preparations for the battle of Spion Kop at the beginning of the second episode was interrupted to reacquaint viewers with the moral bankruptcy of British war aims: 'I think at this point we should remind ourselves here that the gold that was under Johannesburg was a long distance away. I think at this point we should still remind ourselves of the awful businessmen and politicians who had demanded that gold and that power – Cecil Rhodes, Milner, Chamberlain'.[74] A veteran's recollection of losing five close friends during the ensuing fighting was greeted with the mordant response: 'I hope the gold under Johannesburg was worth the effort'. An acerbic aside made abundantly clear the real reason for British

---

72   BBCWAC, TFVR/72/462, Audience Research Report, 8 September 1972.
73   *Radio Times*, 9–15 September 1972, p. 64.
74   *Against the Empire: The Boer War*, Part 2, 'Why Are We Here?' (BBC2, 1999).

reluctance to negotiate with the Boers after the fall of Bloemfontein: 'and, of course, the Johannesburg gold was considerably nearer'. The Boers may have been defeated, Griffith predictably concluded, but this was a hollow victory: 'the British Empire had won at a ghastly cost in human suffering and all for British material profit'.[75]

The British commanders in South Africa received similarly damning treatment. Sir Redvers Buller was 'inflexible and ill-informed' in his preparations for Spion Kop, while Lord Methuen was 'innocently confident' as he attempted to relieve Kimberley. But the greatest opprobrium was reserved for Lords Roberts and Kitchener. It was, viewers were told, these two senior officers who, as commanders-in-chief of the British forces in South Africa from the beginning of 1900 onwards, were responsible for the counter-insurgency policies that resulted in the 'virtual genocide' of the Afrikaner people. 'The Boers', Griffith lectured the audience, 'had great moral heroes and we had none'.[76]

Yet, as the script ground out a message of British imperial hubris, it was made clear that the rank and file of the British army should be excused blame. Unfailingly introduced by Griffith as 'my friend', a succession of elderly British veterans attested to their revulsion at the tactics they were ordered to adopt and their powerlessness to resist in the face of a rigid military authority. Oppressed by the 'social class arrangements of imperialism', these men were presented as being as much the victims of the war as were the Boers.[77] After one veteran's recollection that the pay of the dead was docked the price of the blanket their body was wrapped in, an indignant Griffith rejoined, 'That doesn't speak too well for England does it?'[78] Neither the high level of middle-class volunteerism in the aftermath of Black Week nor the debate over working-class engagement with the imperial mission was made reference to in the script.[79] This was colonial warfare reshaped for the political agenda of the late twentieth century; a history of the 'ignored or suppressed'.[80]

Despite the overtly polemical nature of Griffith's script, *Against the Empire* was a critical success. Although virtually all reviewers noted the anti-imperial agenda that underpinned the programme, few if any chose to disagree with the views being perpetuated. Andrew Billen in the *New Statesman* described

---

[75] *Against the Empire: The Boer War*, Part 2, 'Why Are We Here?' (BBC2, 1999).
[76] *Against the Empire: The Boer War*, Part 2, 'Why Are We Here?' (BBC2, 1999).
[77] *Against the Empire: The Boer War*, Part 2, 'Why Are We Here?' (BBC2, 1999).
[78] *Against the Empire: The Boer War*, Part 2, 'Why Are We Here?' (BBC2, 1999).
[79] Blanch, 'British Society and the War', in Warwick (ed.), *The South African War*, pp. 210–230; Miller, *Volunteers on the Veld*; Price, *An Imperial War*; S. Surridge, '"All You Soldiers Are What We Call Pro-Boer": The Military Critique of the South African Wars 1899–1902', *History*, 82 (1997), pp. 582–600; Clare Griffiths, 'Questioning the Abstract Morality of War: The Use and Abuse of Imperial Rhetoric in Soldiers' Letters during the Second South African War, 1899–1902', unpublished MA dissertation (University of Sheffield, 2009).
[80] Griffith, *Fool's Pardon*, p. 184.

the series as a 'two part, anti-British rant', but concluded that, 'Still, the hyper Griffith had a good war, in as much as he made vivid, morally involving television out of it'.[81] Paul Hoggart from *The Times* took a similar line. Griffith might be 'extraordinarily one-sided', he told the paper's readers, but that didn't stop him being 'clearly right that a greedy, conniving British oligarchy provoked the war to seize the Transvaal gold mines'.[82] It was, argued Christopher Dunkley, *Arts* magazines' TV critic, Griffith's power as a performer that accounted for this willingness to accept such a 'powerfully opinionated version of events'. 'Griffith', he wrote, 'is like some Byronic storyteller from the depths of time, posing by the camp fire and not just telling the tale, but captivating his audience by drawing them in to his enactment of the entire saga'.[83]

Yet, Dunkley's review also hinted at another reason why Griffith's proselytising resonated with the late twentieth-century viewing public. 'What emerges most powerfully from the series', the piece concluded:

> is the contrast between the confidence, indeed arrogance, of the British concerning their imperial cause in 1899 and the complete absence of such confidence in 1999. You begin to wonder whether – barring the Second World War with the attempted annihilation of the Jews – there is any war that posterity will not eventually come to see as wrong-headed.[84]

For Dunkley, therefore, the essential truth of *Against the Empire* lay not in its precise interpretation of the conflict between Briton and Boer but rather in the wider message it disseminated about the futility of war in general. Here the programme was neatly reflecting the contemporary public mood. To a post-imperial, post-Cold War Britain, the wars of a century ago with their high rhetoric of 'honour', 'sacrifice' and 'glory' seemed to a public schooled in the 'good' fight against Nazism to epitomise waste and stupidity.[85]

To a large extent this jaundiced modern memory of the conflicts of the nineteenth and early twentieth century had been established by studies of the First World War. A glut of populist books, films and television documentaries since the war had been rediscovered in the 1960s had led to the construction of what has been termed the 'Myth of the War'.[86] By the 1990s this 'myth', revolving around heartlessly incompetent generals sending naively idealistic soldiers to pointless deaths, had become firmly embedded in the public

81 *New Statesman*, 4 October 1999.
82 *The Times*, 2 October 1999.
83 *Arts*, 2 October 1999, p. 7.
84 *Arts*, 2 October 1999, p. 7.
85 Gary Sheffield, *Forgotten Victory: The First World War: Myths and Reality* (London: Headline, 2001), p. xix.
86 Samuel Hynes, *A War Imagined: The First World War and English Culture* (London: Bodley Head, 1990), pp. ix–x; Todman, *The Great War*, pp. xi–xii.

consciousness. Thus, it was hardly surprising that Griffith's account of the sacrifice and suffering of British troops on the veldt found a receptive audience. Indeed, even though *Against the Empire* made no attempt at comparative history, the parallels between the two wars did not go unnoticed by some reviewers. For Christopher Matthew of the *Daily Mail*, 'The slaughter of the young men of the Highland Brigade on Spion Kop on January 24th 1900, thanks entirely to dithering leadership, was a horrifying preview of a far greater slaughter to come'.[87] Similarly, for Simon Rockall of the *Bath Chronicle*, the shift from the jubilant send-offs of 1899 to shameful operations of Kitchener's counter-insurgency held echoes of the death of the spirit of 1914 on the battlefields of the Somme in 1916.[88] To Christopher Dunkley of *Arts* magazine, Griffith had shown that it was the South African War as much as the Great War that had ushered in the modern age. After the deaths of so many British soldiers at the hands of the Boers, what had become, he rhetorically asked his readers, of 'the idea of the war that is honourable, glorious, fought to Queensbury rules?' It had, he continued, been revealed for what it really was: 'A myth, intended to keep young men flocking to the colours and singing patriotic songs before dying in agony on foreign mountainsides'.[89]

For the viewing public, *Against the Empire* had firmly established the South African War in the same mould as the Great War. Fuller's claim that the war had been conducted in a time-honoured chivalrous code, that it had been the last of the gentlemen's wars, had been revealed by the series to be nothing more than outdated imperialistic nostalgia. For late twentieth-century Britain, the imperial rhetoric that underscored *The Times History*, or the messages about king and county, duty and honour, that lay at the heart of memorial iconography, no longer legitimised the human costs, on both sides, of the war. In the closing shot of *Against the Empire*, Griffith, walking away from the National Women's Memorial in Bloemfontein where the ashes of Emily Hobhouse are interred, pauses to remind the audience of the true significance of the war in South Africa: 'Oh, and incidentally, I repeat that the Second Anglo-Boer War was the beginning of the end of the British Empire'. It would appear that such an observation no longer elicited any sense of regret.

87   *Daily Mail*, 24 September 1999.
88   *Bath Chronicle*, 1 October 1999.
89   *Arts*, 2 October 1999, p. 2.

Conclusion

By the end of the nineteenth century, Britain was a nation fascinated by the military world. Although, for some of the working class, this fascination may have been darkened by a lingering sense of apprehension, for the vast majority of the population the army served as a symbol for national and imperial pride. In part, the roots of this burgeoning popularity can be found in the Victorian cult of personality. Already well established by the time of Gordon's death in Khartoum in 1885, the focus on the individual hero reached new heights during the South African War as the new mass daily newspapers seized on it to market the conflict and increase sales.[1] Yet, coeval with this development was a growing interest in, and idealisation of, the ordinary soldier. The popular image of Tommy Atkins, propagated through a variety of media, was of a stoic and increasingly abstemious imperial warrior sacrificing himself in the cause of a Christian mission.[2] Steve Attridge has argued that such imagery became even more pressing during the early stages of the South African War when public confidence in the armed forces took a knock as news of the reverses at Stormberg, Magersfontein and Colenso filtered through.[3] Representations of the ordinary soldier, which came to rival in popularity those of the officer, provided a romanticised vision of army life in which the enlisted man was idealised as the embodiment of Anglo-Saxon virtues. However, for this to work, the war itself had to be sanitised and reshaped into a traditional heroic narrative in which the subjugation of the Boers was a moral as well as military victory. This, of course, became increasingly difficult to do as the war entered into the drawn-out guerrilla stage.

---

[1] Paula M. Krebs, *Gender, Race and the Writing of Empire: Public Discourse and the Boer War* (Cambridge: Cambridge University Press, 1999), pp. 14–15; Cynthia Behrman, 'The After-Life of General Gordon', *Albion*, 3: 2 (Summer 1971), pp. 47–61.

[2] John Springhall, 'Up Guards and At Them', in J. Mackenzie, *Imperialism and Popular Culture* (Manchester: Manchester University Press, 1986), pp. 69–71; Anderson, 'The Growth of Christian Militarism'.

[3] Steve Attridge, *Nationalism, Imperialism and Identity in Late Victorian Culture* (Basingstoke: Palgrave, 2007), pp. 64–68.

These themes and challenges were reflected and crystallised in the war memorial movement that followed the cessation of hostilities in South Africa. While the individual hero was still central to much of the commemorative activity, especially where a community felt slighted by the perceived maltreatment of a local celebrity, there was a growing shift towards the memorialisation of the ordinary soldier.[4] This democratisation of memory was indicative of not only Edwardian civil society's greater acceptance and understanding of the military world, but also its idealisation of the qualities that underpinned army service. By holding up the ordinary soldier as the paragon of British manhood, civilian communities were able to address their fears about national efficiency and racial degeneracy. The war was seen as redemptive. Thus, monuments honouring the service of their peers would, it was felt, help to jolt the public schoolboy out of his indolence and remind the industrial worker of the importance of patriotism. This vision of war as a moment of salvation very much reflected the Edwardian mindset and was to feature prominently in the rituals of remembrance following the First World War.[5]

Memorial iconography and dedication ceremonies also served as celebrations of an aspirational set of national character traits. Figurative monuments depicting heroic charges or self-sacrificing last-stands were frequently complemented at unveiling ceremonies by speeches focusing on abstract virtues and concepts. More than anything else, this was a reflection of the civic, regimental or institutional pride that underpinned much of the commemorative activity in this period. Those being honoured were put forward as the ideal representatives of their parent communities. This was especially, but not exclusively, true for those who had volunteered for active service. The war records of these citizen-soldiers were regarded as personifying and defining the values that the wider community held dear. Occasionally, such was the contentious nature of the conflict's origins, officiating dignitaries felt it necessary to divorce the qualities that the fallen were thought to enshrine from the specifics of the war. This was the case in Rochdale and Llanelli where opposition to the war had been markedly pronounced.[6] However, for the vast majority of communities, no such doubts were allowed to creep in and the struggle against the Boers was portrayed as a necessary step in the nation's great imperial mission. The didacticism of South African war memorialisation was augmented by the relatively peripheral role the bereaved played in the remembrance process. Although grief was in evidence, particularly at the intimate level of family commemoration, it was rarely the predominant or overriding emotion. As a result, dedication ceremonies were celebrations of collective values and achievements, frequently carnivalesque in

---

4   See monuments to Buller and Wauchope, pp. 114–20 above.
5   See Glenn R. Wilkinson, '"The Blessings of War": The Depiction of Military Force in Edwardian Newspapers', *Journal of Contemporary History*, 33: 1 (January 1998), pp. 97–115.
6   See pp. 24–25 and p. 43 above.

mood, in which the needs of the bereaved were not allowed to cloud the tone of self-congratulation. This was to change in the 1920s when the substantially higher death rate and more emotionally charged atmosphere of the Great War were to see a much greater emphasis placed on mourning in the construction of memory sites.[7]

The two dominant, contemporary written histories of the war, *The Times History of the War in South Africa* and Maurice's official history, buttressed the triumphal typography of the memorial movement. Leo Amery, though more inclined than those charged with overseeing the memorialisation process to highlight shortcomings in the conduct and management of military operations against the Boers, nonetheless presented readers of *The Times History* with an equally sanitised version of events. His certainty about the sanctity of Britain's imperial mission and his admiration for the fighting spirit of the Boer Republics reinforced the vision of a necessary and heroic struggle fought along gentlemanly lines. Further mirroring the monumental commemoration of the fighting, the work also served a didactic function. By presenting the image of a hide-bound military establishment unable to cope with the demands of modern warfare, a forceful case was made for army reform. This representation of the conflict, dominated by the twin themes of chivalry and incompetence was, albeit inadvertently, bolstered by Frederick Maurice's official history. Firstly, the War Office's insistence that Maurice had to excise all material that might give offence to the Boers helped to confirm the notion of a gentleman's war by validating the public's perception of an honourable struggle waged against a noble adversary. Secondly, allegations in the press about censorship pointed to an establishment cover-up and thus appeared to corroborate Amery's claims about administrative mismanagement and military ineptitude.

More importantly for the memory of the war, in both histories the ordinary soldier continued to be represented as the embodiment of national values and virtues. Amery, although critical of the army's performance, went to great lengths not to disparage the spirit or character of the fighting man. The shortcomings in Britain's military prowess that the war had revealed were, he argued, nothing to do with a lack of moral fibre within the ranks of the army but rather the product of years of complacency from the authorities and civil society in general. Such luminaries as Rudyard Kipling fully appreciated this distinction. The moral to be drawn from the criticisms of Volume II was, he observed, 'that the nation lost Spion Kop'.[8] Others, however, were less sure. One veteran of the Natal campaign, convinced that the history was little more than a 'damnable libel on the British Army', chose to pursue his grievance through the law courts.[9] The

---

[7]   Winter, *Sites of Memory*, chapter 2.
[8]   ChCA, Leopold Amery papers, AMEL 2/5/4, Kipling to Amery, 4 May 1905.
[9]   Amery, *Political Life*, p. 366

vigour with which the case was defended, and won, attests to the importance that Amery attached to the issue.[10]

The representation of war enshrined in the pages of Amery's and Maurice's histories and through the iconography of the war memorials dominated the public image for next half century. Not until Kenneth Griffith reintroduced the conflict to the wider public through three BBC television documentaries between 1967 and 1999 was the orthodoxy of a gentlemen's war seriously challenged. A passionate if somewhat eccentric campaigner against perceived injustice, Griffith moulded the conflict to fit his worldview of an on-going struggle between the privileged and the oppressed. In this new interpretation, it was the ordinary British soldier as well as the Boer commando who was presented as the victim of imperial hubris. Misgivings about the legitimacy of British war aims, which had been largely expunged from the collective memory during the memorialisation process and the writing of the histories, were now given centre stage. In the televised version of the war, the civilising mission of British imperialism was replaced by the egregious materialism of a corrupt plutocracy. The military authorities received equally damning treatment. A succession of elderly veterans, Boer and British, testified on camera not only to the professional incompetence of the British army's high command but also to their callous disregard for the lives of combatants and non-combatants from both sides. This revised configuration of events mirrored the changing cultural landscape. The rediscovery of the Great War and the growing interest in the human face of battle had established, to borrow once again Ashplant, Dawson and Roper's phrase, new templates of war remembrance.[11] Not only did military operations against the Boers fit neatly into these reworked templates but they also, as Bill Nasson has pointed out, resonated with a liberal anti-war public who could see in them a parallel with America's conflict in Vietnam.[12] Yet, in one crucial way, the televised war of Griffith's documentaries remained true to the representation of events constructed through the war memorial movement and histories. Notwithstanding his righteous outrage, Griffith still presented the war as a heroic narrative, with the ordinary soldier centre stage. The personal qualities of what Griffith called 'these poor bloody footsloggers' were being held up, as they had been in so many of the remembrance rituals in the immediate post-war years, as worthy of emulation.[13] Yet, an important shift had occurred. The focus was now on the humanity of the combatants not their national

[10] See Amery, *Political Life*, pp. 366–367.
[11] Ashplant, Dawson and Roper, *The Politics of War Commemoration*, pp. 34–36. See also pp. 00–00 above.
[12] Bill Nasson, 'Waging Total War in South Africa: Some Centenary Writings on the Anglo-Boer War, 1899–1902', *Journal of Military History*, 66: 3 (July 2002), p. 828.
[13] BBCWAC, T41/535/1, Kenneth Griffith to Robin Scott, 11 September 1972, p. 5.

devotion. For Griffith, the war was a lesson in the resilience of the human spirit, a celebration of a common humanity that crossed national boundaries.

The South African War has both shaped and reflected the remembrance of the Great War. The intense commemorative activity that followed the signing of the Peace of Vereeniging established new approaches and themes in memorialisation. A potent admixture of frontline journalism, stirring militarism and mass volunteerism had not only transfixed civil society during hostilities against the Boers but had also provided the impetus for a diverse range of individuals and communities to engage actively in the post-war construction of memory. This latter phenomenon was to be repeated, though on a much larger scale, after 1918. As Britain entered the second half of the twentieth century, with the popular perception of what constituted a moral war having been redefined by the defeat of Nazism, it was the turn of the South African War to be refashioned in the mould of the Great War. Futility, incompetence and horror, the central tenets of a new historiographical trend from the 1960s onwards, seemed to serve as the perfect shorthand for the last of Victoria's colonial wars. Yet, what remained unchanged in this reconfiguration of the memory of the war was the idealisation of the frontline soldier. Although serving different purposes according to the divergent agendas of controlling agencies, the memory of the ordinary soldier remained sacrosanct throughout. This thread of continuity points towards a democratisation in war remembrance, the beginnings of which can be traced to the conflict in South Africa. In this respect, as in so many others, the South African War can be identified as an important moment of transition.

Bibliography

Unpublished Primary Sources

Ashton-under-Lyne, Manchester Regiment Archives
MR1/3/1/3 A History of the Manchester Regiment, anonymous, undated pamphlet
MR3/18/11 *The War Memorial at Manchester* (Portsmouth: Gale and Polden Ltd, 1908)

Bedford, Bedfordshire and Luton Archives (BLA)
L/c/Cha, Bedford County Lieutenancy, county meeting minutes

Bury, The Fusilier Museum (TFM)
The Lancashire Fusiliers' Annual, 1903–1905

Bury St Edmunds, Suffolk Record Office
GB554/23/1 Supplement to the *Bury and Norwich Post*, 22 November 1904

Cambridge, Churchill College Archives (ChCA)
AMEL 1/1/6–11 Leopold Amery papers

Canterbury Cathedral Archives (CCA)
CC/AC/23 Parks Committee minutes, 1904
CC/AC/23/1 Canterbury City Council minutes, 1904
CC/BB149 Canterbury City Council minutes, 1923

Canterbury, Howe Barracks, Royal East Kent Regiment Archives
Dragon

Charterhouse School Archive (CSA)
Carthusian, 1900–1905
83/8/2 Sir Richard Jebb's unveiling address, 1903

Chatham, Royal Engineers Museum (REM)
RO270 Royal Engineers War Memorial Committee Book, Corps meeting minutes, 1902–1903
RE Journal
Sapper

Cheltenham College Archive
Cheltonian, 1901–1903

Chichester, West Sussex Record Office (WSRO)
Par301/4/31, Holy Trinity Cuckfield parish magazine, 1903–1904
RSR/MS/11/6, Royal Sussex Memorial Fund, minutes, 1902–1903

Crewe Local Studies Centre
CP/Crew/O Crewe Memorial Unveiling Programme
C/Crew/C *Programme for the Crewe Patriotic Carnival and Demonstration to Celebrate the Unveiling of the Crewe (South Africa) Volunteers' and Reservists' Memorial*

Dover, East Kent Archives (EKA)
Do/AMS/3 Queen Victoria Memorial Committee, minutes
Do/CA/10/5/7 South African War Fund Committee, minutes
Do/CA17/1/17 South African Memorial Committee, minutes, 1904

Dulwich, Dulwich College Archive (DCA)
Alleynian, 1901–1903

Eton College Archive (ECA)
Eton College Chronicle, 1902–1908
Misc/EME/1 Eton Memorial Fund Balance Sheet, 1903
Misc/EMF/1 'Eton Officers Memorial 1902', committee meeting minutes
Misc/EMF8 'Eton Memorial'
Misc/EMF/8/1 'List of Etonians who served in the South African War between October 11th 1899 and May 31st 1902'

Exeter, Devon Record Office (DRO)
ECA 12/20, Exeter City Council Estates Committee Reports
2065Madd28/Z9, *Official Souvenir of the Unveiling of the Buller Memorial*

Forfar Local History Library
25:B/OGI, 'Inscription on the Airlie Monument, Tulloch Hill, Cortachy'

Glasgow, Royal Highland Fusiliers Museum (RHFM)
Highland Light Infantry Chronicle, 1906

Harrow School Archive (HAS)
Harrovian, 1901–1903

Ilford, Redbridge Local History Library
Ilford Urban District Council Minutes, 1904–1905

Ipswich, Suffolk Record Office (SRO)
352.1409/Ips, Ipswich Town Council Minute Book, 1904–1906
GB554/W/13–16, *Journal of the 2nd Battalion XIIth (Suffolk) Regiment*, 1903

Leicester, Leicester and Rutland Record Office (LRRO)
DE171, The Leicestershire South African War Memorial Committee minutes,

London, Honourable Artillery Company Archive (HACA)
Court Minutes, Vol. JJ, 1899–1905
Moeller Papers

London, British Library
Field Marshal Sir George White papers, Grant Richards Archive

London, King's College, Liddell Hart Centre for Military Archives
The papers of Sir Frederick Maurice

London Metropolitan Archives
P84/JUD/58 St Jude, Kensington, vestry minute book, 1901

London, News International Archive
Moberly Bell papers, Bell Letter Book 23

London, The National Archives (TNA)
WO132/14 Lord Methuen's Despatches
WO32/4755–4763 Official History of the War in South Africa, correspondence
WORK 20/55 Royal Marines' Memorial, 1901–1911
WORK 20/57 Carabiniers' Memorial, 1905–1906.
WORK 20/59 Royal Artillery Memorial, 1905–1912

Maidstone, Royal West Kent Regiment Archives
Queen's Own Gazette, 1902

Middlesbrough, Dorman Memorial Museum Archive (DMMA)
Proceedings of Middlesbrough Town Council 1903–1904

Pembrokeshire Record Office (PRO)
HDX/94/1, *Booklet on the Pembrokeshire South African War Memorial*, 1908

Reading, BBC Written Archives Centre (BBCWAC)
Kenneth Griffith papers

Simon Langton Boys' School Archives
Langtonian, 1902–1903

Tonbridge School Archives
Tonbridgian, 1905

Wellington College Archive (WCA)
The Wellingtonian, 1900–1901
Wellington Year Book 1900

Winchester College Archive (WinCA)
J10/3 Circular: Wykehamist South African War Memorial Fund, 1901
J10/5/1 Circular: Wykehamist South African War Memorial Fund, 1903
Wykehamist, 1900–1902

Woking, Surrey History Centre (SHC)
QRWS/1/8/2/22, Queen's Royal West Surrey Regiment, unveiling programme

Journals and Newspapers

Alyth Guardian
Army and Navy Gazette: Journal of the Militia and Volunteer Forces
Arts
Bath Chronicle
Bedfordshire Times and Independent
Birmingham Daily Mail
Birmingham Daily Post
Brighton Herald
Bury Free Press
Bury and Norwich Post
Chatham News
Chester Chronicle
City Press
Crewe Chronicle
Daily Mail
Daily Mirror
Daily Telegraph
Darlington and Stockton Times
Devon and Exeter Gazette
Dundee Courier and Argus
Dover Express
East Anglian Daily Times
East Ham Echo
Edinburgh Evening News
Evening News
Folkestone Express
Forfar Herald
Glasgow Herald
Globe and Laurel. The Journal of the Royal Marine Light Infantry
Graphic
Guardian
Halifax Courier
Hampstead Advertiser
Hampstead and Highgate Express
Household Brigade Magazine
Huddersfield Chronicle
Huddersfield Examiner
Ilford Recorder
Independent
Islington Daily Gazette
Jewish Chronicle
Kensington News
Kentish Gazette and Canterbury Press
Kentish Observer
Leicester Daily Post

Lenton Times: The Magazine of the Lenton Local History Society
Liverpool Mercury
Llanelli Mercury
London Gazette
Manchester Courier
Manchester Evening News
Manchester Guardian
Midland Counties Tribune
New Statesman
Northern Echo
Norwich Mercury
Nursing Record and Hospital World
Observer
Pall Mall Gazette
Penny Illustrated Paper and Illustrated Times
Prescot Reporter
Radio Times
Regiment: An Illustrated Military Journal for Everybody
Rochdale Observer
Salford Chronicle
Salford Reporter
Scotsman
Slough Observer
Spectator
Standard
Star
St Helens Advertiser
Sun
The Sunday Times
Thistle
The Times
The Times Literary Supplement
Tonbridge Free Press
Warrington Guardian
Warrington Observer
Weekly Scotsman
Westminster Gazette
Westminster and Pimlico News
Wigan Examiner
Yorkshire Evening Post
Yorkshire Weekly Herald

Primary Published Material

Amery, Leo, *My Political Life, Volume One: England before the Storm, 1896–1914* (London: Hutchinson, 1953)

Amery, Leo (ed.), *The Times History of the War in South Africa* (London: Sampson Low, 1900–1909)

Barker, H. R., *West Suffolk Illustrated* (Bury St Edmunds: F. G. Pawsey, 1907)

Boyle, L. R. C., *Two Years at the Front with the Mounted Infantry. Being the Diary of B. Moeller. With a Memoir by Lieutenant-Colonel L. R. C. Boyle, HAC* (London: Grant Richards, 1903)

A British Officer, 'The Literature of the South African War, 1899–1902', *American Historical Review*, 12 (1907)

Churchill, Winston S., *My Early Life: A Roving Commission* (London: Odhams Press Ltd, 1930)

Churchill, Winston S., *The World Crisis* (London: Penguin, 1938, first published 1927)

Conan Doyle, Arthur, *The Great Boer War* (London: Smith, Elder and Co., 1900)

Conan Doyle, Arthur, *The War in South Africa: Its Cause and Conduct* (London: Smith, Elder and Co., 1902).

du Moulin, Louis Eugene, *Two Years on Trek: Being Some Account of the Royal Sussex Regiment in South Africa* (London: Murray and Co., 1907)

Fuller, J. F. C., *The Last of the Gentlemen's Wars: A Subaltern's Journal of the War in South Africa, 1899–1902* (London: Faber and Faber, 1937)

Gildea, J., *For Remembrance and in Honour of Those Who Lost Their Lives in the South African War, 1899–1902* (London: Eyre and Spottiswoode Ltd, 1911)

Gleichen, Edward, *London's Open-Air Statuary* (London: Longmans, Green and Co., 1928)

Historical Record of the 3rd County of London (Sharpshooters) Imperial Yeomanry, 1900–1905 (London: no imprint, 1905)

Hamilton, Ian, *Compulsory Service: A Study of the Question in the Light of Experience* (London: John Murray, 1910)

Hamilton, Ian and Sampson, Victor, *Anti-Commando* (London: Faber & Faber, 1931)

Lloyd George, David, *War Memoirs* (London: Nicolson and Watson, 1936)

Maurice, Frederick, *History of the War in South Africa, 1899–1902* (London: Hurst and Blackett, 1906–1910).

McDonnell, Michael F. J., *A History of St. Paul's School* (London: Chapman and Hall, 1909)

Neve, A. H., *The Tonbridge of Yesterday* (Tonbridge: Tonbridge Free Press, 1933)

Queen's Royal West Surrey Regiment Unveiling Souvenir (Guildford: Surrey Advertiser and County Times, 1904)

Suffolk County Handbook, 1906 (Ipswich: East Anglia Daily News, 1906)

Tanner, Lawrence, E., *Westminster School: Its Buildings and their Associations* (London: Philip Allan and Co., 1923)

Webb, A. H., *A History of the 12th (Suffolk Regiment)* (London: Spottiswoode and Co., 1914)

Secondary Published Material

Anderson, Olive, *A Liberal State at War: English Politics and Economics during the Crimean War* (London: Macmillan, 1967)

Ash, Chris, *The If Man: Leander Starr Jameson, the inspiration for Kipling's Masterpiece* (Solihull: Helion and Company, 2012)

Ashplant, T. G., Dawson, G. and Roper, M. (eds), *The Politics of War Commemoration* (London: Routledge, 2000)

Attridge, Steve, *Nationalism, Imperialism and Identity in Late Victorian Culture* (Basingstoke: Palgrave, 2007)

Audoin-Rouzeau, Stephanie and Becker, Annette, *1914–1918: Understanding the Great War* (London: Profile, 2000)

Barnes, John and Nicholson, David (eds), *The Leo Amery Diaries, Volume 1: 1896–1929* (London: Hutchinson, 1980)

Beckett, Ian, *Riflemen Form: A Study of the Rifle Volunteer Movement, 1859–1908* (Aldershot: Ogilby Trust, 1982)

Bennett, Will, *Absent-Minded Beggars: The Volunteers in the Boer War* (Barnsley: Leo Cooper, 1999)

Bergin, T., *Salford: A City and its Past* (Salford: City of Salford Cultural Services Department, 1975).

Bond, Brian, *The Unquiet Western Front: Britain's Role in Literature and History* (Cambridge: Cambridge University Press, 2007)

Borg, Alan, *War Memorials: From Antiquity to the Present* (London: Leo Cooper, 1991)

Bowman, Timothy and Connelly, Mark, *The Edwardian Army: Recruiting, Training, and Deploying the British Army, 1902–1914* (Oxford: Oxford University Press, 2012)

Boyle, Andrew, *The Riddle of Erskine Childers* (London: Hutchinson, 1977)

British Sculpture, 1850–1914 (London: Fine Arts Society, 1968)

Caldwell, T. C., *The Anglo-Boer War: Why Was it Fought? Who Was Responsible?* (Lexington: D. C. Heath, 1968).

Cannadine, David (ed.), *History and the Media* (London: Palgrave Macmillan, 2004)

Cash, Mary, *A History of Islington* (London: Historical Publications Ltd, 2005)

Castle, Ian, *Majuba 1881: Hill of Destiny* (Colchester: Osprey, 1996)

Cavanagh, Terry, *Public Sculpture of Leicestershire and Rutland* (Liverpool: Liverpool University Press, 2000)

Cavanagh, Terry, *Public Sculpture of Liverpool* (Liverpool: Liverpool University Press, 1997)

Chaplin, H. D., *The Queen's Own Royal West Kent Regiment, 1881–1914* (Maidstone: Queen's Own Regimental History, 1959)

Cole, John, *Rochdale Revisited: A Town and its People, Volume II* (Littleborough: George Kelsall, 1990)

Connelly, Mark, *The Great War: Memory and Ritual: Commemoration in the City and East London, 1916–1939* (Woodbridge: Boydell and Brewer, 2002)

Craig, F., *British Parliamentary Election Results, 1885–1918* (Chichester: Parliamentary Research Services, 1989)

Cunningham, Hugh, *The Volunteer Force: A Social and Political History, 1859–1908* (London: Croom Helm, 1975)

Cuthbertson, Greg, Grundlingh, A. and Suttie, M.-L. (eds) *Writing a Wider War: Rethinking Gender, Race and Identity in the South African War, 1899–1902* (Athens, OH: Ohio University Press, 2002)

Dennis, Peter and Grey, Jeffrey (eds), *The Boer War: Army, Nation and Empire* (Canberra: Army History Unit, 2000)

Donaldson, Peter, *Ritual and Remembrance: The Memorialisation of the Great War in East Kent* (Newcastle: Cambridge Scholars Press, 2006)

Dorman Memorial Museum: History and Guide (Middlesbrough: County Borough of Middlesbrough, 1959)

Dorment, R., *Sir Alfred Gilbert* (London: Weidenfeld and Nicolson, 1986)

Farwell, Byron, *The Great Anglo-Boer War* (New York: Harper and Row, 1976)

Feldman, David, *Englishmen and Jews: Social Relations and Political Culture, 1840–1914* (New Haven and London: Yale University Press, 1994)

Gaffney, Angela, *Aftermath: Remembering the Great War in Wales* (Cardiff: University of Wales Press, 1998)

Gifford, Denis, *The British Film Catalogue 1895–1970: A Guide to Entertainment Films* (Newton Abbot: David & Charles, 1973)

Gill, Robin, *The Myth of the Empty Church* (London: SPCK Publishing, 1993)

Girouard, Marc, *The Return to Camelot: Chivalry and the English Gentleman* (New Haven and London: Yale University Press, 1981)

Goebel, Stefan, *The Great War and Medieval Memory: War, Remembrance and Medievalism in Britain and Germany, 1914–1940* (Cambridge: Cambridge University Press, 2007)

Gooch, John (ed.), *The Boer War: Direction, Experience and Image* (London: Frank Crass, 2000)

Green, Andrew, *Writing the Great War: Sir James Edmonds and the Official Histories, 1915–1916* (London: Frank Cass, 2003)

Gregory, Adrian, *The Silence of Memory: Armistice Day, 1919–1946* (Oxford: Berg, 1994)

Grey, A. Stuart, *Edwardian Architecture: A Biographical Survey* (London: Duckworth, 1985)

Griffith, Kenneth, *The Fool's Pardon: The Autobiography of Kenneth Griffith* (London: Little Brown and Co., 1994)

Hanna, Emma, *The Great War on the Small Screen: Representing the First World War in Contemporary Britain* (Edinburgh: Edinburgh University Press, 2009)

Harris, Jose, *Private Lives, Public Spirit: A Social History of Britain, 1870–1914* (Oxford: Oxford University Press, 1993)

Hichberger, J., *Images of the Army: The Military in British Art, 1815–1914* (Manchester: Manchester University Press, 1988)

The History of The Times: *The Twentieth Century Test, 1884–1912* (London: *The Times*, 1947)

Hodson-Pressinger, Selwyn, *Adrian Jones, 1845–1938, British Sculptor and Artist* (London: Sandilands Press, 1997)

Hodson-Pressinger, Selwyn, *Captain Adrian Jones, 1845–1938: Military and Equine Works* (London: Sandilands Press, 2004)

Holt, Edgar, *The Boer War* (London: Putnam, 1958)

Holt, Richard, *Sport and the British: A Modern History* (Broadbridge: Clarendon Press, 1990)

Hynes, Samuel, *The Soldiers' Tale: Bearing Witness to Modern War* (London: Pimlico, 1997)

Hynes, Samuel, *A War Imagined: The First World War and English Culture* (London: Bodley Head, 1990)

Inglis, Ken, *Sacred Places. War Memorials in the Australian Landscape* (Melbourne: Melbourne University Press, 1998)

Jalland, Pat, *Death in the Victorian Family* (Oxford: Oxford University Press, 1996)

Kessler, Stowell, *The Black Concentration Camps of the Anglo-Boer War, 1899–1902* (Bloemfontein: War Museum of the Boer Republics, 2012)

King, Alex, *Memorials of the Great War in Britain: The Symbolism and Politics of Remembrance* (Oxford: Berg, 1998)

Koss, Stephen, *The Rise and Fall of the Political Press in Britain* (London: Hamish Hamilton, 1984)

Krebs, Paula M., *Gender, Race and the Writing of Empire: Public Discourse and the Boer War* (Cambridge: Cambridge University Press, 1999)

Kruger, Rayne, *Goodbye Dolly Gray: The Story of the Boer War* (London: Cassell, 1959).

Laity, Paul, *The British Peace Movement, 1870–1914* (Oxford: Oxford University Press, 2002)

Lowry, Donal (ed.), *The South African War Reappraised* (Manchester: Manchester University Press, 2000)

Luvaas, Jay, *The Education of an Army: British Military Thought, 1815–1940* (London: Cassell, 1965)

Maclean, Chris and Phillips, Jock, *The Sorrow and the Pride: New Zealand War Memorials* (Wellington: GP Books, 1990)

Mangan, J. A., *The Games Ethic and Imperialism* (Harmondsworth: Viking, 1986)

McCracken, Donal P. (ed.), *Ireland and South Africa in Modern Times* (Durban: Southern African–Irish Studies, 1996)

Mileham, Patrick, *Wellington College: The First 150 Years* (London: Third Millennium Publishing, 2008)

Miller, Stephen, *Lord Methuen and the British Army: Failure and Redemption in South Africa* (Abingdon: Frank Cass, 1999)

Miller, Stephen, *Volunteers on the Veld: Britain's Citizen-Soldiers and the South African War, 1899–1902* (Oklahoma: Oklahoma University Press, 2007)

Mosse, George, *Fallen Soldiers: Reshaping the Memory of the World Wars* (Oxford: Oxford University Press, 1990)

Nasson, Bill, *The Boer War: The Struggle for South Africa* (Cape Town: Tafelberg, 2010)

Nasson, Bill, *The South African War, 1899–1902* (London: Arnold, 1999)

Nead, Lynda, *Victorian Babylon: People, Streets and Images in Nineteenth-century London* (New Haven and London: Yale University Press, 2000)

Omissi, David and Andrew S. Thompson, *The Impact of the South African War* (Basingstoke: Palgrave, 2002)

Pakenham, Thomas, *The Boer War* (London: George Weidenfeld and Nicolson, 1979)

Parker, Peter, *The Old Lie: The Great War and the Public School Ethos* (London: Hambledon Continuum, 1987)

Porter, Bernard, *The Absent-Minded Imperialists: Empire, Society and Culture in Britain* (Oxford: Oxford University Press, 2004)

Porter, R. (ed.), *The Myths of the English* (Cambridge: Polity Press, 1992)

Price, Richard, *An Imperial War and the British Working Class: Working-class Attitudes and Reactions to the Boer War, 1899–1902* (London: Kegan Paul, 1972)

Pugh, Martin, *State and Society: A Social and Political History of Britain since 1870* (London: Hodder, 1994)

Reader, W. J., *At Duty's Call: A Study in Obsolete Patriotism* (Manchester: Manchester University Press, 1991)

Rice, Michael, *From Dolly Gray to Sarie Marais: The Boer War in Popular Memory* (Noordhoek: Fischer Press, 2004)

Sanderson, M., *Education and Economic Decline in Britain, 1870 to the 1990s* (Cambridge: Cambridge University Press, 1999)

Sheffield, Gary, *Forgotten Victory: The First World War: Myths and Reality* (London: Headline, 2001)

Sherman, Daniel, *The Construction of Memory in Interwar France* (Chicago: University of Chicago Press, 1999)

Simon, Brian and Bradley, Ian (eds), *The Victorian Public School: Studies in the Development of an Educational Institution* (Dublin: Gill and Macmillan Ltd, 1975)

Smith, Paul (ed.), *The Historian and Film* (Cambridge: Cambridge University Press, 1976)

Spiers, Edward M., *The Army and Society, 1815–1914* (London: Longman, 1980)

Spiers, Edward M., *The Late Victorian Army, 1868–1902* (Manchester: Manchester University Press, 1992)

Spiers, Edward M., *The Scottish Soldier and Empire, 1854–1902* (Edinburgh: Edinburgh University Press, 2006)

Spiers, Edward M., *The Victorian Soldier in Africa* (Manchester: Manchester University Press, 2004)

Strong, Roy, *And When Did You Last See Your Father? The Victorian Painter and British History* (London: Thames and Hudson, 1978)

Thompson, P., *Socialists, Liberals and Labour: The Struggle for London, 1885–1914* (London: Routledge and Kegan Paul, 1967)

Todman, Dan, *The Great War: Myth and Memory* (London: Hambledon Continuum, 2005).

Usherwood, Paul, Jeremy Beach and Catherine Morris, *Public Sculpture of North-East England* (Liverpool: Liverpool University Press, 2000)

Van Hartesveldt, Fred R., *The Boer War: Historiography and Annotated Bibliography* (Westport CT: Greenwood, 2000).

Victoria History of the County of Cambridgeshire and the Isle of Ely, Volume IV (London: Institute of Historical Research, 1953)

Victoria County History of Lancashire, Volume V (London: Institute of Historical Research, 1911)

Victoria County History of Middlesex, Volume VIII (Oxford: Oxford University Press, 1985)

Walton John, K. and Walvin, James (eds), *Leisure in Britain, 1780–1939* (Manchester: Manchester University Press, 1983),

Warwick, Peter (ed.), *The South African War: The Anglo-Boer War, 1899–1902* (Harlow: Longman, 1980)

Whaley, Joachim (ed.), *Mirrors of Mortality: Studies in the Social History of Death* (London: Europa, 1981),

Wilkinson, Alan, *The Church of England and the First World War* (London: SPCK, 1978)

Winter, Jay, *Sites of Memory, Sites of Mourning: The Great War in European Cultural History* (Cambridge: Cambridge University Press, 1995)

Winter, Jay and Robert, Jean-Louis (eds), *Capital Cities at War: Paris, London, Berlin 1914–1919* (Cambridge: Cambridge University Press, 1997)

Wyke, T., *The Public Sculpture of Greater Manchester* (Liverpool: Liverpool University Press, 2004)

Young, M. and Willmott, P., *The Symmetrical Family: A Study of Work and Leisure in the London Region* (London: Routledge and Kegan Paul, 1973)

Chapters, Journal Articles and Theses

Adams, R. J. Q., 'The National Service League and Mandatory Service in Edwardian England', *Armed Forces and Society*, 12: 1 (October 1985)

Anderson, Olive, 'The Growth of Christian Militarism in Mid-Victorian Britain', *English Historical Review*, 86 (1971)

Badsey, Stephen, 'The Boer War as a Media War', in Peter Dennis and Jeffrey Grey (eds), *The Boer War: Army, Nation and Empire* (Canberra: Army History Unit, 2000)

Bailes, Howard, 'Technology and Imperialism: A Case Study of the Victorian Army in Africa', *Victorian Studies*, 24: 1 (Autumn 1980)

Baker, Dennis, 'Griffith, Kenneth Reginald (1921–2006)', *Oxford Dictionary of National Biography* (Oxford: Oxford University Press, 2004)

Beaumont, Jacqueline, 'The Times at War, 1899–1902', in Donal Lowry (ed.), *The South African War Reappraised* (Manchester: Manchester University Press, 2000)

Beckett, Ian, 'Buller, Sir Redvers Henry (1839–1908)', *Oxford Dictionary of National Biography* (Oxford: Oxford University Press, 2004)

Beckett, Ian, 'The Historiography of Small Wars: Early Historians and the South African War', *Small Wars and Insurgencies*, 2: 2 (1991)

Behrman, Cynthia, 'The After-Life of General Gordon', *Albion: A Quarterly Journal Concerned with British Studies*, 3: 3 (Summer 1971)

Bergoff, H., 'Public Schools and the Decline of the British Economy, 1880–1914', *Past and Present*, 129: 1 (1990)

Best, Geoffrey, 'Militarism in the Victorian Public School', in Brian Simon and Ian Bradley (eds), *The Victorian Public School: Studies in the Development of an Educational Institution* (Dublin: Gill and MacMillan, 1975)

Blanch, M. D., 'British Society and the War', in P. Warwick (ed.), *The South African War: The Anglo-Boer War, 1899–1902* (Harlow: Longman, 1980)

Brook, Anne C., 'God, Grief and Community: Commemoration of the Great War in Huddersfield c. 1914–1929', unpublished Ph.D. Thesis, Leeds University (2009)

Bury, M., 'The Royal Scots Greys Monument', *Eagle and Carabine*, 16 (May 1986)

Bushaway, B., 'Name upon Name: The Great War and Remembrance', in R. Porter (ed.), *The Myths of the English* (Cambridge: Polity Press, 1992)

Cannadine, David, 'War and Death, Grief and Mourning in Modern Britain', in Joachim Whaley (ed.), *Mirrors of Mortality: Studies in the Social History of Death* (London: Europa, 1981)

Connelly, Mark, 'The Great War, Part 13: The Devil Is Coming', *Historical Journal of Film, Radio and Television*, 22: 1 (2002)

Connelly, Mark and Donaldson, Peter, 'South African War (1899–1902) Memorials in Britain: A Case Study of Memorialization in London and Kent', *War and Society*, 29: 1 (May 2010)

Danchev, Alex, 'Bunking and Debunking: The Controversies of the 1960s', in Brian Bond (ed.), *The First World War and British Military History* (Oxford: Oxford University Press, 1991)

Griffiths, Clare, 'Questioning the Abstract Morality of War: The Use and Abuse of Imperial Rhetoric in Soldiers' Letters during the Second South African War, 1899–1902', unpublished MA dissertation, University of Sheffield (2009)

Hendley, Matthew, '"Help Us Secure a Strong, Healthy, Prosperous and Peaceful Britain": The Social Arguments of the Campaign for Compulsory Service in Britain, 1899–1914', *Canadian Journal of History*, 30: 2 (August, 1995)

Honey, J. R. de S., 'Tom Brown's Universe: The Nature and Limits of the Victorian Public School Community', in Brian Simon and Ian Bradley (eds), *The Victorian Public School: Studies in the Development of an Educational Institution* (Dublin: Gill and Macmillan Ltd, 1975)

Jones, Meurig, 'The Yorkshire County War Memorial: A History of the Yorkshire County Memorial, York, for the Second Anglo-Boer War, 1899–1902', *York Historian*, 12 (1995)

Kuehl, Jerry, 'History on the Public Screen', in Paul Smith (ed.), *The Historian and Film* (Cambridge: Cambridge University Press, 1976)

Mangan, J. A., 'Images of Empire in the Late Victorian Public School', *Journal of Educational Administration and History*, 12: 1 (1980)

Marks, S., 'Imperial Nursing and the South African War', in G. Cuthbertson, A. Grundlingh and M.-L. Suttie (eds), *Writing a Wider War: Rethinking the South African War, 1899–1902* (Athens, OH: Ohio University Press, 2002)

McFarland, E. W., 'Commemoration of the South African War in Scotland, 1900–1910', *Scottish Historical Review*, 89 (October 2010)

Morgan, Kenneth, O., 'The Boer War and the Media (1899–1902)', *Twentieth Century British History*, 13: 1 (2002)

Moriarty, Catherine, 'Christian Iconography and First World War Memorials', *Imperial War Museum Review*, 6 (1991)

Moriarty, C., 'Private Grief and Public Remembrance: British First World War Memorials', in M. Evans and K. Lunn (eds), *War and Memory in the Twentieth Century* (Oxford: Berg, 1997)

Nasson, Bill, 'Waging Total War in South Africa: Some Centenary Writings on the Anglo-Boer War, 1899–1902', *Journal of Military History*, 66: 3 (July 2002)

Porter, Bernard, 'The Pro-Boers in Britain', in P. Warwick (ed.), *The South African War: The Anglo-Boer War, 1899–1902* (Harlow: Longman, 1980)

Redfern, Allan, 'Crewe: Leisure in a Railway Town', in John K. Walton and James Walvin (eds), *Leisure in Britain, 1780–1939* (Manchester: Manchester University Press, 1983)

Schama, Simon, 'Television and the Trouble with History', in David Cannadine (ed.), *History and the Media* (London: Palgrave Macmillan, 2004)

Springhall, John, 'Up Guards and At Them', in J. Mackenzie, *Imperialism and Popular Culture* (Manchester: Manchester University Press, 1986)

Staunton, Martin, 'Boer War Memorials in Ireland', in Donal P. McCracken (ed.), *Ireland and South Africa in Modern Times*, Vol. 3 (Durban: Southern African-Irish Studies, 1996)

Surridge, S., '"All You Soldiers Are What We Call Pro-Boer": The Military Critique of the South African Wars 1899–1902', *History*, 82 (1997)

Wilkinson, Glen R., '"The Blessings of War": The Depiction of Military Force in Edwardian Newspapers', *Journal of Contemporary History*, 33: 1 (January 1998)

Electronic/Digital Sources

Amos, Denise, 'The Boer War', www.nottsheritagegateway.org.uk/events/boerwar/boerwar-structural.htm (accessed 19 October 2011).

Cawston Historical Society, www.cawstonparish.info (accessed 7 March 2011)

Jones, Meurig, 'A Survey of Memorials to the Second Anglo-Boer War in the United Kingdom and Eire', *Journal of the Africana Society*, 1999 reproduced on the Anglo-Boer War Memorials Project website, http://members.aol.com/abwmp/briefing.htm (accessed 20 June 2012)

Schellhammer, Richard, 'How the Boer War Saved the Movies: The Depiction of the Boer War in Early British Cinema', http://westalabama.academia.edu/RichardSchellhammer/Papers (accessed 22 June 2010)

Index